Narrating from
the Archive

Narrating from the Archive

Novels, Records, and Bureaucrats in the Modern Age

Marco Codebò

Madison • Teaneck
Fairleigh Dickinson University Press

© 2010 by Rosemont Publishing & Printing Corp.

All rights reserved. Authorization to photocopy items for internal or personal use, or the internal or personal use of specific clients, is granted by the copyright owner, provided that a base fee of $10.00, plus eight cents per page, per copy is paid directly to the Copyright Clearance Center, 222 Rosewood Drive, Danvers, Massachusetts 01923. [978-0-8386-4205-4/10 $10.00 + 8¢ pp, pc.]

Associated University Presses
2010 Eastpark Boulevard
Cranbury, NJ 08512

The paper used in this publication meets the requirements of the American National Standard for Permenance of Paper for Printed Library Materials Z39.48-1984.

Library of Congress Cataloging-in-Publication Data
Codebò, Marco, 1952–
  Narrating from the archive : novels, records, and bureaucrats in the modern age / Marco Codebò.
    p. cm.
  Includes bibliographical references and index.
  ISBN 978-0-8386-4205-4 (alk. paper)
  1. Archives in literature. 2. Fiction—History and criticism. I. Title.
 PN3352.A73C63 2010
 809.33'939—dc22   2009031049

PRINTED IN THE UNITED STATES OF AMERICA

A Giulietta

Contents

Acknowledgments	9
Introduction	13
1. The Novel and the Archive: Prehistory	21
2. The Novel and the Archive: Legitimation and Challenge	38
3. *I promessi sposi (1840). Storia della colonna infame* by Alessandro Manzoni: The Power of the Archive	60
4. Balzac's *La Comédie humaine* or the Epic of the Archive	79
5. *Bouvard et Pécuchet* by Gustave Flaubert: The Brilliant Stupidity of the Archive	101
6. *La Vie mode d'emploi* by Georges Perec: The Archive as a Game	119
7. *Libra* by Don DeLillo: The Archival Novel in the Autumn of the Paper Archive	137
Epilogue	158
Notes	161
Works Cited	183
Index	193

Acknowledgments

WRITING THIS BOOK HAS BEEN LIKE BUILDING A BRIDGE THAT spans not between two pillars, but two persons: Sven Spieker and Magdalena Edwards. Sven taught me that archives exist and played a major role in twentieth-century art. More importantly, since the first seminar I took with him at UCSB up to the writing of my PhD dissertation under his direction, Sven showed me what being a scholar in the humanities means. Every single word in this book is inspired by his teaching and example. As the patient, implacable, and insightful editor of the manuscript, Magdalena has helped me to give this book its final shape. In addition to cleaning my native tongue's legacy from my prose, she engaged me in a provocative intellectual dialogue: if this book has achieved some coherence, this largely depends on our conversations.

Throughout the years I have worked on this project, many people, in different capacities, have contributed to give my archives their proper form. I am indebted to all of them, and this book is as much theirs as mine. In particular, I would like to thank Lucia Re for enthusiastically supporting my research, first as a cochair of my dissertation committee and then as a mentor and a friend. I am also thankful to all the brilliant scholars I met at UCSB: Jorge Castillo, Susan Derwin, Suzanne Jill Levine, Sidney Levy, Didier Maleuvre, and Catherine Nesci. I also want to thank Katherine Hayles for helping me clarify my ideas in the initial phase of my research. I am indebted to Tom Harrison, Michele Marra, Luigi Ballerini, Massimo Ciavolella, and Elissa Tognozzi, for many stimulating talks and for having being wonderful colleagues at UCLA. Heartfelt thanks go to my friends on the two sides of the Atlantic Ocean, Alessandro Carrera, Sandy Waters, Carole Viers, Nando Fasce, and Manlio Calegari, whose contributions to this book are greater than they know. My sincere appreciation, finally, goes to the anonymous reader who, on behalf of Fairleigh Dickinson University Press, reviewed my manuscript with intelligence and passion and provided me with invaluable suggestions.

My love and my deepest gratitude go to my wife Giulietta and my daughters Agnese and Carlotta who have always believed in this project and supported me through its ups and downs, all the while withstanding my shortcomings as husband and father. My father Gio Batta who was a great bookkeeper and a dedicated bureaucrat will not be able to read this page. But I have often felt his presence while writing about clerks, files, and records, and while remembering how skillful he was at aligning numbers and keeping folders in order. I have not inherited his skills, but I am thankful for everything else he gave me.

Chapter 3 is a revised version of "Records, Fiction, and Power in Alessandro Manzoni's *I promessi sposi* and *Storia della colonna infame*." Copyright © 2006 The Johns Hopkins University Press. Reprinted with permission of the Johns Hopkins University Press. This article first appeared in *MLN*, 121:1, 2006, pp. 187–206. I am greatly obliged to the courtesy of the editors for their kind permission to reprint this material.

Narrating from
the Archive

Introduction

THIS BOOK DISCUSSES THE RELATIONSHIP BETWEEN THE NOVEL and the archive from early modernity to the dawn of the digital age in the late twentieth century. It focuses on the archival novel, a fictional genre where the narrative stores records, bureaucratic writing informs language, and the archive functions as a semiotic frame that structures the text's content and meaning. In archival fiction, the archive provides the reader with a conduit to reality, defined as both the novel's textual environment and the external world it comments upon.[1] The archive's ability to mediate our approach to reality means (1) that the events of our lived experience become intelligible when they are recorded and (2) that records keep their value as proof of lived life only if they are stored in compliance with protocols tested through the historical practice of the archive. The kind of archive I discuss and analyze in my study is a repository for records that share three traits: they are created by individuals or organizations; they are preserved because of the enduring value of the information they contain; and they are arranged by dint of "the principles of provenance, original order, and collective control."[2] Throughout modernity, in addition to storing society's foundational papers, the archive has carried out crucial tasks, such as building and preserving public memory, providing governments with the tools needed for the identification of citizens, as well as elaborating and testing viable methods for the management and retrieval of knowledge. I view the archive as a discourse, or, to paraphrase Foucault, as a practice that systematically forms the objects of which it speaks.[3] The Foucauldian objects shaped by the discourse of the archive include not only typical archival items such as record series, files, and folders, but also professional figures such as the archivist and the archival scholar, and, to the extent that they rely on archives in their activities, the historian, the lawyer, the notary, and the policeman, to name just a few; the ultimate purpose of my study is to add the archival novel to this list of objects. While functioning in a fictional mode, archival novels perform the same kind of meaning-making operations executed by the records, files, and inventories that characterize bureaucratic archives' practices. The archival novel's and the archive's epistemic projects share a consistency guaranteed by their common vision that knowledge is the result of the systematic arrangement of records.

As John Frow has argued, the structural dimensions of a genre include its formal organization, rhetorical framework, and thematic content.[4] Given both the novel's and the archive's flexibility, to pinpoint the defining traits of the archival novel in formal terms appears to be an elusive task. Within this cautionary frame, I propose one element that without question distinguishes the archival novel in a formal manner, independent of specific texts' contents and historical situations: the storing of records in the text. The actualization of this constituent may occur in a number of distinct ways, and yet there must be room in an archival novel for copying records and inserting them in the narrative even though such insertion may significantly affect the novel's structure by interrupting or sidetracking the plot. Indeed, a latent conflict between the storing of records and plot, or between the archival and narrative dimensions of the text, simmers underneath the surface of the archival novel. Records are severed from a network of spatial relations, a.k.a. the archive, in order to be inserted in texts whose key structural component is (chrono)-logical plot, from which a certain contradiction originates. Postmodern writers of archival novels have played with this conflict and allowed themselves the greatest freedom of disrupting the plot of their novels; they have inserted complex archival objects—catalogues, lists, calendars—into the narrative and, at times, attempted to shape the text according to the spatial order of the archive.

The archival novel's rhetorical structure—which concerns the position from which the text is delivered and the kind of reactions it aims to prompt in the reader—is set apart by the fact that the sender of the novel is an archival authority who uses his/her knowledge as a tool for structuring the receiver's experience of the world. In the fictional world of the novel, this expert may assume the traits of a narrator, a character, an authorial voice speaking in the text, or an implied author. In all of these cases, the novel is provided with an epistemic center of gravity, namely a depositary of the archival expertise that is necessary for turning the text into a coherent cognitive tool. Because of the dialoguing nature of this representative of archival discourse in the text, the archival novel invariably engages the reader in a discussion concerning the truth-value of records and/or the reliability of the archive's procedures. Even though the results of this debate may vary from the eager endorsement of the epistemic value of archival discourse to its overt criticism, archival novels are committed to the search for truth. While such an approach can assume, at times, the form of the strongest challenge to the archive's epistemic soundness, it always gestures toward a nonfictional core of archival practices that gives structure, meaning, and purpose to the text.[5]

As for their thematic content, the "shaped human experience that a genre invests with significance and interest," archival novels deal with the search for documentation, the appraisal of records, the taking of notes, the storing and arrangement of papers, in short the bureaucratic labor that nonarchival texts leave in the writer's workshop.[6] They describe archives, narrate archival research, and/or discuss issues of relevance in archival discourse. Their heroes are archivists, clerks, researchers in archives, analysts of records, and notaries; they can also be laymen who find themselves involved in archival adventures, such as legal arguments over personal identity, disputes over an inheritance, or investigations into their families' past.

By approaching the archival novel as a genre, we can reconsider the map of prose writing in modernity; suddenly new demarcations emerge that cross both the borders separating fictional from nonfictional texts and the internal boundaries of novelistic discourse that lead to divisions among, for example, historical, realist, modernist, and postmodern novels. Because a genre is to be invoked "less as a law, a rigid taxonomic landscape, and more as a self-obsoleting system, a provisional set that will always be bent and pulled and stretched by its many subsets," these lines fluctuate by definition: the writing of a new text, the fresh reading of an old one, or the introduction of an original critical category can determine the rearrangement of the entire map.[7] It is this kind of reordering that I am advocating by proposing the genre of the archival novel, an operation that appears by no means new, as it has already occurred whenever critics have highlighted the connections between the novel and other established discourses, for example, history or the law.

Texts can have affiliations with different genres, as they do not belong to, but participate in, the latter.[8] Within this theoretical frame, the archival novel emerges as a field bordering, and at times overlapping, several, (non)fictional genres: historical, realist, epistolary, and testimonial novels, as well as historiography, memoirs, the law, and journalism. To these stabilized genres of prose writing, I would like to add texts that defy canonical classification such as Domingo Sarmiento's *Facundo* (1845), Euclides da Cunha's *Os Sertões* (1902), Elena Poniatowska's *La noche de Tlatelolco* (1971), and Dubravka Ugresic's *The Museum of Unconditional Surrender* (1999), which all utilize the resources of fiction, journalism, historiography, and memoirs to narrate stories originating in and foregrounding essential archival documentation. The application of tools elaborated by archival discourse to the apprehension of reality is the trait that archival novels written across ages and different linguistic traditions share. This characteristic, Wai Chee Dimock's *likeness* partaken by texts affiliated with the same literary kinship/genre, ensures the nonexclusive link of a text to the archival novel tradition, as a text can be archival and at the same time historical, realist, modernist, or Oulipian.[9] Multiple affiliation does not dilute the identity of the archival novel in the *mare magnum* of prose writing. To the contrary, it aids in comprehending how texts interact with each other, as well as with genres. The heuristic tool for understanding how this network of relations works is Frow's reflexive model, "in which texts are thought to use or to perform the genres by which they are shaped."[10] As performers of generic conventions, archival novels are defined by their preferential use of the norms of archival fiction, but can comfortably utilize the protocols of other genres without weakening their identity in the process.

In the historical context that frames the experience of the archival novel, the three hundred years spanning from the eighteenth century to postmodernism, an agency stands out as the most significant practitioner of archival discourse, the bureaucratic archive. This type of archive applies archival theory and technology to the production of truth in the form of documents. It can achieve this goal because the practice of appraising, registering, sorting, and retrieving records represents a reliable system for giving knowledge coherence, while the archivist's method of verifying claims of identity, property, and power against properly stored original papers appears as an effective truth-finding procedure. Albeit rooted in the archival operations carried out by the absolute monarchies since the sixteenth century, this repository of papers is a historical construction contingent on the age following the French Revolution, which reflects the kinds of records that the archivists of that time worked with—textual/written government records produced by the classic Weberian hierarchical bureaucracies of the European nation state.[11] As a cognitive tool historically determined by the epistemic and material constraints of the paper age, the bureaucratic archive reached its technological sunset with the advent of the digital database in the 1970s. The bureaucratic archive played such an important role throughout the modern age as the official memory of Western(ized) societies that it was viewed as the quintessential storeroom of all that might be recorded, which left other forms of archivization—including the private collection of letters, diaries, or memoirs—at the margins. In short, it became the archive by definition and did not need to be accompanied by any adjective (bureaucratic, public, or state-run), a tradition I intend to follow in this book. I will define other kinds of archival practices with specific terms (personal archives, archivization through letters or diary writing) when they are relevant to my study.

Identifying the archival novel as a genre is an abstraction that functions *a posteriori*, following the fact that a sufficient number of novels in possession of certain traits (i.e., the storing of records alongside the introduction of archive-based structures in the narrative, archival knowledge as the epistemic core of the text, and/or stories of archivists, researchers, and clerks as diegetic material) have been published and read by many. In addition to the works discussed in depth or cited in this book, I am referring to texts such as Augusto Roa

Bastos's *Yo/el Supremo* (1974), Vincenzo Consolo's *Il sorriso dell'ignoto marinaio* (1976), Umberto Eco's *Il nome della rosa* (1980), Milorad Pavic's *Dictionary of the Khazars* (1989), Sebastiano Vassalli's *La chimera* (1990), Harry Mathews's *The Journalist* (1994), Tomás Eloy Martínez's *Santa Evita* (1995) and *El cantor de tango* (2004), and José Saramago's, *Todos os Nomes* (1997), all important novels by any means, which attest to the ability of postmodern archival fiction to cross the borders separating linguistic areas, as well as subgenres. What is more, these texts display not only the defining traits of archival fiction, but also their authors' awareness of operating at the junction between the discourse of the novel and that of the archive. The archival novel's visibility is a product of postmodern culture; it originates in the idea (itself drawing on both the myriad of archival practices that inform our bureaucratized lives and the works of scholars such as Michel Foucault, Jacques Derrida, and Giorgio Agamben) that the archive has become the epistemic tool *par excellence* in the organization, validation, and transmission of knowledge. By being situated at the end of the historical curve of the paper archive, hence in the most advantageous position for taking stock of the crucial role it has played in our culture, we postmodern readers of novels can detect the archive's presence in fiction and realize that archival novels do exist and represent a significant strand of literary prose. This process is akin to what occurred in early nineteenth-century Europe, when Europeans, as Georg Lukács taught us, learned to appreciate the molding power of history over individual existences after witnessing how historical events had affected their lives during the French Revolution and the Napoleonic Wars.

To apply the critical category of archival fiction to the analysis of literary works that were published as early as 1720, almost three centuries ahead of the postmodern appreciation of the archive's position in society, means to confront the obvious risk of anachronism. This kind of danger seems inevitable in any investigation that focuses on the novel as its object: after all, a good amount of the texts we nowadays brand as novels were written by authors who had no idea of operating within the convention of the novelistic genre. In order to avoid anachronism, I will not outline the history of the archival novel (viewed as a defined-from-the-start and immutable form). Instead I will analyze the mediating strategies, aimed at building narrative structures and achieving cognitive goals, novelists implemented whenever they applied the archive's epistemology to the production of fictional works. Because these strategies functioned within distinct cultural environments—to use a kind of shorthand, early eighteenth-century England, realism, and postmodernism—my investigation will not progress linearly from Defoe to DeLillo. Rather, as it moves through specific historical contexts, it will be interrupted by necessary discontinuities. Within this interpretive framework, the six texts I discuss in depth illustrate two aspects of the archival novel: (1) its generic dimension, or the way its textual features and its links to other (non)literary genres frame the reader's approach to the text, and (2) its affiliation with history, i.e., the specific encounters between its generic properties and the historical situations within which they operate.

All six novels I discuss in this book embody significant features of the archival novel while tying the tradition to some of its neighbor genres. These texts epitomize the hybridity inscribed in the very term "archival novel," in the fact that by simply naming the genre we invoke the miscegenation of two distinct and cooperating discourses. In chapter 1, I begin to analyze this hybrid by discussing the development of the archival novel in eighteenth-century England. In chapter 2, I examine the two paradigms of archival fiction, legitimation and challenge. In chapter 3, I look at historical writing, records, and fiction in Alessandro Manzoni's *I promessi sposi (1840)* and *Storia della colonna infame;* in this chapter, I also take on an issue of relevance to the entire book, the relation between archival and historical novels. Chapter 4 deals with the archival components of Honoré de Balzac's *La Comédie humaine* (1842–47) and explores the interaction between the archival novel, the law, and the identification of citizens in nineteenth-century nation states. Chapter 5 takes on Gustave Flaubert's criticism of nineteenth-century knowledge in *Bouvard et Pécuchet* (1881), along with the relation between the archival novel, the encyclopedia, and literary realism. Chapter 6 examines Georges Perec's approach to the archive as a game, along with the relations between archives, libraries, and memory in *La Vie mode d'emploi* (1978). Chapter 7 analyzes Don DeLillo's *Libra* (1988) as a discussion of the archive's senescence in a context defined by the achievements of post-Newtonian science and the inception of the digital database.

1
The Novel and the Archive: Prehistory

IAN WATT'S 1957 FIELD-SHAPING STUDY INTRODUCED THE TERM "Rise of the Novel" to refer to the first half of the eighteenth century, the period in English fiction's history when the novel emerged as both a key tool for the comprehension of modernity and the dominant genre in the narrative field. Watt's "rise" is an effective metaphor if one considers the end result of the process it signifies, namely the novel's ascendance and ultimate supremacy over the competing narrative genres of the time. However, in spite of its visual effectiveness, I find the metaphor of the rise misleading. It suggests the idea of the novel as a somehow well-defined entity that maintains its identity throughout its elevation to the top of the narrative field: how else could the novel have risen without being itself, the novel, from the very beginning of its rising? To this essentialist vision of the novel as a form that remains one and the same throughout its irresistible ascendancy, I would like to oppose a more dynamic model in which the definition of the novel is the end result of a century long process of positioning among neighbor discourses (novel, romance, history, journalism). At the end of this process the novel appears as the fittest genre to carry out the task that narrative is asked to perform in modernity: producing reliable records of the modern individual's lived experience. The novel emerged as the leading narrative genre in modernity because of novelists' and critics' ability both to define the novel's generic conventions and to locate its specific position in the larger field of written prose. The uneasy emergence of the term "novel" in the critical lexicon of the age attests to the complexity of this development.

While the novel's rise is equated with the early to mid 1700s, a working definition of the novel was already in circulation in 1692, only to be obfuscated in the literary conversation that took place in the following decades. In that year, William Congreve writes: "Novels are of a more familiar nature [than romances]; Come near us, and represent to us Intrigues in practice, delight us with Accidents and odd Events but not such as are wholly unusual or unpresidented, such which not being so distant from our Belief bring also the pleasure nearer us."[1] The fact that only one important eighteenth-century novelist, Tobias Smollett, employed the term "novel" to define one of his works testifies to the discrepancy between the vision of the rising novel and contemporaries' ability to see it as an independent genre.[2] Indeed, although twentieth-century scholars correctly maintain that the novel's "distinctive character" had emerged "at least by the 1750s in the wake of Fielding and Richardson," the scholarly lexicon of the age did not register that emergence.[3] In 1783, in "the *locus classicus* of eighteenth-century criticism of prose fiction," James Beattie's *Dissertations Moral and Critical,* the novel does not exist as a generic category in its own right.[4] Beattie lumps the texts we now define as novels into the Modern Romance, which he also calls Poetical Prose Fable, in turn divided into Comic (Fielding) and Serious (DeFoe, Richardson).[5] It is only in the early nineteenth century that authors such as Sir Walter Scott and Jane Austen could refer to the novel without providing further specifications about its features, which demonstrated how a well-defined set of formal traits was by then tied to the novelistic genre.[6] To understand what was at stake in the eighteenth-century debate on the novel, the following consideration is crucial: the lexical confusion that followed Congreve's definition depended on an epistemic rather than literary problem, notably on scholars' and the laity's inability to pin down the specific protocols that the distinct, albeit contiguous, discourses of the novel, history, and journalism had to follow in order to achieve truth. Readers did not know how to associate a certain genre, such as the novel or the newspaper article, with the particular type of truth that its generic features made it possible to convey.

Ultimately, the entire issue boiled down to proofs. Once they had situated the romance in the realm of unbridled imagination, eighteenth-century readers remained with the problem of how to verify the novel's claim to be a truthful account of reality. Nobody seemed to know which regime of truth had to frame the operations of the novel, an ambiguous genre that straddled the divide between fiction and factuality without purportedly crossing into the terrain of untruth. Michael McKeon, who rigorously situates the investigation into the eighteenth-century novel on epistemic ground, argues that the novel became a stable genre by giving an effective answer to the "categorical instability" that had affected the early modern experience since 1600.[7] Post-Renaissance England had lived through a period of cognitive and social uncertainty that was characterized by a "transition in attitudes toward how to tell the truth in narrative" and "a cultural crisis in attitudes toward how the external social order is related to the internal, moral state of its members."[8] In other words, the novel grew out of an age in which the articulation of two fundamental oppositions—between the concepts of true and false and right and wrong—inevitably led to insurmountable problems of signification. In this study, I am concerned with the former set of problems, those affecting the epistemic status of narrative, at the core of which lies a crucial question for the development of the archival novel: "what kind of authority or evidence is required of narrative to permit it to signify truth to its readers?"[9] In the seventeenth century, various kinds of narratives (apparition stories, travel journals, biographies of martyrs) attempted to enhance their truth-value by claiming the absolute historicity, or the exact adherence to the world of our lived experience, of the stories they narrated. Formulated in this manner, historicity appeared as a product of "naïve empiricism," thus amounting to an untenable assertion unable to withstand the criticism coming from "extreme skepticism," an epistemic agnosticism of the sort that ended up suggesting "the unavailability of narrative truth as such."[10] McKeon argues that the novel could escape the predicament of other truth-claiming narratives by adopting literary realism, a mediating concept that defines the type of truth that literary creation can reach once its claim to absolute historicity has proven to be an elusive goal.[11] In literary realism, a literary creation asserts to be not history but history-like, "true to external reality . . . but also sufficiently apart from it (hence 'probable' and 'universal') to be true to itself as well."[12] As the history-*likeness* of a narrative is ultimately determined by the rhetorical and narrative structures of that very narrative, the question of what authority can support the truth claim of a given text is answered by invoking a process of self-validation. What perplexes me in McKeon's argument is its being tainted by a vein of anachronism, by the fact that it replies with a postmodern rejoinder (self-validation) to an interrogation emerging from the epistemic ground of early modernity.

In the light of the cultural climate that surrounds eighteenth-century fiction, I instead wonder whether there were novels that looked for validation not in their own narrative and rhetorical configuration, but in the archive, the discourse that had historically concerned itself with the authentication of written records. In this respect, I would like to point out two distinctive traits of early modern England's culture, i.e., the feeling that the printing press provided the nearly instant replay of human experience, as well as the urgent sense of "now," which equated a unique value to the tiniest and most present increment of time: "By the 1690s, the culture became so obsessed with the potential significance to human consciousness of any single moment that an immediate written record needed to be created, and the preoccupations with news and novelty in fact coalesced in the popular consciousness much as Dunton [a pioneer of journalism] suggests."[13] The obsession with records occurred in an epistemic environment, itself a product of the scientific revolution of the seventeenth century, in which knowledge depended on the analysis of data. In particular, it was only by being written down rather than being memorized and transmitted orally that the events concerning a human being's biography could become material for cognitive investigations. In a mix of scientific rigor, protestant anxiety, and mercantile bookkeeping, introspection could function only if life was systematically turned into a record. Recording the life experience of an individual allowed for the observation of otherwise undetectable details, as well as the discovery of patterns, operations that were initially typical of diaries and (auto)biographies and then became decisive constituents of the novel's cognitive strategy. As J. Paul Hunter argues, "without the impulse to record, sort out, and conclude, there is no novel as we know it."[14] In Hunter's sequence of recording, sorting out, and concluding, one can already read the answer the archival novel will give to the question of validation. In archival fiction, it is the very act of creating a record, i.e., putting notes, memos, and/or oral reports on paper according to certain procedures guaranteed by the archive, that validates a work; record creating can do so because it takes the account of an event out of the unverifiable flow of orality and submits it to the sole purveyor of truth in the post-Galileian world: scientific examination. An archival novel weaves this dual process of record creation and verification into the fabric of its text, thus functioning as a record all the while narrating the unfolding of its own archivization.

One of the oldest examples of this practice is Daniel Defoe's *A Journal of the Plague Year* (1722), in which the author validates the truth claim of his text by offering a narration crafted as a record backed by the authority of a well-managed archive. Written when the threat of a new outbreak of the plague loomed over England after the epidemic in Marseille in 1720, the *Journal* deals with the historical circumstances of the mass disease that ravaged London in 1665. A first person narrative, the *Journal* is narrated by H. F., a saddler living in Aldgate who has survived the Plague and recounts the events that he witnessed.[15] An accomplished author, journalist, and publisher, Defoe applied a few literary and editorial tricks to the task of presenting H. F. as the actual author of the *Journal*. Defoe did not sign the book and opened the text with a title page reading thus:

A
JOURNAL
of the
Plague Year:
BEING
Observation or Memorials,
Of the most Remarkable
OCCURRENCES,
As well
PUBLICK as PRIVATE,
Which happened in
LONDON
During the last
GREAT VISITATION
In 1665.
Written by a Citizen who continued all the
while in London. Never made publick before."[16]

On the next page, the story of the epidemic begins with another title, "Memoirs of the Plague," on top of the text, and ends with the signature of H. F. at the conclusion.

In *Robinson Crusoe* (1719) and *Moll Flanders* (1722), texts introduced with anonymous editorial prefaces that attested to their authenticity, Defoe had already disguised himself as an editor who published other writers' stories and vouched for their factuality.[17] In the *Journal*, where no editorial preface introduces the text, H. F.'s unframed narrative purports to be an even more authentic document then those written by Robinson Crusoe and Moll Flanders, that is an eyewitness's unedited account of the Plague kept in its pristine genuineness some sixty years after the facts.[18] The linguistic fabric of the text aided in conveying the idea that the *Journal* was a fresh and unaltered document—namely the numerous repetitions and deferrals, and the abundance of formulaic phrases such as "I have said" or "I say"—and seemed to "imply a lack of assurance in the writer."[19] In other words, the *Journal* looks indeed as if it was penned by a poorly educated merchant who labored to carry out a task, turning memories still laden with emotional power into a coherent narrative, that exceeded his writing skills. It is no wonder that contemporary readers believed H. F. was indeed the author of the *Journal* until 1768, when the antiquarian Richard Gough first unveiled Defoe's authorship of the work.[20]

Judging from the three-century-long history of the reception of the *Journal*, it appears that Defoe was quite successful in his strategy of denying the fictional nature of his work. Starting with Sir Walter Scott's definition of the *Journal* as "one of that particular class of compositions which hovers between romance and history," and ending up with F. Bastian's claim (in 1965) that Defoe's work "stands closer to our idea of history than to that of fiction," the *Journal* has quite often been classified as a non fictional, or partly fictional work.[21] As Robert Mayer argues, interpretations of the *Journal* as strictly historical discourse continued to come out way after the eighteenth century, up to Watson Nicholson's 1919 definition of the Defoe's text as "a faithful record of historical facts."[22] In the rest of the twentieth century, while the reading of the *Journal* as fiction became mainstream in the scholarly community, it was often complemented by hints at the text's historicity: Defoe's work could also be viewed as either a historical novel or a hybrid of history and fiction.²³ Both definitions of the Journal as a fiction/novel and as a historical work do not seem to stand the criterion of textual evidence. The two interpretations actually subvert each other: if the majority of what the *Journal* narrates is historical facts, it is no less true that all this material is selected and organized by a fictional agent, H. F., which invalidates the text's claim to historicity. Approached as a historical novel, finally, the *Journal* lacks the ability to insert characters' adventures into the unfolding of history that characterized Scott's, Manzoni's, and Balzac's classic historical fiction. For instance, after comparing H. F.'s rational, prudent, and tolerant approach to both the plague and the simmering issue of religious dissent, one if left wondering how this attitude can be motivated historically in the text, given a cultural environment that appears rife with superstition and intolerance. Lukács's argument that "the derivation of the individuality of characters from the historical peculiarity of their age" represents the historical novel's defining principle does not apply in the *Journal*.²⁴

The above attempts to define the *Journal* fall shy of their goal because they classify Defoe's text through categories drawn from discourses that had yet to achieve their stabilization in 1722. As discussed, the novel gained generic coherence and a formal definition only toward the end of the century, while historiography became a scientific discipline, in the sense that we moderns gave to the term, only with the inception of academic history, à la von Ranke, in the first half of the nineteenth century. Perhaps, rather than trying to forcibly fit the *Journal* into our modern taxonomies, as the game of defining inevitably ends up doing, it makes more sense to attempt to gain a satisfactory comprehension of what Defoe's text is about, of its subject matter, comprising the substories that complement H. F.'s adventures. With respect to this, there is a key component of the *Journal* whose importance scholarly approaches to Defoe's work somehow overlook. I am referring to the fact that one of the *Journal*'s crucial concerns is the very process of turning a heap of papers, news, and rumors into a record. Indeed, in the economy of the text, while the archivization of the narrative becomes a theme as important as narrating the plague, H. F.'s adventure consists in assembling the documentation of his own ordeal as much as in surviving the disease; and ultimately H. F. as the record creator appears historically more credible than the man who survives the plague.[25] There are numerous sections in the *Journal* in which "H. F.'s history reads more like a romance in which he is a charmed soul, who can walk anywhere and speak to anyone—all the while remaining mysteriously immune to infection."[26] On the contrary, H. F. the record creator is an entirely believable historical figure, a true Lukácsian world-historical individual. He represents the spirit of an age that, because of a series of factors (the Reformation, the scientific revolution, the printing press, and the increased availability of paper), turned to the creation of records as a promising cognitive instrument for making sense of our lived experience.

The recording spirit of early modernity begins to inform the *Journal* since the text's *incipit*, when H. F. narrates the circumstances of the first two casualties of the plague. Despite an attempt to cover-up the two deaths, the secretaries of state are informed of the fact and send two physicians and a surgeon to inspect the house where the two men died. The three doctors' opinion, which establishes the plague as the cause of the deaths, "was given in to the Parish Clerk, and he also return'd them to the Hall; and it was printed in the weekly Bill of Mortality in the usual manner, thus, *Plague 2. Parishes infected 1*" (6). Situated in a strategic position, this episode both sets the tone of the text and represents its metonymy. Since the narration of a historical event coincides with the account of its archivization, the story of the two deaths points out the *Journal* as a text in which recording a narrative is one and the same with narrating the creation of a record. Within this context, the first two victims in London do not really die of the plague until their deaths are recorded and printed in the "Bills of Mortality" as caused by it.[27]

The ultimate meaning of Defoe's text can be grasped by bringing in Paul Ricœur's notion of *"mise en archive."*[28] Ricœur views the archive as the site where oral testimonies turn into written records, thus allowing the discipline of history to carry out the epochal transition from orality to writing: by establishing the documentary proof, the *mise en archive* sets historiography in motion. Ricœur's argument applies nicely to the comprehension of Defoe's work, in the sense that it both illuminates the context for the writing of the *Journal* and aids in understanding the historical dimension of the character H. F. In the first page of his narrative, Defoe's hero states that they "had no such things as printed News Paper in those Days," thus situating the time of the plague in opposition to the unspecified time of his final writing of the *Journal*. In so doing, he represents the former as an age still dependent on orality and the latter as the modern epoch of newspapers and other printed media.[29] As the rest of the *Journal* discovers that the progression from orality to writing follows an uneven development that does not fit into the bipolar model invoked in the *incipit*, Defoe's work tells of the uneasy negotiation between these two media.[30] In its attempt to represent this historical media shift, the *Journal* conveys the picture of an age in which a combination of previous epistemic and technological gains has turned the creation of records into a truth-finding activity carried out on an unprecedented scale.

If the *Journal* is the narrative of the *mise en archive*, then H. F., the memorialist who pens rumors, gossip, and oral stories, all the while witnessing with uncanny curiosity the unfolding of the plague, is the perfect protagonist for Defoe's work. H. F. is a writing hero, in the sense not only that he is the fictional writer of his own story, but also that writing the *Journal* represents his key problem as novelistic character. As H. F. continues to portray himself in the act of writing, he becomes the forerunner of the record maker working with pen and paper that is a fixture in the novels I discuss in this book, until, as occurs in *Libra*, a computer replaces the paper age tools. H. F also accurately informs his readers that two levels of writing, each one corresponding to distinct positions in time, combine in the text. Underneath a first layer, the final compilation of the *Journal* situated in the "present" of the text, there lies a second stratum of writing, the redaction of H. F.'s memorandums of the plague located in 1665.[31] As the various phases of creating, storing, and revising records appear in the text, writing achieves the temporal dimension of a never-ending practice of adjusting and recycling preexisting materials. And the final touch to this representation is added by the impromptu appearance, toward the end of the *Journal*, of a third textual level, the anonymous, and until then hidden, editor who is responsible for this note: "N.B. The Author of this Journal, lyes buried in that very Ground, being at his own Desire, his Sister having been buried there a few Years before" (181).

Published in the age in which the novel was inching toward its stabilization as a genre, the *Journal* demonstrates how the urge to record that pervaded culture in early eighteenth-century England became indeed part and parcel of novelistic discourse. The *Journal* affirms that records are a key constituent of the novel, a notion that the history of the novelistic genre throughout the nineteenth century and the first half of the twentieth—the time in which Western societies felt what Peter Brooks calls an "extraordinary need or desire for plots"—may have contributed to obfuscate.[32] However, the development of the novel since 1950 has taken directions that has given a new shape to our definition of the genre. Our critical vocabulary now hosts terms such as nonfictional novel, like Truman Capote's *In Cold Blood* (1965), or testimonial novel, like Elena Poniatowska's *La noche de Tlatelolco* (1971), that refer to texts whose cut-to-the-bones fictional component exhibits an underlying massive accumulation of archival records.[33] Once situated in the larger context of the novel's historical development, the *Journal* both anticipates the development of the archival novel as a genre and contributes to the insertion of archival themes in novelistic discourse. Indeed, some of the archival novel's key generic components, from displaying the archival base of the narrative to weaving records into the fabric of the text, are already present in the *Journal*. Four elements, in particular, are worthy of closer analysis: the character H. F. as archivist/eyewitness, the use of bureaucratic language, the insertion of heterogeneous, nonnarrative materials into the novel, and the presence of a master record as the archival authority in the text.

H. F. is the depositary of archival expertise in the novel in that he performs the basic archival operations that are instrumental in giving the *Journal* its proper shape as a narrativized record. Some of these operations, such as the storing and the arrangement of memorandums and the assembling of a collection of official records, are implicit, albeit vital for the final success of H. F.'s project.[34] In other words, even though the text does not expand on this information, H. F. must have been a skilled archivist who knew the basics of his trade in order to compose the *Journal*.[35] Most importantly, H. F. conveys to his readers the feeling of what living a historical episode as an archival experience means. He makes clear that somebody must take care of society's papers if we want to remain in touch with history, given the fact that without official documents the past vanishes. As the archive's voice in the text, H. F. shows us an archivized world where any attempt to make sense of our experience must pass through the mediation of the record. H. F.'s role as a novelized archivist is consistent with the *Journal*'s very language, its comprising repetitions, "feckless phrases," and worn out formulas.[36] As it suits more a dull clerk than a creative novelist, the unimaginative language of the *Journal* is a perfect fit for H. F., a merchant used to the bureaucratic prose of bookkeeping: who else beside a bureaucrat could write that way?

By adopting blatantly bureaucratic language for his text, Defoe carried out a more significant operation than simply choosing a style that suited the cultural profile of the *Journal*'s hero. He adopted the communicative instrument that marked the divide between the prestigious tradition of the romance and the promising development of the novel. Gianni Celati has argued that the novel could overcome the romance by observing and registering the experiences of empirical individuals and that bureaucratic writing was the tool that made this recording possible. "Writing as an instrument for putting experience into documents is what interests Defoe as well as the Royal Society and the entire culture of observation."[37] The novel observes and bureaucratically records the areas of marginality, excess, and madness that escape the control of the early modern rational subject. But if this is the case, then bureaucratic writing means "exercising power by dint of documents," and the novel represents the dream of circumscribing marginality by turning it into a paper record.[38] There is no better executor of this strategy than H. F. who decides to remain in London to record the plague, an event that he narrates as the unchaining of human madness: debauchery, violence, and unbridled egoism swirl as all the untamed brutality that lies underneath the tiny veneer of civilization bursts into the open and threatens to take over the city. Some four centuries before Defoe wrote the *Journal*, Boccaccio had narrated how ten well-to-do young men and women fled from Florence during the 1348 black death to go the countryside and enjoy the pleasure of storytelling. Through their stories, Boccaccio's ten narrators try to frame the world of their lived experiences even though it is the plague they left in the city that is actually framing them. By contrast, H. F. can decide to live through the plague because he possesses an instrument, bureaucratic writing, through which he can confront the radical disorder of the disease. Boccaccio's storytellers, although by far better educated than Defoe's hero, lack his tools for reading madness; their own instrument, orality, cannot be applied to that slow accumulation of patiently observed details that represents the secret of H. F.'s ability to narrate the epidemic. Helpless, as narrators, in the face of the black death, Boccaccio's characters must flee from it and turn to an evasive kind of narrating that deals with any topic but the plague. Through H. F.'s remarkable achievement, he out-writes the plague after all, Defoe narrates the conclusive phase of the media shift set in motion by the rise of the clerk in shops, banks, and public administrations and inscribes bureaucratic writing in the core of the fledging novelistic genre.

H. F.'s bureaucratic writing also carries out a task that will become a fixture in the archival novel: the insertion of heterogeneous materials in the text, from the mayor of London's orders concerning the plague to the records of Thucydides-like dialogues. All these writings are not amalgamated into H. F.'s account, but pasted on the page as supporting evidence for his rendition of the events. In so doing, the *Journal* gives an archival turn to one of the defining traits of the novel, its "promiscuous inclusivity."[39] The various records the *Journal* comprises need, of course, to be copied in order to be inserted in the text, and only a writer bureaucrat like H. F. can transcribe, without remorse, any type of written material in a narrative. What is remarkable in H. F.'s copy frenzy, which anticipates that of Flaubert's Bouvard and Pécuchet, is the frequent use of paste-ins, i.e., textual fragments that maintain their original typographical layout event after being transferred to a new text. Defoe inserted sixteen paste-ins in the

1: THE NOVEL AND THE ARCHIVE: PREHISTORY

Journal, thus carrying out a practice that was not strange to eighteenth-century novels and that resurfaced again in postmodern fiction, as my discussion of Perec's *La Vie mode d'emploi* will prove.[40] Most of Defoe's paste-ins concern numerical data on the plague, but one can also find the following case, which anticipates twentieth-century (from Marinetti to Perec) typographic games:

> as if the Plague was not the Hand of God, but a kind of a Possession of an evil Spirit; and that it was to be kept off with Crossing, Signs of the Zodiac, Papers tied up with so many Knots; and certain Words, or Figures written on them, as particularly the Word *Abracadabra*, form'd in Triangle, or Pyramid, thus.
>
>
> A B R A C A D A B R A
> A B R A C A D A B R
> A B R A C A D A B
> A B R A C A D A
> A B R A C A D
> A B R A C A
> A B R A C
> A B R A
> A B R
> A B
> A   (32)
>

As signs of H. F.'s desire to narrow the distance between his account of the plague and the records he is handling, the *Journal*'s paste-ins enhance the archival nature of Defoe's text. They represent the most vivid evidence of both the *Journal*'s archival foundation (if not in an archive, where were those materials stored before being copied?) and of the type of writing, scrupulous and dull to the excess, that put the text together.

Through bureaucratic writing and archival practices, H. F. assembles a text that gives the following answer to McKeon's question about which authority or evidence could support a narrative's claim to truth: a combination of private and public records created through a methodology that privileges eyewitness accounts and verifies oral reports, which are systematically checked against each other and stored by a trusted clerk. In this sketch of the archival novels' epistemology, a key role is played by the "Bills of Mortality."[41] As the episode of the first two victims of the plague has shown, by registering "the number of deaths per parish and the estimated number of deaths caused by plague," the weekly "Bills of Mortality" is the ultimate record of the disease.[42] In the *Journal*, the "Bills" functions as a master record, i.e., a document that either by being an official record guaranteed by the archive's authority, or by being stored in a way that confers an aura of historicity upon it (as occurs with the found manuscript in several historical novels), is endowed with authenticating power over the narrative. As the "Bills" turns the unfolding of the plague into a weekly, numeric balance, it smoothly fits into the modus operandi of H. F., a merchant whose first approach to writing must have been the daily maintenance of his books. The "Bills" becomes the backbone of H. F.'s narrative by guaranteeing the reader that the text he or she is reading corresponds to the official truth stored in the archive. In the *Journal*, it is the periodic citation of the "Bills" that provides the basic information on the growth curve of the epidemic, as well as on how it is spreading geographically. But the "Bills" can also validate an individual's story, as occurs with the episode of an unknown gentleman who escapes from the house where he is confined only to die in a nearby inn, thus infecting all its residents. H. F. can confirm the truth of this story by verifying that the "Bills" presents evidence of an increased mortality in the parish where the episode occurred shortly after the unknown gentleman's death (62). By systematically translating the events on the ground into numbers recorded in the "Bills," the *Journal* fosters the perception of the plague as an occurrence that can only become visible upon its being recorded as a string of numeric data. Readers end up approaching the epidemic the same way as the people in London did: "And the weekly Bills shewing an Encrease of Burials in St. *Giles's* Parish more than usual, it began to be suspected, that the Plague was among the People at that End of Town.... This possessed the Heads of the People very much" (6). From this episode at beginning of the plague up to the end of the disease, it is by reading the regular editions of the "Bills" that people are able to track the plague's doings and eventual demise. Perceiving a historical period as a sequence of recorded data is the inevitable counterpart of the urge to record that obsessed early modern England: if the very existence of an event depends on its being recorded, then identifying a historical occurrence with its record becomes a quite effective cognitive move.

In spite of the structural role the "Bills of Mortality" plays in Defoe's *Journal*, by no means is the city government's bulletin treated as an uncontested source of truth.[43] H. F. repeatedly questions the credibility of the "Bills" by showing how the official numbers of deaths are lower than those he notices through his private observations. In H. F.'s, and Defoe's, narrative strategy, the "Bills" is meant to vouch the methodological soundness of the *Journal*; it proves that the text was composed by a writer who did not base his work on imagination, but on personally gathered testimonies and official records. In other words, the "Bills" supports the historicity of H. F.'s narrative by demonstrating that its author proceeded as a reliable historian when he wrote the text. As far as the reliability of the numeric data it provides, however, even the "Bills of Mortality" can become fair game as target of H. F.'s fastidious examination: it is the methodical checking that only records allow, and not the records in and of themselves, that functions as the support of a truth-bearing story. H. F.'s debunking of the Bill's reliability bespeaks the social tensions that threatened to pull apart the social fabric during the plague. As they shook the city government, these conflicts inevitably affected the way official documents were perceived and ended up undermining their authority. What I would like to underline is the fact that H. F's inquisitive approach to the "Bills" is a defining trait of the genre exemplified by Defoe's *Journal*, a forerunner to the archival novel. The scrupulous analysis of the truth-value of all records is a typical feature of archival fiction: archival novels are second-degree documents that never accept records at face value, in particular those that convey official discourse.

With its archivist as a character in the text, the presence of a master record, and the use of bureaucratic language, Defoe's *Journal* lies squarely in the prehistory of the archival novel. Critics' bewilderment facing Defoe's work, their inability to situate it unquestionably in the field of fiction or history, originates exactly in the *Journal*'s archival component. By straddling the divide between truth and invention, the

Journal's archival core defies scholars' attempts to arrive at an unequivocal definition of Defoe's work. The *Journal* is a fictional dossier, a collection of records (their being authentic or not does not matter here) assembled together by a fictional agent, H. F. While the historicity of many of the events narrated in the book can be questioned, there is no doubt that the method H. F. applies to the compilation of his dossier is historically true: the operations that H. F. carries out in order to gather documents, record testimonies, and organize his papers into a coherent whole are exactly those that a real archivist living in the late seventeenth century would have carried out. The conundrum of the *Journal*'s historicity depends on the inextricable ambiguity of H. F., who completes an utterly fictional operation (the compilation of the dossier called the *Journal*) through a series of practices that appear faithful to the truth of history.

In spite of being so implicated in the archive's epistemology, the *Journal* still remains situated in the prehistory of archival fiction. The reason for this positioning lies in the archive's historical situation in the first half of the eighteenth century, when storing and arranging records still did not rely on a set of theoretical principles independent from the specific situations in which they functioned. Archival discourse made this step in the nineteenth century, as a consequence of both the new demand for archival services that was arriving from the nation state after the French Revolution and the process of centralization and organization of the archives that was engendered by that very upheaval. I discuss this development in the next three chapters, but here I would like to point out H. F.'s epistemic solitude in his handling of public records. Without the option of entrusting his task to public powers, the responsibility for checking all the records falls solely on H. F., a skillful and reliable archivist, but a private citizen nonetheless. As I noted over the course of this chapter, even the highest archival authority in the text, the "Bills of Mortality" enjoys a shaky prestige, to say the least. The "Bills" is clearly the product of an age when the procedures for the collection, transmission, and storage of data did not abide by consistent protocols and were prone to subjective deviances, depending on the context in which they were implemented. Aware of this situation, H. F. collects information by way of his own personal channels, which are reliable enough to allow him to challenge the authority of a document, the "Bills," authored by the same city leaders he generally praises for their handling of the plague. There is no trace in Defoe's narrative of the same deference toward central archives and official documents that one can find in novels written in the first half of the nineteenth century, after the great reform of public archives that followed the French Revolution. In the emblematic author of that age, Balzac, one can read a state of mind that is lacking in the *Journal*, notably the consciousness that by storing an enormous mass of records on individuals' lives and arranging them through rigorous procedures, state-run archives have achieved uncontested epistemic authority.

The shortcomings of the archive in the eighteenth century weaken the very archival discourse that should aid the reader in comprehending the text and, in turn, prevent Defoe from creating a true archival fiction. In this context, what makes the *Journal* a crucial text is its position in reference to the discourse of the novel. In the age in which the novel defines its communicative tools and epistemic goals, Defoe's text represents a moment of self-reflection for the fledging novelistic genre. The *Journal* functions as a mirror where the novel can make out its own roots in the archive, with which it shares medium, materials, and the same urge to create records out of the fleeting moments that compose our lives. Robert Mayer has argued that, "the *Journal* constitutes the most forceful assertion in the whole discourse of the novel in English that the nexus of history and fiction is a constitutive feature of the form."[44] But by demonstrating how this nexus operates through the mediation of archival records, the *Journal* shows that the connection with the archive, too, is a key constituent of the novel form. The archival novel is the genre that narrates how, when, and where the archive and its records mediate between history and fiction; it is also the genre that narrates these mediations' instruments, successes, and failures. This generic tradition began with a saddler's decision to stay home (the court, the noble and rich families, and the scribes living with them were fleeing to the countryside) and keep a faithful record of the calamity that was approaching his city. At the root of the novel's urge to record lies a need to see and testify that is first and foremost ethical.

2
The Novel and the Archive: Legitimation and Challenge

AFTER DEFOE'S UTILIZATION OF ARCHIVAL RECORDS AS GUARANtors of a fictional text's historicity, it was Henry Fielding who made decisive steps toward a modern conception of the archival novel. A literary generation younger than Defoe, Fielding acknowledged to writing fiction and did not pretend to be the editor of diaries or dossiers compiled by other writers: "it is with Fielding that fictional narrative of the outright variety was born."[1] Although he may raise our suspicions as moderns by calling his *Tom Jones* (1749) a "history," Fielding possessed a clear understanding of his text's position among the various discourses that lay along, and often straddled, the divide between fact and fiction in early modernity. In the eighth book of *Tom Jones*, after suggesting that every writer should always keep within the bounds of possibility, Fielding classifies authors according to the relationship their texts establish with probability, or the likelihood that a narrative is true to facts. While deserting probability means trespassing into romance, a choice that does not appeal to Fielding, narrating probable events is the task of both the historians "who relate publick transactions" and the historians "who deal in private characters."[2] Translated into our critical language, Fielding's classification amounts to a distinction between historians (without adjectives), the former, and novelists, the latter. Contrary to what one might think, historians of public events are those who enjoy larger latitude in abandoning probability and shaping their narratives according to the more tolerant norms of possibility. Indeed, since humankind's history is full of improbable or even absurd events, historians of public events are not only allowed, but even required to expand the scope of their narratives to the larger field of possible events. What is interesting in Fielding's argument is the reason why historians of civic affairs can benefit from the freedom of narrating unlikely events: the support of official records. Historians concerned with society are the only writers who can recount incredible stories because their narratives' claims to truth are sponsored by official documents. Compared to the privileged position of historians who deal with public affairs, Fielding says, those who narrate private lives face a "more dangerous" situation: "As we have no publick notoriety, no concurrent testimony, no records to support and corroborate what we deliver, it becomes us not only to keep within the limits of possibility, but of probability too."[3] Limited as they are by their inability to find records that could back their stories, authors like Fielding are bound to narrate only events that have a high probability of happening.

Albeit formulated within a premodern, Aristotelian framework, Fielding's argument stands out as an original answer to the ambition of writers we now call novelists to legitimize their works as truthful discourse. What could guarantee a narrative's truthfulness was no longer its pretended affinity with a more prestigious literary genre, such as historiography (a position that most eighteenth-century writers upheld), but the support of official records. Furthermore, if the history of public events could base its narratives on records while that of private lives could not, the fault was in the archive. It was because the archival institutions were not storing documents of private lives that Fielding could not find the proofs he needed. Fielding's conception of the archive was affected by a humanistic approach to the preservation of society's vital documents that had him blend the archive and the library. He believed that a record was a historian's account of a public event, for example of Alexander's expedition or the battle of Agincourt, and thus considered historical books as primary sources in historiography. Accordingly, he thought that there were no documents of private lives available for writers wanting to support their works with written proofs. Despite Fielding's dated approach to archival theory, one can read in his complaint about the lack of documentation on private lives a hint of what the novelists to come would need in order to establish a firm relation between their text and truth: a viable archive of ordinary citizens' lives, a repository that could store various kinds of records, including those of births, marriages, deaths, adoptions, disinheritances, travels abroad, changes of residences, bankruptcies, and foreclosures. That archive, the storeroom of the bourgeois life, was in the making and was to obtain legal sanction some forty years after the writing of *Tom Jones*.

By considering public records the only documents that could prove a text to be true, Fielding shunned exactly that type of archive that in early modernity appeared most closely related to the novel, i.e., the collection of private letters. In the context of eighteenth-century literature, Fielding's view that public records were the sole purveyors of truth equated to a switch from private to public archives as guarantors of a narrative's trustworthiness. In those years, there was widespread agreement among writers that literary works needed to be related to, or disguised as, some nonfictional discourse in order to be accepted as truthful texts. Fielding's greatest rival, Samuel Richardson, employed every editorial device available in order to present himself as the editor and not the writer of the letters comprising novels such as *Pamela* (1740) or *Clarissa* (1747).[4] His solution to Fielding's problem, the lack of records of private lives, was to camouflage his works as personal archives of correspondence: it was another manner of anchoring a fictional text to records, albeit these records lacked the guarantee offered by archival institutions. Fielding's visionary move was instead to seize the archival strand that played such an important role in defining novelistic discourse, as proven by the success of Richardson's epistolary novels, and relocate it into a new context, the public archive. What is more, in *Tom Jones*, Fielding was able not only to discuss the relation between records and novels from a theoretical point of view, but also to combine the narration of a fictional story with the compilation of historical records. Even though he acts in a much subtler way than Defoe in the *Journal*, Fielding still manages to turn sections of *Tom Jones* into collections of records stored by a writer/bureaucrat.

As Lennard J. Davis has argued, Fielding "did attempt what no novelist before had ever attempted. He wove into his work an actual, ongoing political and historical event—the Jacobite Rebellion of 1745."[5] He accomplished this feat by coordinating segments of the fictional plot of *Tom Jones* with the chronology of the Rebellion and by having all the main characters "take strong stands on the issue of Jacobitism."[6] In this textual framework, both Tom's insubordination against Allworthy and Sophia's challenge to her father's authority mirror, in the private sphere, the revolt that is unfolding in the larger historical context of 1745 England. Furthermore, *Tom Jones* presents sufficient textual evidence to suggest the hypothesis that the novel became, at times, an actual record of the uprising. After making his first reference to the rebellion in book seven, Fielding felt obliged to justify his delay in informing the reader of that historical event: "The serjeant had informed Mr. Jones that they were marching against the rebels, and expected to be commanded by the glorious Duke of Cumberland. By which the reader may perceive (*a circumstance which we have not thought necessary to communicate before*) that this was the very time when the late rebellion was at the highest" . . . [my emphasis].[7] Davis maintains that "this sounds like an attempt to patch up the fact that Fielding had just been struck by the idea of including the current uprising into the ongoing work."[8] If this hypothesis is true, then the references to the Jacobite insurgency were registered as the rebellion was progressing, thus turning the text into a historical record and Fielding into a record creator. Or, to use Fielding's terminology, the historian of private characters and that of public life become one and the same in book seven of *Tom Jones*. The language used by Tom Jones to inform the Man-of-the-Hill of the historical events that are occurring in the country foregrounds the novel's ability to function as an archive: "I will tell you a fact which is not yet recorded, and of which I suppose you are ignorant. There is actually now a rebellion on foot in this kingdom."[9] In the very moment in which Fielding states that the rebellion is not yet recorded, he starts recording it, in an ironic reversal of the performative capacity of language.

Fielding's method for converting parts of *Tom Jones* into the record of a historical event can be understood by drawing a comparison between *Tom Jones* and *A Journal of the Plague Year*. While the latter pretends to be a document in order to narrate the plague, it is as a fictional work that *Tom Jones* can record the Jacobite rebellion.[10] Because Defoe chooses to hide himself as the author of the *Journal*, he must situate the record creator H. F. in the text's diegesis. In other words, since Defoe pretends to be the editor, H. F. must step up and become the agent in charge of storing records in the novel. In *Tom Jones*, on the contrary, Fielding plays the role of record creator as the author of a fictional tale. The difference in the archivist's position in each work makes for a paradoxical contrast. Because in *Tom Jones* the storing of records takes place in the real word (the one in which Fielding sits at his desk to write the novel), the text that embraces its fictional status up front ends up being much more factual than the *Journal*, the work that claims strict factuality.

Positioning the storing of records on the level of the text's composition, as occurs in *Tom Jones*, allows authors to choose among a wide range of options: operating as record creators, appearing as copyists, record managers, and/or archivists, turning a character into an archivist in the text, or even a mix of the above solutions. In the historical development of the archival novel, it is possible to identify key formal features of the genre in the said options, which in turn help to define the various types of archival fiction that have appeared ever since. In *Tom Jones*, Fielding allows the reader only a quick glimpse at how the text and the archive are bound together, but the modus operandi he adopts, situating the archive in the author's workshop where it can inform the structural and narrative fabric of the novel, functions in a crucial line of archival novels including works by realist authors such as Balzac, and postmodern novelists like Perec and DeLillo. Instead, Defoe's *Journal* can be viewed as the remote model for all the archival novels that utilize the literary device of the found manuscript, from Manzoni's *I promessi sposi* to Eco's *Il nome della rosa,* or in novels that base their pretended historicity on textual remains surviving from the past, such as Pavic's *Dictionary of the Khazars*. Although Manzoni's, Eco's, and Pavic's novels share with the *Journal* the same formal principle, these four texts are separated by a semiotic divide: disguising the author as an editor gestures toward historicity in the *Journal*, while it becomes an unmistakable mark of literariness in the other works, as well as in all the novels of this kind that were written after the end of the eighteenth century.

Fielding appears to be the only writer of his age who could conceive of the relation between the novel and the archive in terms that anticipated modernity. Even though archival discourse had yet to achieve stabilization in 1749, Fielding was able to envision the novel as a genre firmly situated in the fictional field and the archive as the institution for storing the foundational materials (a.k.a. records of private lives) of the modern individual. The archive that Fielding coveted is the result of a historical rupture in the storing and arranging of records that took place toward the end of the eighteenth century. Because of that change, the archive became one of the key agencies in the modern nation state, thus assuming an importance comparable to that of the police, the judiciary, or the fiscal apparatus. As occurred with several strategic innovations that paved the way for the establishment of modern administrations, this decisive event in the history of the archive occurred during the French Revolution. On the seventh of Messidor II (June 25, 1794), the revolutionary convention approved legislation that granted the national archives jurisdiction over all public records in the whole territory of the French republic.[11] For the first time at the national level in a major country in the Western tradition, "an organic administration of archives covering the whole extent of existent depositories of older materials and of record-producing public agencies was established."[12] France's national archives, which in the following decades became a model for record management throughout Europe, relied on three principles: they were centralized, open to the public, and geared toward the protection of private property.[13]

With the law of the seventh of Messidor II, archives entered modernity. In addition to centralization, which enabled governments to supply their national archives with plenty of material and intellectual resources, two other pillars of the modern management of records came along in the nineteenth century: the employment of a body of professional archivists and the availability of sound archival theory. The latter reached a turning point when the French archivist Natalis de Wailly stated the principle of "Le Respect des fonds" in 1841.[14] He recommended arranging records in a way that complied with their unique connection to the office that had produced them. This was the first formulation of a norm that became later known as the principle of provenance, the cornerstone of modern archival theory, which prescribed "respect for every original order, for every original designation."[15] By formulating "Le Respect de fonds," Natalis de Wailly determined the obsolescence of the principle of pertinence that had ruled over eighteenth-century archives. While the principle of pertinence requires archivists to classify records by subject, thus following an order reminiscent of encyclopedias in the age of enlightenment, that of provenance states that documents generated by the same agency are to be placed in one record series and lie side by side on the shelves.[16] It dictates that homogeneity of source rather than of subject matter constitutes the criterion for grouping records.[17] As the origin is an intrinsic feature of a record, the criterion for arranging the archive emerges from within the records themselves. It is not the result of a preexisting, transcendental order, as occurs with the encyclopedia-based principle of pertinence, which relies on the idea that human sciences are *a priori* rationally enchained.

The formulation of "Le Respect des fonds" and the principle of provenance represented the completion of a true revolution, which could be compared to what would occur in the classification of books if libraries started to shelve volumes on the sole basis of their authors. If this were the case, all the texts written by, for example, Umberto Eco, would be stored together regardless of their being novels, philosophical treaties, or handbooks for writing dissertations. Once arranged in such way, libraries would outline a universal roster of writers (updatable with geographical and historical data) that would make it impossible to separate books on the basis of the different fields of knowledge that comprise our encyclopedia. By switching to provenance as its guiding concept, the archive brought about a similar outcome. It relinquished its encyclopedic ambition, but achieved a previously unknown ability to reproduce both the history and the geography of record-creating administrations: record arrangement became a form of mapping. As Sven Spieker argues, "The PP [principle of provenance] reminds us that in an archive, it is never just a question of what is being stored bur rather of what is being stored *where*. Archival storage has something to do with topology, and the authority of the archivist derives from his or her ability to interpret texts in relation to both their place in the archive and to the place from which they emerged."[18] What I would like to emphasize is that in tying each record to its own origin, the archive undertook a process of individualization. When a record must be linked to the unique agency that created it, it can be stored in only one position: records are treated as individuals defined by both their specific relation to their origins and the unique place they occupy on the shelves.

Assisted by sound scholarship and tested by the daily practice of preserving, arranging, and retrieving papers, nineteenth-century archivists elaborated and verified the epistemic paradigm that would inform archival theory until the 1970s. Keeping governments' and corporations' documents, saving society's memory through the conservation of its vital records, and preserving the original papers against which the authenticity of legal deeds could be checked, all became possible because a well-defined epistemology was leading the practice of the archive. Two principles backed the archivist's work: (1) truth exists in the form of an original record that has been safely stored through procedures in compliance with the archive's established protocol; (2) a record achieves sense only within the series where it belongs. Since series are arranged by assembling together documents created by the same agency, from this principle it follows that a researcher can correctly understand the meaning of a record only by relating it to the original source of its creation. I believe that this method, which I would like to call "apprehension through localization," is also one of the defining traits of the novels that refer to the realist tradition. The archival paradigm leads to a type of truth that is original, contextual, and serial. The pragmatic and bounded nature of this truth is evident; it is also no less clear that, since its inception, it has functioned well for millions of people working in offices, police stations, courts of law, and history departments all over the world.[19]

Parallel to its methodological development, the newly empowered archive of the nation state experienced a significant expansion of its tasks. A drive toward individualization, too, characterized this process, as the archive, in a development that Fielding would have certainly appreciated, became increasingly involved with the private lives of common citizens. Once more, the piece of legislation that set this process in motion came into force during the French Revolution. The constitution of September 3, 1791 states that "the legislative power will establish for all the citizens, without distinction, a system for recording births, marriages, and deaths; it will appoint public officials who will receive and store the records."[20] For governments, creating permanent records of citizens' lives answered the challenge presented by the new relations between individual and territory that the French Revolution had determined.[21] In the ancien régime, people were both subjects, quite often by birth, to local political entities—such as the town, the rural commune, the *seigneurie*—and members of intermediate civic bodies, such as corporations and *confréries*. As Balzac writes in *Une Fille d'Ève*, "Dans le dix-huitième siècle chacun avait une position sûre et definie" [In the eighteenth century everybody had a firm and defined position].[22] Ancien régime subjects' very clothes hinted at their trades, social statuses, and domestic dwellings. By abolishing feudal rights, corporations, and cities' privileges, the revolution cut all the links that tied individuals to their own traditional positions and created a nameless and worrisome, from the point of view of the elites in power, multitude. In the following decades, the social upheaval engendered by the Industrial Revolution and the ensuing migration from the countryside to the metropolitan areas compounded the problem by amassing an anonymous crowd of wage-workers in the suburbs. For the modern state, it became imperative to substitute bureaucratic identification for the territorial, inherited identity that had characterized the ancien régime society.

The systematic identification of citizens was an archive-based project that only modern administrations relying on efficient systems for storing, cataloging, and retrieving records, could take on. No government could have instituted either the register of births, marriages, and deaths or the nationwide archive of criminal records without turning to archival scholars' theoretical knowledge and archivists' practical expertise with records, files, folders, and calendars: it was the archive that enabled rulers to apprehend the individual. To use a digital age metaphor, the archive represented both the software of the new individualized power, its ubiquitous nervous system whose terminals collected basic data, and the hard disk where long-term memory was stored and kept available for future use. Nineteenth-century writers who wanted to base their works on proven records of individuals' existences found in this powerful and reliable archive the discourse that could legitimize their novels as truthful texts. Only four decades prior to the French Revolution, a writer in search of documentation, such as Fielding, had to choose between the tales of heroic *res gestae* and the collections of personal correspondence, i.e., between narrating histories of kings and generals or epistolary novels of love and seduction. With the advent of the modern archive, even narratives of private events could receive the support from official records that used to be reserved to the narration of public affairs in the previous ages. What is more, the chief object of novelistic representation during the nineteenth century, the citizen of industrial society, largely appears as an archival construct. The bureaucratization of the individual was the result of a process that once again started at the outset of modernity, within the context of the radical changes in the features of power that framed the reform of the archive. By achieving an increasing capacity to grasp the single item through the understanding of its milieu, the archive paralleled power's growing ability to identify, and thus govern its subjects. At the time when the ancien régime was collapsing, as Michel Foucault has taught us, a break in the nature of power led to a greater individualization of all the relations submitting subjects to authority in society: "Power [in the ancien régime] had only a weak capacity for 'resolution,' as one might say in photographic terms; it was incapable of an individualizing, exhausting analysis of the social body. But the economic changes of the eighteenth century made it necessary to ensure the circulation of effects of power through progressively finer channels, gaining access to individuals themselves, to their bodies, their gestures and all their daily activities."[23]

The drive toward grasping finer and finer traits of its subjects defines power in the entire modern age. It has evolved from the written descriptions of passport holders' physical features in the nineteenth century to the collection of data regarding bank accounts, DNA profiles, and fingerprints that we are experiencing today. The fashioning of increasingly sophisticated instruments for identifying citizens has gone hand in hand with the "incorporation" of authority, a Foucauldian term describing power's ability to access the bodies of its subjects. This process developed in concert with the evolution of the human sciences toward the gathering of new knowledge on human behavior. The epistemological leap these disciplines made toward the end of the eighteenth century, when they began formalizing their language and defining the object of their practices, was crucial to this development. What was the role of the archive in the truth-finding operations of anthropology, criminology, and sociology, in addition to all the branches of knowledge whose name includes the root "psycho," as Foucault wanted to call them?[24] Saying that it was essential would sound like an understatement, at the very least. The archive has provided the human sciences with techniques, theories, and experiences that have been essential to the definition of their object, the individual human being. At the core of the human sciences, in the method for carrying out experiments, verifying hypotheses, and inferring laws, there lies the archive:

> Thanks to the *whole apparatus of writing* that accompanied it, the examination opened up two correlative possibilities: firstly, the constitution of the individual as a describable, analyzable object . . . and secondly, the constitution of a comparative system that made possible the measurement of overall phenomena, the description of groups, the characterization of collective facts, the calculation of the gaps between individuals, their distribution in a given "population."
> These small techniques of *notation, of registration, of constituting files*, of arranging facts in columns and tables that are so familiar to us now, were of decisive importance in the epistemological "thaw" of the sciences of the individual.[25] [my emphasis]

The modern individual began to appear in the records regarding soldiers, inmates, employees, and pupils that armies, prisons, hospitals, asylums, factories, and schools were storing. This practice enabled those institutions to accumulate data on how human bodies' behaved under the methodical pressure of disciplinary power; it created the context in which a *"pouvoir d'écriture"* that "modeled itself after traditional methods of administrative documentation" materialized.[26] It was because of the archive's ability to seize the single datum and arrange it into overarching, meaningful units—the file, the series, and the entire collection—that archival discourse could lend its methods to human sciences. Archival know-how made the apprehension of the human being possible: it was instrumental in collecting data on individuals and situating this information into coherent frames of reference. In the modern age, gathering knowledge on humans is an archival process. Its first step, the examination, places individuals "within a field of surveillance" and "situates them within a network of writing; it traps them in a mass of documents that capture and fix them."[27] Bureaucrats who had learned how to gather and arrange data from their experience in archives were able to make individuals' names, physical features, and psychological traits emerge from obscurity.

In nineteenth-century realism, characters are fictional interfaces of these bureaucratically conceived individuals. Realistic characters can coalesce into credible human figures because archival and novelistic discourses participate in the same project: making the industrial city dweller visible through the storing of individualized knowledge. This program is political, as it provides power with cognitive tools that can help in governing the post-ancien régime society. It functions through the circulation of skills, notions, professional figures, media, and data. It accumulates one knowledge, which might originate in different sources (the pages of a realist novel, the police's archive, or the records in the register of births, marriages, and deaths), but still remains archival as far as its object, its epistemology, and its goal are concerned. This project is archival because the principle of "apprehension through localization" represents its key epistemic asset. It relies on the particular archive*ness* that pervades the industrial society in response to the anonymity fostered by the collapse of the ancien régime. The very shift of the archival institution from the "principle of pertinence" to that of "provenance" demonstrates how a particular, more individualized archive*ness* effected the theory of the archive and ultimately its functioning.

The bureaucratization of the modern individual as an archive-backed project frames the emergence of the paradigm of legitimation in the genre of the archival novel. Within this paradigm, the archive functions as a guarantor of truth for novelists seeking to legitimate their works as reliable accounts of facts. As practitioners of a genre with no literary pedigree, early modern novelists had strived to enhance the status of their works by presenting them as truthful texts, as Fielding's meditation demonstrates. To this purpose, they often titled their novels "histories" and "memoirs," or disguised themselves as editors. They situated their texts within discourses that society endowed with truth-bearing ability, such as historiography or (auto)biography. After being reformed during the French Revolution, the archive enhanced its ability to be one of the discourses that could support the novel's claim to truth. Adopting the paradigm of legitimation enables realist writers to highlight their works' consonance with the larger archival discourse of the age. In this operation, what matters is the presentation of the novel's defining traits as elements belonging to a veridical discourse. By referring to the prestigious institution that helps the nation state to know its past, define its subjects' identities, and ascertain the legitimacy of individual claims to private property, practices such as storing records in the text, shaping the textual structures after the archive, and anchoring plot turns to the discovery of archival documents support the novel's claim to truth. For writers who operate within the paradigm of legitimation, copying documents into the text shows that their works tell true stories, adopting the archive as a structural model guarantees their narratives' epistemic rigor, and basing the building of characters on archival proofs links their novels' diegesis to instruments that science is applying to the understanding of the human being. Furthermore, nineteenth-century writers' practice of establishing a nexus between novelistic characters' personal features, their familial situations, and the contexts of their upbringings, corresponds to the classic archive's principle of relating the meaning of a document to the source of its creation. Novelists wanting to support the truth-claim of their narratives on hard evidence could find in this archive the proofs they needed: the certified records of private lives that Fielding craved. As it fits into the epistemic frame of realism, the paradigm of legitimation belongs squarely to the nineteenth century and finds its most successful practitioners in authors such as Manzoni and Balzac. Consequently, its hegemony declined in correspondence to the crisis of literary realism, as is proved by Gustave Flaubert's *Bouvard et Pécuchet* (1881), which exposes the realist novel's and the archive's truths as the products of dubious, politically motivated procedures rather than of coherent and epistemically sound operations.

In order to function, the paradigm of legitimation needs the concomitant presence of two conditions: (1) The archive and the novel apply homogeneous tools to their core business, the apprehension of the individual, and (2) the polity regards the archive as a trustworthy institution. While the former condition had been in place since the French Revolution, it began to fade away in the last two decades of the nineteenth century. The key factor in the opening of an epistemic distance between the archive and the novel was the fact that the written report gradually ceased to be the chief instrument for the identification of individuals. In the course of the 1880s, a physician working for the police in Paris, Alphonse Bertillon, perfected an identification system that combined "photographic portraiture, anthropometric description, and highly standardized and abbreviated written notes on a single *fiche*, or card," and organized "a comprehensive, statistically based filing system" for the management of these data.[28] As the mechanical substituted for the human in the identification of citizens, "the witness of the former age was replaced by the memory of instruments": it goes almost without saying that novelists who adopted the paradigm of legitimation were first and foremost witnesses of their society.[29] After Bertillon's *fiche signaletique*, writing the story of an individual (a procedure that had been applied to the making of passports for over a century) in order to identify him or her became an obsolete practice. As Matt Matsuda notices, "rather than considering the subject a story, the fiche was a record of the subject as an arrangement of descriptive parts."[30] It is true that the *Bertillonage* did not bring about the complete dismissal of writing as a medium in identification procedures. In Bertillon's system, side by side with a series of anthropometric measurements and a photograph, a *portrait parlé*, which, incidentally, represents the clearest definition of realist writers' technique for describing characters, still played a crucial role in the identification of criminals. In spite of this, a crack, initially negligible but in the long run decisive, began to open up between writing as a medium and the representation of physical bodies: "The revolution of '*Bertillonage*'... did not lie chiefly in the invention of a new instrument of identification but rather in the disruption of the established ways to conceive a relation to the body, a problem that was tied to the emancipation of the sign from its physical substratum."[31]

Freeing the sign from a direct relation to the body struck at the core of the project of realism. What matters here is that writing ceased to represent the cutting edge technology for the definition of individuals, a reality that was reinforced with the introduction of fingerprinting in Europe and the United States at the beginning of the twentieth century.[32] A significant consequence of the diminished role of writing in identification procedures was the fact that, after functioning for a century as the laboratory for experimenting techniques of description, the novel was free to deal with other, more intriguing objects than the physical features of human beings, buildings, and cities. But much more important was the end of the consonance between the archive's epistemology and the novel's, an agreement that had enabled realist writers to craft reliable portraits of recorded individuals. The type of relation that the novel established with the archive in the age of realism, whereby novelistic writing belonged in the larger archival endeavor of the bourgeois society, became a thing of the past.

As for the archive's prestige as a trustworthy institution, it met formidable challenges throughout the twentieth century. This erosion of trust began with the perception that the archive was simply sinking under the excessive weight of its own records. In the twentieth century, because paper was available almost without limits and machines were helping clerks to drastically reduce the labor needed to reproduce originals, bureaucracies created an amount of documents and copies that was unthinkable in previous ages. As Sir Hilary Jenkinson argued, while the archives of the past had to be protected from destruction, those of the future had to be saved by preventing the accumulation of records at the source: a sensible administrator "must preserve as little as possible."[33] In this context, the modern archivist's main problem is appraisal, i.e., how to select the records to be stored out of the huge mass of material coming from public and private institutions.[34] While Jenkinson situates the beginning of the archive's hypertrophy in the First World War, all the technological innovations that increased bureaucrats' ability to create and reproduce records compounded the problem throughout the twentieth century.[35] As Alexander Stille notices, storage consumes nearly half of the United States National Archives' budget so, "ironically, the more information it keeps, the less money is has to spend on making it available to the public."[36] Nowadays, a true information explosion is taking place, to the point that "six rows of shelves on a single floor hold all of the documents generated by the U.S. Supreme Court in its first 140 years, while it takes the rest of the floor, the equivalent of about half a city block, to house the papers from the last sixty years."[37] Even though this mass of paper can be enormously reduced in size through an appropriate use of digital technology, it still "presents problems of control and access.... The problem is information overload."[38]

In the twentieth century, having to destroy almost all of the records that arrive to its repositories undermines the original reason for the archive's prestige, its being the institution that receives society's papers in consignment and guarantees their safe storage. As the archive's epistemology displays other inconsistencies (in terms of the archive's connections to political power, as well as its inability to keep its holdings in order), the once smooth agreement between the archive's and the novel's cognitive projects falters. The epistemic obsolescence of the written report as an instrument for the identification of individuals, the perception of the archive's hypertrophy, as well as the sense of archivists' inability to properly manage the records sent to their repositories, all created a favorable context for the gradual coalescence of the paradigm of challenge. The emergence of a new matrix for archival fiction in the twentieth century amounts to a shift in the key concern of the archival novel: the validation of the text's truth in the paradigm of legitimation is replaced by the demonstration of the archive's conventionality, and ultimately literariness, in the paradigm of challenge.[39] Within this critical framework, the set of practices applied to the composition of an archival novel remains the same as in the nineteenth century: copying records, shaping the text as a dossier, and defining characters and plots through archival procedures. What changes is the orientation of these instruments, or, to use an electric metaphor, their polarity. Within the paradigm of challenge, novelists relate their work to archival practices not to support the verisimilitude of their texts, but to detect the errors, frauds, and/or (ab)uses of power that have led to the creation and storage of records. While significant features of the paradigm of challenge already appear in certain modernist works, a proper example being William Faulkner's *Go Down Moses*, it is in postmodernism that archival novels meant to question the archive's epistemology achieve true formal definition.[40] One of the first novels to be fully shaped along the lines of the paradigm of challenge is Leonardo Sciascia's *Il consiglio d'Egitto* (1963).

Set in eighteenth-century Palermo, *Il consiglio d'Egitto* tells the story of abbot Giuseppe Vella—a historical figure whose life and action are documented—and how he forges a medieval Arabic codex, "Il consiglio d'Egitto." Vella's fake manuscript reconstructs the origin of feudal privileges in Sicily at the time of the Norman invasion of the island in the eleventh century AD. Since it "proves" that Sicilian barons usurped their prerogatives by infringing upon the ancient rights of the Crown, it ends up supporting viceroy Caracciolo's program of curtailing the privileges of the aristocracy. For more than ten years, Vella's papers are considered authentic, but this occurs only because they narrate Sicily's history in a manner that legitimizes the program of the political leaders in power. Accordingly, in 1795, when the fear of the French Revolution puts a halt to the reforms started by Caracciolo, the authenticity of Vella's forged documents is questioned. Aware that his position has become unsustainable in the new political climate, Vella gives up and confesses his fraud to his superior.

In and of itself, Vella's forgery is nothing more than a highly evolved prank. As he himself reveals when he confesses his crime, the watermark indicating the place where the paper of his "Arabic" codex was made reads "genova," by any means the name of a Christian city. Given the sophistication of eighteenth-century instruments for inspecting archival proofs, Vella's manuscript could not have survived a careful examination conducted according to the rule of diplomatics, the science that deals with the authenticity of documents. One of the fundamental assertions of the treatise that established diplomatics, Jean Mabillon's *De re diplomatica* (1681), was that "the context of a document's creation was made manifest in its physical and intellectual form."[41] An average investigator would have easily inferred from its material constitution that Vella's codex had been created in a fraudulent context. But in *Il consiglio d'Egitto*, an entire social group, Sicily's nobility and clergy, rather than a professional archivist, is responsible for verifying the authenticity of Vella's codex. In other words, while Mabillon took for granted the investigator's impartiality, Sciascia contextualizes the investigation. It is the shifting of political and economic interests within the elite in power that determines the status of the manuscript. By showing that the authenticity of a record is contingent on the political climate of the moment, Sciascia demonstrates how the core operations of the archive can be biased. And this appears even more significant since Vella's counterfeit records deal with the origin of law and power, that elusive ἀρχή which is inscribed in the archive's etymology, as Jacques Derrida reminds us.[42] However, the pristine document that levitates high above all human struggles does not, cannot exist. In the archive, we can only find proofs of practices of power that are rooted in conflicts. The epistemic consequences are devastating: if a forgery of the dimension of Vella's is accepted for more than a decade and then unmasked on political rather than philological ground, then the truth of the archive is exposed as opinion.

As *Il consiglio d'Egitto* proves, the key move in the paradigm of challenge is contextualization. In Sciascia's novel and in other texts that adopt the same approach to archival discourse, archivists, record creators, and record analysts are critically observed in the very moment they carry out their operations, as if they were performing an experiment in a laboratory. Ultimately, this operation corresponds to situating the public archive in its historical context: it is by grasping the complex interaction of social forces fighting for power during the decline of the ancien régime that Sciascia can understand the role played by the archive in that transition and turn this understanding into novelistic material. Within the paradigm of challenge, novelists rectify the approach to public records that had defined the encounter between novelistic and archival discourses at the dawn of the novel's golden age. Rather than supporting their texts' truthfulness by way of public records, as Fielding advocates, these writers see in the historicization of the archive's procedures the sole method that can lead to the production of honest, trustworthy prose. This approach foregrounds the context for the creation and the arrangement of records in a way that is absent in archival novels written within the paradigm of legitimation. In the latter, what chiefly matters to writers is the exhibition of the novel's foundation in the archive. Instead, novels like *Il consiglio d'Egitto* investigate the cognitive operation that is embedded in that foundation; in a sense, by showing the base of the base, i.e., the epistemic archive of the archive, they are archival to the power of two.

The thrust to place the practice of the archive, from the creation of records to their arrangement via the principle of provenance, in its social, cultural, and political context is also present in archival discourse after 1970. Terry Cook, an eminent Canadian archival scholar and archivist, characterizes "archival postmodernism as focusing on the context behind the content; on the power relationships that shape the documentary heritage; and on the document's structure, its resident and subsequent information systems, and its narrative and business-process conventions as being more important than its informational content."[43] The digital age and the ensuing change in the conditions for the creation, transmission, appraisal, and storage of records are responsible for this shift in archival discourse. As Dan Zelenyj puts it, "the difficulties of managing and preserving electronic records, arising principally from the growth and physical character of digital information, necessitate a thorough re-examination of the essential functions and activities of the record-keeping professions, and of their underlying theoretical, methodological, and practical bases."[44] To take on these difficulties, in dealing with records generated by bureaucracy, archivists should concern themselves "more with the analysis and management of functions and processes than with physical records."[45] Contextualization represents the archivist's response to the fact that a record displayed at the computer terminal "might exist in 2,000 different versions each year"; or, in other words, to the disappearance of the document, that artifact which was expected to establish unequivocal relations to both its creators and the events it recorded.[46]

In both postmodern archival novels and archives, to focus on context implies dealing with the intentionality of archival practices. Novels show how various social groups, each one supporting specific agendas and enjoying different amounts of power, struggle to take control of the archive. Deciding which documents are to be stored, which relations between records are to be fostered, how, when, and why to destroy papers, all these practices affect the distribution of power/knowledge in society.[47] Archival novels put tags on these decisions by identifying the individuals and groups that benefit from them. Then, archival procedures lose their *super partes* aura and appear to be as partial and subjective as any human endeavor. What is at stake in postmodern archival theory is the appraisal of documents, the crucial phase in which archivists decide which papers are worthy of being stored in the archive. In one of the most innovative cases of this practice, the macroappraisal model adopted in the national archives of Canada, archivists decide what to keep and what to destroy through "a functional analysis of the interaction of citizen with the state."[48] This method aims at documenting not so much the activity of the government's agencies as their impact on society, including citizens' reactions to the state's policies; it "deliberately seeks to give voice to the marginalized, to the 'Other,' to losers as well as winners, to the disadvantaged and underprivileged as well as the powerful and articulate."[49] The Canadian macroappraisal model suggests that postmodern archives and novels implement one strategy: foregrounding the political nature of archival operations. While the archive achieves this goal by opening up its facilities to the demos knocking at its doors, the novel does so by denouncing the aberration that the archive might reach should its project coincide with that of political power.[50]

Realism and postmodernism, the two ages in which the novel and archive develop their most significant affinity as far as their cognitive projects and the tools for realizing them are concerned, share a common characteristic: in both epochs, significant innovations change the theory and the practice of the archive. In the nineteenth century, the centralization of the archives in Western Europe, the key role they play in the identification of citizens, and their contribution to the development of human sciences, all pushed toward a quantum leap in archival discourse. The evolution of archival theory that led to the definitive formulation of the principle of provenance demonstrates this point. In the last three decades of the twentieth century, instead, both the digital age and the political pressure from social groups up until then excluded from the archive have brought about another revolution in archival practices. The record's material and conceptual nature, as well as key concepts (record group, provenance, and appraisal, to name just a few) in the discourse of the archive, has moved from their classical definition into a new paradigm that emphasizes context, immateriality, multiple agency, and endless reproducibility. Consistent with its nature as a literary genre whose only ethics is knowledge, as Milan Kundera wrote, the novel displays a keen interest in the archive when the latter becomes a laboratory for experimenting with epistemic tools, testing cognitive theories, and figuring out imaginative methods for managing information, as occurs in the nineteenth century and in the last thirty years of the twentieth century.[51]

The interpretive metaphor for this relationship is not dependence, whereby one of the two discourses relies on the other for elaborating the epistemic instruments it needs, but osmosis. A continuous stream of ideas and tools circulates through archives and novels, a flow of theoretical and practical notions that springs from their participating in one cognitive enterprise: the hoarding of knowledge on society and its preservation in the form of written paper.[52] In 1924, Arthur G. Doughty, as quoted by Hugh Taylor, argued, "Of all national assets archives are the most precious. They are the gift of one generation to another, and the extent of our care of them marks the extent of our civilization."[53] By documenting society's endless development, archives become its structured memory, a heritage that is passed across generations so as to tie together the dead, the living, and the unborn.[54] As for the novel, it is common knowledge that one of its keenest interests, too, is the narration of society, or better, the narration of the discourse that presides over a given society. As Lennard J. Davis wrote, "novels do not depict life, they depict life as it is represented by ideology."[55] Just as in the novel the representation of a given ideology becomes most effective when it takes place at the level of the text's narrative and symbolic structure (the ways the text tells its story and organizes an experience of the world), so too in the archive, where it is the order that enables archivists and researchers to make sense of records that conveys ideology. The system for arranging an archive invariably bespeaks the world vision, the attendant power structures, and the cognitive projects of the archivist, which in turn are a function of those dominant in society at large.

The ironic nature of the cognitive partnership developed by the archive and the novel in their endeavor to document ideology cannot be stressed enough. While the former, by creeping into the novel's fabric, helps in displaying the bureaucratic strand that cuts across modern fiction, the latter points to the many personal, societal, and political motivations that turn the most ancient veridical discourse of humankind's history into a provisional and historically conditioned practice. In so doing, the two discourses invalidate each other: the debasing of the novel's self-representation as the product of unbound creativity accompanies the dismissal of the archive's ethics of objectivity and sole commitment to the preservation of records. In a final twist of irony, the end result is helpful to both parties: it turns the novel into a less genial artifact that is more firmly grounded in the materiality of social practices, and the archive into a more fallible, and thus definitely human, enterprise.

3
I promessi sposi (1840). Storia della colonna infame by Alessandro Manzoni: The Power of the Archive

THE ARCHIVAL NOVEL SOLIDIFIES FURTHER AS AN EMERGING genre with the publication of Alessandro Manzoni's *I promessi sposi* (1840), a historical novel that claims to be true on the basis of its relation to the archive, all the while establishing a clear distinction between record and fiction. As Manzoni purported to have adapted the novel from an old manuscript, it may appear that *I promessi sposi* still operates on the ambiguous ground of Defoe's *Journal*, where the boundaries between the fictional work and the record blur. Having been employed in scores of gothic novels published in Manzoni's time, however, the artifice of the found manuscript was a patently literary device indicating not the text's absolute historicity, but its fictionality; indeed, no contemporary of Manzoni's believed *I promessi sposi* to be the actual rendition of an authentic document.

The methodological revolution that historiography undertook in the first decades of the nineteenth century was vital to the success of Manzoni's project of writing a novel that combined truth-bearing fiction and scrupulous historical research. As a newly founded academic discipline, history based its methodology on the rigorous examination of archival sources, which allowed Manzoni to narrate the historical past as a construct whose constituents had to be found in the archive.[1] But even though Manzoni's type of fiction and historiography shared the same reliance on the record as fundamental to discerning the truth-bearing paths to the past, the two discourses were unquestionably distinct as far as their cognitive methods and goals were concerned: the novel remained fiction and historical works continued to be veridical texts. The very fact that the novel, historiography, and the archive were different and autonomous discourses allowed Manzoni to think of a text where the relation between the novel, historical writing, and the archive could function as the generative core of a fictional work. In *I promessi sposi* the record represents the mediation between the text and the past, thus allowing readers to approach history as a discourse framed by the archive. The Manzonian novel is historical as far as its subject matter, but archival as far as the methodology that presides over the construction of the text and ultimately guides readers' experience of it. In Manzoni's historical fiction, the novel both approaches the past as a construct based on archival records and foregrounds the investigation that brings about this construct. In works that take this constructive process for granted—Scott's and Dumas *père*'s fiction for instance—the novel is simply historical, as a text that is built outside of the archive and not within, as occurs in *I promessi sposi*.

Establishing a clear-cut distinction between the archive and fiction allowed the archival novel to gain decisive ground with respect to its prehistoric phase. As fiction, the novel can be like an archive, thus applying the cognitive power of metaphor to the representation of archival discourse. At the same time, being fiction does not prevent the novel from functioning as a real archive: once records are transcribed into a fictional text, the latter stores them and becomes an archive by all means. As it functions within two discursive contexts at the same time, the archival novel entertains a continuous negotiation between two distinct methodologies for the apprehension of our lived experience. This epistemically rich dialogue allows readers to experience a constant shuttling between the archive and the novel, each time enjoying the privilege of knowing these discourses from both an internal and an external point of view; this cognitive negotiation is suggestive of what occurs to great actors playing for great playwrights (Pirandello for example) who require them to enter and exit from their roles during the performance itself.

The cognitive capacities of the Manzonian model of archival fiction became available to readers in 1840, when Manzoni published a book that contained two texts, *I promessi sposi*, a historical novel, and *Storia della colonna infame*, the history of a judicial error.² The volume carried two title pages; while in the first the title was *I promessi sposi*, in the second it read *I promessi sposi; storia milanese del secolo XVII scoperta e rifatta da Alessandro Manzoni. Edizione riveduta dall'autore. Storia della colonna infame; inedita.*³ No sign of separation interrupted the flow of the two texts, as the word "End" appeared only at the conclusion of *Storia della colonna infame*, at the bottom of the last page of the book. By adopting these criteria for publishing the most important work of his literary career, Manzoni seemed to suggest that *I promessi sposi* and *Storia della colonna infame* are to be considered a single entity, i.e., as "a coherent and undivided object articulated in a novel and a historical work."⁴

Both *I promessi sposi* and *Storia della colonna infame* are set in seventeenth-century Lombardy. *I promessi sposi* tells the story of two young peasants, Renzo and Lucia, who struggle to get married against the will of the local lord, Don Rodrigo. As no legitimate power can protect the two fiancés, they must leave their village and find separate shelters. During Renzo and Lucia's separation, their adventures intertwine with the historical events of the time: the Milan uprising of November 11, 1628, the famine of the following winter, the war over the succession to the duchy of Mantua, and the plague of 1630. Only when the plague kills Don Rodrigo, who is succeeded by a respectable Marquis, can Renzo and Lucia reunite, and finally celebrate their marriage. *Storia della colonna infame* recounts the trials against the anointers, scapegoats accused of spreading the plague in Milan. It focuses on the case of Guglielmo Piazza and Giangiacomo Mora, two defendants who lied under torture and accused themselves and other innocent people of nonexistent crimes. In *Storia della colonna infame*, Manzoni aims to prove not so much Piazza and Mora's innocence as their judges' culpability. By achieving this goal, he can argue that evil originates in human beings' perverse passions and not in the sociocultural environment where historical events occur. This argument allows Manzoni to both uphold the principle of personal responsibility and deny that divine providence might be involved in earthly injustice.

For those familiar with his thought, it may come as a surprise that an author like Manzoni, who always considered fiction and historiography as two fundamentally different types of writing, would even consider combining a novel and a historical investigation into one volume. I would like to argue that what connects *I promessi sposi* and *Storia della colonna infame* is the role that both texts assign to archival records as key instruments for a truthful representation of history; they articulate Manzoni's project of making the examination of documents the centerpiece of any historical narrative, whether fictional or not. Both texts can be viewed as experiments in which Manzoni attempts to verify if, and how, he can apply the document and the narrative to a truthful rendition of the past. Publishing *I promessi sposi* and *Storia della colonna infame* together in the same edition proposes an archival solution, so to speak, to Manzoni's theoretical problems. The volume published in 1840 is not a single work that can be viewed as the epitome of his thought regarding truth and invention in historical writing, rather two sequential texts resulting from nearly two decades of his pondering this issue; it is not the book but the dossier that can convey Manzoni's meditation. The same mix of autonomy and physical contiguity that defines the relationship between records in a record series also characterizes the connection tying *I promessi sposi* to *Storia della colonna infame* in their final edition. Records belonging to the same series can be letters, memos, or circulars, to name just a few examples; they can concern different events, or take distinct approaches to the same event. However, by "being related as the result of being created, received, or used in the same activity," they help in constituting a more general entity, the series comprising them.[5] Although both *I promessi sposi* and *Storia della colonna infame* belong to distinct genres and take different approaches to the plague of 1630, they are also parts of a more general, overarching unit, the dossier collecting Manzoni's records on seventeenth-century history.

The fact that archival tools represent Manzoni's solution to a crucial theoretical issue, such as the relation between truth and invention in historical writing, is consistent with the key role in the representation of the past that he has always attributed to archival records. Since his first attempt as a novelist, Manzoni made a commitment to resting his account of the past on solid documentation. In a letter to Gaetano Cattaneo (probably written in the first months of 1821), Manzoni jokingly stated that, after finishing the work that was keeping him busy, he would write only lyric poems, which did not need *notizie positive* (documented facts) but simply inspiration.[6] At the likely time of the letter, Manzoni was writing *Adelchi*, a historical tragedy set in the middle ages, as well as doing the preliminary investigation for the writing of *I promessi sposi*. Thus, what differentiates the writer of works set in the historical past, be they tragedies or novels, from the poet is the former's need to find proofs in historical records. The obligation to found his writing on solid documents is a constant in Manzoni's career. In 1850, he wrote that the only concern of historical writing was the *fatto positivo*, the same "documented" fact that he had mentioned almost thirty years earlier in his letter to Cattaneo. As his argument unfolded, Manzoni defined the ultimate source of historical proofs, the *fatto positivo*, as a piece of information *cavato da tal documento* [taken from a certain document].[7] At the root of historical knowledge—that *vero* [truth] which, according to Manzoni, ought to be the subject matter of morally and aesthetically sound literature—there is the record. Only the archive can certify that our knowledge of the past is sound.

Manzoni upheld an idea of literature that relied on documented evidence rather than on the author's inspiration and genius. Under this approach, by turning records into readable texts, literature behaved as an interface to the historical archive. In *I promessi sposi* in particular, the documents Manzoni was investigating became the source of his narrative of Renzo and Lucia's adventures. The pattern of exploring the archive, finding a record of interest, and turning it into a novelistic event recurs repeatedly throughout the novel. Manzoni's paradigm, the archival historical novel, does not allow him to create long chains of fictional episodes unsupported by archival documentation, as occurs, for instance, in Alexandre Dumas *père*'s works. In Manzoni's novel, fiction cannot roam freely over the fields of the literary imagination: records must keep novelistic invention in check. They provide fiction with its raw materials and establish the epistemic boundaries that imagination must not cross. Within this framework, in the two texts comprising *I promessi sposi/Storia della colonna in-*

fame, Manzoni pursues different agendas. In *I promessi sposi*, he sets out to prove that documents can mix with invention and produce a credible historical novel, provided the writer follows certain protocols in the treatment of archival materials. In *Storia della colonna infame*, he attempts to demonstrate how only a rigorous analysis of records can lead to a trustworthy narrative of the historical past.

The first step in Manzoni's archival strategy is a vintage novelistic device: the discovery of a hidden old manuscript. In the introduction to *I promessi sposi*, he pretends to have found a *dilavato e graffiato* [defaced and faded] manuscript regarding Renzo and Lucia's adventures, a clear allegory of the novel's origins in the archive. Rather than describing this aging document as a foreign object that mysteriously appears at the beginning of the story, as in the tradition of the gothic novel, Manzoni treats the manuscript as a historical artifact, a typical product of seventeenth-century culture. To this purpose, he exhibits an excerpt of the old document, obviously of his own making, written in the convoluted style of seventeenth-century prose. As Salvatore Silvano Nigro demonstrates, this excerpt is an accurate imitation, almost a cento, of Daniello Bartoli's "Introduction" to *Geografia trasportata al morale*.[8] Through a proper use of philology, Manzoni can historicize the manuscript and eschew the exoticism that usually surrounds the retrieval of old papers in nineteenth-century historical fiction. Thus, he can analyze the manuscript as an authentic record through the insightful questions of the narrator, his proxy in the novel. The narrator's questions portray the manuscript's anonymous author as someone who espouses certain defining traits typical of seventeenth-century culture such as the exaggerated respect for noble families. The anonymous writer also qualifies as a committed researcher who has carried out a thorough investigation into the events he narrates. As such, he has met with two of the story's characters, one of whom, Renzo, is the primary source of the narrative.[9]

In dealing with the found document, Manzoni follows a three step legitimizing strategy that involves (1) producing a record (the manuscript) that could appear authentic because of its intrinsic features, (2) attributing this record to a credible source (the anonymous author), and (3) proving that this witness was personally able to verify the story he heard. This method is rooted in legal discourse: a document tells the truth when its author is a reliable witness of the events he/she relates. The manuscript is fictional, but the control of its authenticity is not: it depends on a genuine procedure that would function even in the real world. The validation of the master record of the novel establishes a paradigm for approaching all the other papers stored in *I promessi sposi:* they must be subjected to the same procedure that the original document has undergone. In and of itself, the introduction of records cannot legitimize a novel as a trustworthy text. Proper protocols, taken from the prestigious discourses of the archive, historiography, and law, must function in the handling of archival proofs. They guarantee that documents provide the novel with truth and nothing more than truth.

As they are submitted to rigorous verification, records dictate the contents and the temporal boundaries of *I promessi sposi;* they are instrumental in building the novel's narrative structures. The first episode of the story and the particular structure of the plot represent two fitting examples of how Manzoni created a new paradigm of archival historical fiction by using documents not only as sources of, but also as frame for, narrative. *I promessi sposi* begins by situating the story in its geographical territory, a two-page description in the Nigro edition, and then zooms in on Don Abbondio, Renzo and Lucia's parish priest, who is strolling back home on the evening of November 7, 1628. As the reader suddenly sees the scene from the character's point of view, he/she makes out two *bravoes,* outlaws on some noble lord's payroll, clearly waiting for the priest. Something important is going to occur, an argument, perhaps an ambush, as the *bravoes'* formidable characterization suggests. But all of the sudden the action stops: instead of the encounter between Don Abbondio and the two waiting thugs, the novel offers the reader a three-page long list of the *grida* (edicts) that were approved against *bravoes.* This inventory begins with an edict signed on April 8, 1583, and ends with one published on February 13, 1632. As the narrator specifies, the only purpose of this anticlimactic catalog is to prove that *bravoes* did exist on the day the novel begins.

Manzoni mastered the rules of his trade. He knew how to

catch his reader's attention through a dramatic novelistic beginning, as his masterful shifting of perspective in the initial episode of his novel demonstrates. He was well aware that interrupting the action of *I promessi sposi* in order to copy a file of legal records amounted to a rejection of the novelistic canon. If he did so, it was because he intended to clarify once and for all what rule he was following in writing *I promessi sposi*: no narrative without records. *Bravoes* could become characters in his work because authentic documents proved that they indeed had existed at the time of the novel's setting. But this was not enough for Manzoni who, in defiance to the convention of storytelling, decided to paste in, in the middle of the novelistic action, those very records that could prove the truth of his account. In order to set the tone of the novel, not only did the *fatto positivo* need archival proofs, it had also to display them.

The sudden eruption of extradiegetic documents into the text shatters the illusionism of the first pages of *I promessi sposi*. When a novel stops the story in order to analyze records, it can no longer demand readers to believe in the perfect consistency of the novelistic world. *I promessi sposi* cannot be considered an "illusionist novel," in which "everything aims at creating the illusion of an autarkic world, a totality that readers can enter thus forgetting their own."[10] Archival historical novels verify records in the middle of the narrative, which place them squarely in the category of antiillusionism. Rather than entertaining readers with self-contained universes set in past ages, they aim at stirring up a debate on how history achieves truth. *I promessi sposi* follows a radically different paradigm from that of Sir Walter Scott's novels, the dominant model for historical fiction in the first half of the nineteenth century.[11] In *Waverley* and *Ivanohe*, for example, Scott never interrupts his stories in order to examine historical documents. His realism depends on highly refined illusionism rather than on the self-conscious analysis of records. In Scott's fiction, no intrusion from outside the self-contained world of the novel, such as a quote from nondiegetic papers, can break the illusion of the recreated past. Even illusionist novels, however, cannot avoid reflecting on those documents that represent the hidden foundation of the stories they narrate. Thus, in the revised edition of Scott's works, in 1829, *Waverley* is accompanied by eighty-six endnotes for analyzing the documentary sources that the novel hides. A similar strategy is adopted by Alfred de Vigny in the fourth edition of *Cinq-Mars* (1829), another illusionist historical novel that, according to its author, was more interested in the truth of general ideas than in historical details.[12] At the end of the day, even if this happens behind the screen of an external critical apparatus, illusionist historical novels, too, must recognize their debts to the archive.

An illusionist novel reminds us of a box: a wonderfully constructed container into which the reader is invited to for a while. And Manzoni manufactures a splendid one indeed at the beginning of *I promessi sposi*, complete with countryside landscape, characters, and action, only to break it into pieces when he asks readers to enter his archive and read with him a few legal records written in archaic Italian. He envisions a reader able to switch from the plot to the record series, from the enchantment of novelistic illusion to the task of carrying out an archival investigation.

When the list of the *grida* ends and Don Abbondio can finally move ahead and meet the two *bravoes*, he learns something that he would never have wanted to know, given the coward he is. In threatening language, Don Rodrigo's hatchet men tell the priest that their boss forbids him to marry Renzo and Lucia. This episode is the novelistic rendition of an actual edict, signed on October 15, 1627, which established severe punishments for threatening a priest out of celebrating a marriage.[13] Appropriately, later in the story, Azzecca-garbugli, an ambiguous lawyer that Renzo consults, reads a copy of this edict taken from his personal repository of legal papers.[14] As the story of the heroes' struggle to overcome the prohibition to get married, *I promessi sposi* hinges upon an actual record taken from the legal archive of the seventeenth century.[15] Here, the remark that the novel begins in the archive achieves a double meaning. It means that only upon Manzoni's retrieval of a record, the edict of October 15, 1627, can the writing of *I promessi sposi* start. It also indicates that it is up to an archival record to give the novel its first generative nucleus, in terms of characters, action, and intrigue. Since the retrieval of this old edict plays such an important role in the construction of the novelistic world, the novel must narrate it as its foundational act in the dialogue between Renzo and Azzecca-garbugli.

The long ellipsis interrupting the novel's main story line at the end of chapter 27 presents further proof of the close relation associating *I promessi sposi* to archival records. At this point, with the chronological time of the novel at the late fall of 1628, the narrator informs his readers that no significant changes are going to affect the characters' lives until the fall of 1629 (525). The following chapter consists of a summary of the historical events in that period, notably the famine in the duchy of Milan and the war over the succession to the duchy of Mantua. The novel's fictional characters, but not the two heroes, show up again in chapters 29 and 30, when Agnese, Perpetua, and Don Abbondio have to leave their village before the arrival of an invading imperial army. This digression, which does not affect the novel's main story at all, accomplishes the sole objective of translating a historical event, the invasion of the duchy of Milan in September 1629, into a novelistic episode. Here Manzoni reverses the use of the past as an exotic background for fictional adventures that characterizes popular historical novels in his age. In chapters 29 and 30, instead of substituting imaginary episodes for missing records, he narrates fictional events as pretexts for displaying historical documents: fiction becomes instrumental in discussing an event whose existence is firmly backed up by records. After this digression, the novel dedicates two more chapters to a historical event, the plague that strikes Milan and its territory in 1630. Only at the end of August 1630 can Renzo and Lucia's story resume and continue without further interruption until the end.

This sequence, comprised of ellipses, digressions, and summaries, is needed in order to adjust the plot to the records in Manzoni's possession. The chronology of *I promessi sposi* conforms to a time line connecting only historically proven facts. Manzoni must place the beginning of his narration at some point between October 15, 1627, the date of the edict punishing the threats to parish priests, and November 11, 1628, the day of the uprising of Milan in which Renzo is involved. Then, in Manzoni's archive, the next existing records regard two events: the invasion of the duchy of Milan by the imperial army in September 1629 and the plague of the spring/summer of 1630. Given the principle of narrating only documented evidence, these interruptions in the historical records force the writer to either fill this void by dint of summaries or translate it into ellipses. Other solutions, such as bridging the gaps in the historical archive by means of fictional adventures, become impractical given Manzoni's choice of keeping the story within the boundaries of archival proofs. The openings in the novel's time line correspond to the voids in the author's files: the archive commands the tempo of the plot.

With records functioning as the novel's backbone, the narrator of *I promessi sposi* dons the mask of a copyist/researcher. While copying represents the basic operation for transferring records from the archive into the novel, researching guarantees the selectivity of this process. Tellingly, it is when the narrator portrays himself in the act of copying that he suggests his closest identification with Manzoni. For instance, during an embarrassing dialogue between Don Abbondio and Cardinal Federigo Borromeo, the narrator states that "per dir la verità, anche noi, con questo manoscritto davanti, con una penna in mano . . . sentiamo una certa ripugnanza a proseguire" [to tell the truth, as we sit down with this manuscript in front of us, pen in hand . . . even we feel some reluctance to go on] (493). Later in the novel, the narrator pretends to be afraid of deserving the name of *copiator servile* (servile copier) for having blindly followed the anonymous writer through one of his several digressions (525). The narrator copying from the manuscript is the fictional double of Manzoni, the actual copyist who transferred real historical records from his archive to *I promessi sposi*. The expression "Manzoni's archive" does not assume a metaphorical sense. It refers to the actual collection of documents that the writer put together after researching public and private archives. It is, as it were, an archive to the second degree, similar to the repositories of papers and notes that researchers, in any field of knowledge, must assemble before sitting at their desk and write.

By suggesting a passive reception of archival records, Manzoni's self-representation as a copyist is deceiving. The novelist, as a historian would do, questions the archive: he looks only for those records that, by proving or disproving his hypotheses, can help him make sense of a narrow section of the past. As *I promessi sposi* often represents the author combing through archival papers, the close relation tying the novel to the archive becomes a novelistic theme in its own right. When Manzoni narrates the famine, for instance, he denounces the lack of documents on the government's policy, discusses the limits of available historical works, and concludes by stating that he is going to present readers with "la copia di quel ritratto doloroso" [the copy of that tragic picture] (531). Later in the novel, the chapters on the plague begin by describing Manzoni's investigation into historical texts and official papers. He reminds readers that he has examined and collated all the written memoirs regarding the topic, including those still unpublished, and several official records to boot. The purpose of this research is not the reporting of all these documents but the meaningful arrangement of the most significant events that occurred during the plague: "una notizia succinta, ma sincera e continuata, di quel disastro" [a succinct yet unbroken and authentic account of that catastrophe] (585). Later in the description of the plague, Manzoni twice explicitly mentions the archive of San Fedele, where he found the records regarding the anointers' ordeal (599, 623). Far from being a mere device for translating records into readable stories, fiction represents the heuristic thread connecting the evidence that the researcher/novelist finds in the historical archive. Writing an archival novel means making sense of the archive. To this purpose, novelists are required to both circumscribe the focus of their research and select records that can coalesce into a meaningful story. Here, fiction performs the same role as an interpretive hypothesis in historical investigation. Rather than roaming blindly among files and records, both the novelist and the historian carry out deliberate archival research.

When Manzoni mixes the analysis of records with the fictional story, he boldly shatters the wall between the novel and its critical apparatus.[16] By breaking from the Scottian paradigm that confined archival proofs to the endnotes, Manzoni anticipates methods that would become common only after 1970, with the rise of the "new historical novel."[17] Manzoni's visionary handling of documents within the main body of his work bespeaks of his interest in the tools for making sense of the past rather than in its mere reproduction. He behaved as a forerunner of narrative solutions later adopted by postmodern authors who wanted to discuss the methods for apprehending history rather than luring readers into illusory worlds.[18] It is this approach to historical novels that turns the archive, our chief tool for storing evidence on the past, into a protagonist of fiction. By dealing with history through the mediation of records, archival historical novels narrate the actual work of the historian: researching, choosing, and examining papers taken from archives. Archival historical novels help readers dispel the notion of the past as a sequence of facts already endowed with meaning. They foreground the operations that shape readable narratives out of the historical record. In so doing, they foster a sophisticated approach to history based on the understanding of not so much past events as the various readings of archival documents that different cultures and ages have generated.

Both *I promessi sposi* and *Storia della colonna infame* narrate the entire life cycle of a record, from its creation to its storage into an archive, as an exercise of power. In *I promessi sposi*, writing, the archival medium par excellence, is invariably performed by a person of authority, be it a parish priest, an innkeeper, a scholar, a noble lord, or a cardinal. Likewise, in *Storia della colonna infame*, the judges who write down the extorted confessions of Piazza and Mora perform the purest act of power: the use of torture to obtain self-accusatory confessions from two innocent defendants. Even though the consequences of writing may vary from sending away a monk to a remote convent to fabricating a wrong death sentence, the written word always spells out the unequal confrontation between the powerful and the powerless. As Nigro argues, paper, pen, and inkwell "mark and draw the destiny of the novel's characters."[19] Furthermore, storing a record in the archive preserves forever the power relation engraved in the written word, thus producing lasting consequences in the powerless' lives. Appropriately, *Storia della colonna infame* reminds readers that the names of Piazza and Mora became synonymous with infamy for more than one hundred seventy years, the time that separated their trial from the publishing of Pietro Verri's *Osservazioni sulla tortura* in 1804. In *I promessi sposi*, after his run-in with the law during the uprising in Milan, Renzo has a direct experience with how the police archive can banish outlaws from society by holding onto the records of their socially dangerous deeds.[20] Indeed, in *I promessi sposi/Storia della colonna infame*, the opposition between the powerful and the powerless matches exactly the divide separating the characters who control the archive from those who must endure it. As an intoxicated Renzo declares, significantly in the wake of the rebellion of November 11, 1628, "la penna la tengon loro: e così, le parole che dicon loro, volan via e spariscono; le parole che dice un povero figliuolo, stanno attenti bene, e presto presto le infilzan per aria, con quella penna, e te le inchiodano sulla carta, per servirsene a tempo e luogo" [they (the powerful) hold the pen in their hand; so their words fly away and disappear; instead, if a poor fellow speaks, they listen to him, right away catching his words in midair, and, with their pens, nail them on paper, to use them at the right time and place] (281). A well-defined sequence of archival practices—creating, storing, and retrieving records—allows the dominant elite to accumulate lasting knowledge on the underprivileged.

In *I promessi sposi*, writing affects the lives of the powerless because it is the medium employed by the ruling classes' emissaries to create permanent records. In Renzo's speech, it is by possessing durable knowledge and using it at their will that the powerful gain a decisive edge over the poor. The archive functions in one direction only: it funnels information about ignorant subjects to their rulers.[21] As a dossier, *I promessi sposi/Storia della colonna infame* records how the exercise of power and the practice of knowledge, in their indissoluble nexus, affect society. As it deals with the impact of archival practices on the lives of common people, it provides a type of information that, in Manzoni's time, was lacking in traditional historiography.

By placing *I promessi sposi* and *Storia della colonna infame* in the same dossier, Manzoni juxtaposes two stories that, albeit developing within one legal archive, end up with opposite results. The same judicial system that spares Renzo wipes out Guglielmo Piazza and Giangiacomo Mora, the anointers. The benevolent archive of *I promessi sposi*, where a marquis's word has enough power to cancel a warrant imposing the death penalty, lies side by side with the merciless legal repository of *Storia della colonna infame*, which stores extorted testimonies and never forgets what it keeps. As there is no doubt that Renzo would have faced Piazza and Mora's fate had he been captured, the different relations between narrative and documents ultimately explain the diverging endings in *I promessi sposi* and *Storia della colonna infame*. In the novel, fiction shields readers from the impact of the most unsettling records of the seventeenth-century archive, while in *Storia della colonna infame* the historical account presents them with a complete understanding of the brutal nature of those documents. As Manzoni proceeds from *I promessi sposi* to *Storia della colonna infame*, the truth of the archive counters the fiction of the novel.

By joining two texts in which narrative and documents play distinct roles, *I promessi sposi/Storia della colonna infame* invites readers to appreciate different manners of writing history. It fosters a thoughtful approach to the text(s), one that compels readers to check and compare the peculiar methodologies that inform the writing of *I promessi sposi* and *Storia della colonna infame*. This method is particularly needed as the latter handles the relations between truth, fiction, and the archive in a way that promotes an antifiction agenda. In this text, in order to hold the judges accountable for their egregious violation of the law, Manzoni carefully examines the interrogation of Piazza and Mora. Long sections of *Storia della colonna infame* expand on the *mise en archive* of oral testimonies; they explain how the court translated Piazza's and Mora's jumbled utterances into the written narratives of their supposed crime. As record creators, the judges took advantage of their unchallenged power in order to produce a document that appeared both formally authentic and substantially false: recording Piazza's and Mora's testimonies was tantamount to documenting an obvious lie. It was through the merciless use of torture that the court could force Piazza and Mora to invent their testimonies. But this is not all, as the judges were actively involved in the production of this invention by repeatedly prompting Piazza and Mora to review their versions of the events until their narratives achieved the desired consistency.

In *Storia della colonna infame*, Piazza's and Mora's testimonies are repeatedly defined as *invenzione*. In Manzoni's vocabulary, this term means fiction and, in particular, its pernicious tendency to make up stories. In order to counterbalance invention, by definition largely present in a novel, the publication of *Storia della colonna infame* alongside *I promessi sposi* brings to the fore the historical truth. As a critical double of *I promessi sposi*, *Storia della colonna infame* aims to prove that invention amounts to concocting deceitful narratives that end up hurting innocent people.[22] In this respect, Piazza's first confession appears exemplar. In order to make up an account that will satisfy his tormentors, Piazza attaches "a molte circostanze reali un'invenzione incompatibile con esse" [an incompatible invention to several true circumstances] (797). By mixing facts and invention, Piazza, the judges, and the clerks who record his story behave like historical novelists. Writing novels and lying share the same rhetorical procedure.[23]

Manzoni achieves the goal of denouncing the ethical flaws of novelistic invention at the price of undermining the archive's reliability. *Storia della colonna infame* demonstrates how an unchecked use of power mars the core operation of the archive. The very *mise en archive* of Piazza's and Mora's confessions becomes a fraud, which nonetheless produces a record that people trust for one hundred seventy-four years. At this point, after drastically questioning the objective foundation of the archive, the institution that makes the writing of history possible, Manzoni reaches an ironic crisis. Having attempted to demonstrate that a well-documented historical narrative represents the only ethically acceptable approach to the past, he finds himself denouncing the archive, the basis for any historical research, as a domain of fabrications. *Storia della colonna infame* begins by stating that the events it narrates "in un romanzo sarebbero tacciate di inverosimili" [would be considered unbelievable in a novel] (759). However, the attempt to demonstrate how the atrocity stored in the archive trumps the maudlin inventions of fiction ends up pointing to the creation of records as the real atrocity. *Storia della colonna infame* brings to conclusion premises that were already implicit in the representation of writing as a tool of power in *I promessi sposi*. Manzoni's inquiry into the trial of the anointers shows how the scribes' authority may achieve exponential efficiency in the archive. Since frail, passion-driven human beings enjoy the unchecked power that comes from controlling the creation of records, documents are subject to manipulation, destruction, and arbitrary arrangement. In other words, archives are prone to storing lies. To make the matter worse, as power invariably creates the conditions for its own persistency, the untruth can last indefinitely in the archive. At the conclusion of *Storia della colonna infame,* Manzoni praises Pietro Verri as the first scholar to understand (not until 1777) who had been the true wrongdoers in the trial of 1630 and to demand compassion for Piazza and Mora. This truth, however, had to remain hidden until 1804. Verri's father was the head of the city senate, Manzoni writes, the public body that had been responsible for the trial of the anointers one hundred forty-seven years earlier.[24] Not wanting to damage his father's reputation, Verri did not publish his *Osservazioni sulla tortura,* which was to come out only seven years after his death. Manzoni's investigation reveals that not only does the archive host a core of invention, as occurs to novels, but also possesses a superior ability to protect its lies. As for truth, it is up to a shrewd researcher to wrestle it out of the archive. Truth is not a gift; it is the prize awarded to smart investigators who know how to pierce through the layers of distortions, half-lies, and fabrications that the practices of power have deposited on records.

Manzoni destabilizes the archive by approaching records as if they were texts. This strategy can appear paradoxical for a writer who legitimized his only novel by giving it the features of a document. However, in *Storia della colonna infame,* it is by considering records as instances of textuality that Manzoni can expose their falsehood. This approach stands in opposition to archivists' relentless attempts to "compress" the meaning of the papers in their custody: "The archivist's main purpose is . . . to fix the hitherto undisciplined text—to fix it, and to fix it in place, to cut off any surplus energy within textuality."[25] Classic archival practices aim at imposing one context, the supposedly *original* one, on the record's content. "Archivists deploy provenance to defend the borders of context, to specify *for all time* the time when and place where the creation of meaning began and ended. This is the structure of a record."[26] In other words, archivists refuse to treat records as texts. If this were the case, once inserted in a chain of interpretations and references to other textual entities, records would lose their univocal connotation. As their meaning would change in correspondence to cultural trends, they would achieve the ability to evolve along a temporal axis. It is this susceptibility to transformation, however, that characterizes legal documents in *Storia della colonna infame*. This occurs because Manzoni inserts the record of Piazza and Mora's trial into a web of references: to laws, confessions of other defendants, statements by witnesses, city senate's letters, legal opinions on torture, and historians' judgments on the trial. Seventeenth-century archivists established a correct procedure for storing the record of Piazza and Mora's trial. By tying this record to one source, the tribunal that had tried the anointers, however, they also cut it out from its rich context: it was provenance and "an unblemished line of responsible custodians" at work, as Sir Hilary Jenkinson's archival manual recites.[27] Once prisoner of one context, the account of the trial could only possess one meaning: Piazza and Mora's guilt. Manzoni returns the record content to the many contexts where it belongs. By breaking the archival envelope that sealed the record, he reveals a different truth. Likewise, as he presents the temporal chain of its interpreters, from seventeenth-century historians to Pietro Verri, Manzoni shows how the same record could generate different meanings, each one tied to a specific historical condition. By no means, I must add at this point, did Manzoni want to suggest that truth was a subjective concept adjusting to cultural changes. Manzoni intended to demonstrate how truth, the one that human reason could produce when guided by Christian faith, inexorably emerged from the smoke of contrasting opinions. The slippage of meanings always comes to a halt in Manzoni's texts.[28] A kind of controlled, rather than unbound, textuality is what Manzoni applies to records. For the sanctity of the archive, the result remains equally devastating.

In *Storia della colonna infame*, Manzoni applies textuality to the analysis of records with an ease that may appear astonishing when one thinks that he employed the opposite method for the writing of *I promessi sposi*. In the novel, Manzoni plays the archive against fiction: records deny illusionism, establish the novel's temporal boundaries, and force the direction of the plot. In a word, Manzoni uses record*ness* in order to contain the novel's rich textuality, its ability to play with imagination and to allow for diverging interpretations. Rational Christian truth, which emerges from *Storia della colonna infame* only after shattering the official integrity of the document, belongs to *I promessi sposi* from the beginning: Manzoni put it there. For this reason, the novel needs records: by locating the text in time and space, they give it the one context that archivists covet and truth demands. In short, Manzoni behaves like an archivist when he writes a novel and a novelist when he writes a historical investigation. It seems to me clear, now, the sense of his operation in *I promessi sposi/ Storia della colonna infame.* Neither text can stand alone: the instruments employed to write the novel help in criticizing the historical investigation and vice-versa. *I promessi sposi* and *Storia della colonna infame* could achieve meaning only by belonging to one entity, while maintaining at the same time their own identities. Only in an archive can this occur. *I promessi sposi/Storia della colonna infame* is this archive: a repository of Manzoni's theories, of the practices of power in seventeenth-century Lombardy, as well as of the tensions between record*ness* and textuality in novels and historical investigations. Only an archive can hold together such a diverse array of themes, goals, and cultural forms and allow so many signifying forces to coexist without disintegrating the structure that hosts them. Ultimately, this is an ironic archive: it stores the reasons for its own dismissal, all the while standing tall as the sole instrument for arranging the documents of human experience in this world.

4
Balzac's *La Comédie humaine* or the Epic of the Archive

HONORÉ DE BALZAC'S *LA COMÉDIE HUMAINE* REPRESENTS THE most coherent endeavor to write archival fiction within the coordinates established by the paradigm of legitimation. This occurs in the very historical time when the nation-state is engaged in the project to identify its citizens by means of instruments created in the archive and then adopted by the police and the judiciary system. In this context, Balzac situates his writing workshop at a metaphorical crossroads where the distinct discourses embodied by the French national archives, the Paris police, and the law meet. Balzac's novels not only appear as symbolic forms of the nation-state, as Franco Moretti might argue, but also develop their signifying structures, in terms of plots, stories, and characters, along coordinates that are in sync with that state's program of drawing a cognitive map of its territory via the archivization of its population.[1] Which is to say that the nation-state's archive functions as the key semiotic frame for the readers of *La Comédie humaine*. To them, French society can make sense only because it is submitted to systematic reconnoitering by officials armed with archival expertise, as an unknown region that gradually achieves intelligibility after being observed by explorers' and cartographers' inquisitive gazes. The rhetorical constitution of *La Comédie humaine* increases the intensity of this experience: the sender of the text—an authority in possession of archival knowledge according to the parameters of archival fiction—is Balzac himself, in the form of both the author who signs the "Avant-propos" to *La Comédie humaine* and the omniscient voice that introduces the novels and disseminates piercing, clarifying comments throughout the narrative. By foregrounding the nation-state as a key agent in the textual productivity of the paradigm of legitimation, *La Comédie humaine* demonstrates how the logic of the archival novel and that of the official archive have been actually the same since the former's fledging days. In a reflexive move that is typical of the genre, Balzac's archival fiction unveils the concordance between its urge to record and governmental bureaucracies' need to gather data on the state's subjects. By founding his monumental oeuvre on this agreement, Balzac made a crucial contribution to the development of the archival novel. He proved that the genre could move in new directions besides those explored by historical fiction following historiography's new appreciation of the epistemic significance of the archive.

Balzac introduces *La Comédie humaine* as an archive-based project in a well-known passage of the "Avant-propos," where he maintains that his only duty as a writer is to be the secretary of French society.[2] Then, after calling his work a copy of social reality, as well as an inventory of human vices and virtues, he claims that writing novels amounts to "competing with the état civil." By defining his texts through terms and concepts borrowed from the lexicon of bureaucracy, Balzac situates *La Comédie humaine* squarely within archival discourse. What position, however, does Balzac envision for his novels within the archive? In particular, what relation does *La Comédie humaine* establish with the état civil—the register of births, marriages, and deaths—the most emblematic institution of the new regime of the archive following the French Revolution? Michael D. Garval has cautioned against reading Balzac's words as an affirmation of his ambition to mimic the realities of civil/bureaucratic society. This interpretation proves to be inadequate, Garval argues, "for it proceeds from an insufficient understanding of the état civil itself."[3] Rather than being the passive object of novelistic mimesis, the état civil functions as a model for the writing of *La Comédie humaine* through the latter's incorporation of the institution's particular logic into its representational strategies.[4]

While I agree that the reading of the "Avant-propos" as a restatement of Balzac's mimetic desire misses the point, I also believe that a more complex relation than the one Garval suggests ties *La Comédie humaine* to the archive. The état civil and Balzac's oeuvre are two of the several agents that cooperate in the realization of the modern French state's archival project. By considering the former as a model for the latter's approach to representation, Garval's analysis overlooks the active role played by the realist novel in that undertaking. I argue that the flow between the état civil and Balzac's novelistic architecture goes both ways, namely because Balzac's narrative functioned, during the time of its writing and publication, as an effective paradigm for thousands of clerks employed in the daily practice of the état civil. The bureaucratic institution and the novel play a game of give and take, of trading methods and epistemic principles, that is more elaborate than the mere incorporation of the état civil and its logic into the Balzacian world. Balzac can be viewed as an archivist not only because *La Comédie humaine* "is a civil register of the fictional society it depicts," but also, and more importantly, because a relation of mutual support ties this register to its bureaucratic counterpart.[5] While the fact that Balzac's fictional archive must rely on the real archive in terms of the procedures, records, and professional figures it integrates into its narrative fabric appears commonsensical, what remains less clear is whether the bureaucrat, too, may require the novelist's assistance. With regard to this point, the fictional and the institutional archives, I believe, operate in a regime of osmosis: techniques and conceptual categories, bureaucratic profiles and human types move from one to the other in both directions. This does not amount to the assumption, of course, that Balzac operated as a bureaucrat in the French state's administration, but that *La Comédie humaine* and the bureaucratic archive of its age share goals, means, and position (in terms of their ability to effect certain kinds of change/control/influence) vis-à-vis society. The proof of this epistemic overlapping lies in the very fabric of Balzac's oeuvre.

A horizontal fracture runs across the universe of *La Comédie humaine* so as to divide reality into two superimposed layers. While fictional characters' stories unfold on the surface, a powerful archive functions underneath. It stores records of individuals' successes and failures, deviant behaviors, and wealth. It comprises a plurality of agencies that, albeit operating in distinct fields, are all part of one larger archival endeavor. As occurs in *Modest Mignon*, where Balzac complains that no girl could enjoy a romance without being noticed by curious observers, the archive consists in a pervasive recording network. This ubiquitous control over people's lives, he writes, is typical of a civilization that takes note of the time in which coaches leave and return, registers the sending and delivering of mail, numbers street addresses, and institutes the cadastre.[6] The universe of *La Comédie humaine* is a version of Foucault's, and Bentham's, "Panopticon": for each individual, it determines a permanent and conscious state of visibility that makes possible the automatic functioning of power.[7]

In modern civilization, what matters is that the inquisitive eye invariably helps in creating a record: visual observation works for the archive. In Balzac's Panopticon, one of the most significant archives appears in *Splendeurs et misères des courtisanes:*

> La police a . . . des dossiers, presque toujours exacts, sur toutes les familles et sur tous les individus dont la vie est suspecte, dont les actions sont répréhensible. Elle n'ignore rien de toutes les déviations. Ce calepin universel, bilan des consciences, est aussi bien tenu que l'est celui de la Banque de France sur les fortunes. . . . Cette immense quantité de procès-verbaux des commissaires de police, de rapports, de notes, de dossiers, cet océan de renseignements dort immobile, profond et calme comme la mer.[8]

> The police keep dossiers, almost invariably exact, regarding all the families and individuals whose life may look suspicious and whose actions are reprehensible. The police know every detail of any deviations from the norm. This universal notebook, this budget of the people's conscience, is as well kept as the Bank of France's books on people's wealth. This huge amount of police records, reports, notes, dossiers, this motionless ocean of information sleeps deeply and quietly as the sea.

This archive can even store records on people's conscience, which, incidentally, represents one of the novel's typical fields of interest. A different archive, privately run by a group of loan sharks, but still able to collect records on society at large, is described by the usurer Gobseck in the homonymous novella: "Nous avons une èspece de *livre noir* où s'inscrivent les notes les plus importantes sur le crédit public, sur la Banque, sur le Commerce. Casuiste de la Bourse, nous formons un Saint-Office où se jugent et s'analysent les actions les plus indifférentes de tous les gens qui possèdent une fortune quelconque, et nous devinons toujours vrai" [We keep a kind of *black book* where all the most important notes on the public credit, the banks, and the commerce are recorded. Casuists of the stock market, we constitute a sacred tribunal that judges and analyzes the most indifferent actions carried out by those who own any kind of wealth: we always guess right].[9]

As it registers the movement of money throughout society, the usurers' livre noir outperforms the police's archive in both scope and efficiency: Gobseck and his associate can record data concerning any human action, while law enforcement agencies must limit themselves to collecting information on deviant behavior. In a universe where wealth measures the value of life, a similar role is played by the *Grand-Livre des rentes*, the book that registers government bonds, which becomes Balzac's quintessential archive. Throughout *La Comédie humaine,* a refrain continues to resonate: "*Il avait . . . (cinq, dix, soixante. . . .) mille livres sur le Grand-Livre.*" As this formula registers the successes and failures of Balzac's characters, the *Grand-Livre* equates individual destinies to their alienated value in the bourgeois society: their financial worth. A store of records created by way of a universal sign, money, the *Grand-Livre* becomes society's ultimate repository. Its capacity for grasping the meaning of human lives trumps even that of the law: at the end of legal procedures, it is in the form of money that characters reap their reward or receive their punishment.

A crowd of figures related in different capacities to the storing of records (judges, lawyer, clerks, and notaries) links the submerged archive of *La Comédie humaine* to the work's diegetic surface, the world of Balzac's characters. Although usually confined to minor roles, they constitute the fictional side of bureaucracy and make possible the encounters between major characters and the documents recording their destinies. Among all these bureaucrats, the notary stands out. Authentic mediators between records and human beings,

Balzac's notaries are present in almost all the stories narrated in *La Comédie humaine:* among Balzacian characters, being a notary is the most common profession. Notaries perform a vast range of functions: they register contracts and wills, serve as financial advisors, and operate as mediators in the real estate market. In a world where successes and failures translate into money, those who legalize contracts end up creating reliable records of human lives. As notaries know all the details concerning their clients' private lives, they behave as secular confessors from whom no secret can be concealed: "[notaries] take after priests, judges, bureaucrats, and lawyers."[10]

From a narrative point of view, notaries play a crucial role as active agents in plots: they deal characters their cards and draw the balances of their gains and losses at the end of their stories. A case in point is notary Mathias in *Le Contrat de mariage*. He assists Paul de Manerville in the lengthy negotiation of the financial aspects of his marriage and then receives the confidence of his personal ruin in the epilogue of the novel. In between the two encounters, the novel's three main characters, Paul, his wife, and his mother-in-law, have made different use of the opportunities they received at the signing of the contract of marriage. In this story, a notary's act functions as an implicit plot, a preemptive record of sorts, where all the potential directions that the novel could take are registered in an inchoate form. A symmetric procedure is applied to the writing of *Le Cousin Pons*. At the end of this story, in the office of notary Berthier, Schmuke signs the act that strips him of his right to his friend Pons' inheritance.[11] Here, a notarized paper certifies whether characters have achieved their goals or not; it attests that Mme Camusot has succeeded in her scheme to seize her cousin Pons' patrimony and that Schmuke is a naïve artist in a world of vampires. In Balzac's novels, notaries set up and untie plots by way of their professional relation with records. They prepare, legalize, and interpret documents that either lay the premises or draw the conclusions of narratives. In so doing, they become the fictional embodiment of the relationship tying the Balzacian novel to the archive. It is for this reason that they continue to appear throughout *La Comédie humaine:* novels need notaries to show what they are really narrating, the *mise en intrigue* of the nation state's archive.¹² As the archival foundation of the Balzacian novel irresistibly mixes with its narrative surface, one of the distinctive traits of archival discourse, the impossibility of separating the arranging system from the items it organizes, becomes part and parcel of *La Comédie humaine.*

The basic formula of the realist novel consists in this navigation between archives and fiction. I believe that realist writers could claim to be creating rigorous reproductions of the world at large because they depicted a society in which archival records were already registering the events of citizens' lives. And what allowed archivists to consider these records authentic and reliable was the assumption of a directly signifying connection between the word and the world, which also represents realism's epistemic foundation.¹³ The realist project of generating truthful documents of individual existences relied on the somehow tautological premise that the object of the novelistic representation, the industrial city-dweller, was already a recorded entity.¹⁴ It is in this homogeneity between its project and its object that novelistic realism found the epistemic reason for its success. Balzac's representational strategy achieved its goals by anchoring literary texts in a solid documentary foundation, an operation that often becomes the subplot of his novels. Literary realism did not consist in forging a language that could bridge the gap between signs and extralinguistic reality by virtue of its almost divine ability to grasp the essence of things. Realism thrived because it related written signs to other written signs, the word of the record to that of the fictional text. It seems to me that by way of this approach the debate on literary mimesis can also achieve a satisfying conclusion. As a concept that is logically untenable, because the linguistic sign cannot imitate things, mimesis, at least in nineteenth-century realism, achieves a more plausible sense if conceived as the relation between two homogeneous entities such as the novel and the record.¹⁵

A product of the archival turn that occurred at the end of the eighteenth-century, the realist novel strives to represent an individual who is the product of practices—from the creation of the état civil to the dressage of bodies in military camps, prisons, and factories—that are deeply connected to the archive and its bureaucratic know-how. The entire operation of nineteenth-century realism is self-reflective: with its storage of archival practices, the realist novel functions within the boundaries of a world that the archive is taming and preparing for novelistic representation. Its defining trait in this age, positioning the individual in its own milieu as a precondition for its explanation, squarely matches the modus operandi of an archive that arranges records according to their original provenance.[16] The beginning of *Le Père Goriot*, in which Balzac first delivers a detailed description of Madame Vauquer's boarding house—from the Parisian district and the street where the building is located, to the external façade, the garden, and the interiors of all the rooms, finally settling in the characters' own private quarters—represents a classic case of the novel's archival approach to the definition of its heroes.[17] Throughout the entire *Comédie humaine*, by describing with obsessive precision the physical settings for his stories, Balzac applies an epistemic paradigm that relates the apprehension of individuals to the mapping of their territories. Exactly as in the archive, where archivists can grasp the meaning of records only by relating them to the original context where they were produced, so Balzac outlines characters only in the physical locations, usually homes or work-places, where their identities can be cornered.

Once territorially situated, Balzac's characters are submitted to identification procedures that are in agreement with those employed by the various archival agencies functioning in the New Regime society.[18] Let us take, for example, one of the basic operations in Balzac's novels, the identification of individuals through proper names taken from the context of contemporary life. As Ian Watt argues, using ordinary rather than historical or type names became one of the defining traits of the novelistic form in the nineteenth century.[19] In that age, novelistic discourse attributed such a power of identification to the first and the last, patronymic name that it often used their combination to title novels, as in *Eugénie Grandet* or *Oliver Twist*, a habit that did not exist in the eighteenth century. In so doing, nineteenth century novels were abiding by the rules of their age's archive that prescribed to legally identify people only by way of their first and patronymic names. As occurs with all the identification systems, those implemented after the French Revolution, too, played a significant role in the construction of people's identity, rather than being mere bureaucratic devices for recording their names, physical traits, and nationality. They were instrumental in constructing the individual as we know it in modernity, just as drawing the borders of a country on a map was the first step for calling it a nation.[20] Identity is not a presence that existed before the identification system was created to grasp it; the two come into being together, as occurs with all the operations based on the archive. The methods we use for identifying people inexorably coalesce with the identity they help in producing: "the individual only existed *as an individual* by being identified."[21] Having one, unchangeable name is not a natural phenomenon but the product of decisions taken within a certain historical context; it was a law approved on the 11th of Germinal XI [April 1, 1803] that imposed fixed names for French citizens. During the Napoleonic age, for instance, the rule establishing the patronymic as the only legal name for a French citizen was instrumental in forcing a particular type of identity on Jews, who were used to identifying persons by way of two first names, their own and their father's.[22] When Balzac's novels named characters by way of their first names and patronymics, they surely displayed their author's project: realistically representing contemporary society. But they also helped in spreading the use of a politically charged system for identifying people and, more importantly, in creating a certain type of individual. In so doing, they qualified as agents in the nation-state's project of identifying its citizens on the basis of inescapable rules.

In order to understand the Balzacian novel's role in this project, let us take a closer look at *Le Père Goriot*. Sandy Petrey rightly argues that this novel aims to demonstrate how paternity has lost any referential value. During the Restoration, fatherhood became a convention that could function only under certain conditions. Goriot's two daughters prove this point by repudiating their own father when he can no longer provide them with money. He cannot satisfy the chief condition for paternity in a bourgeois society: the father's ability to transfer wealth to his children. Although I agree with Petrey's analysis, I would like to point out that Balzac's demonstration of the nonreferential nature of paternity in the

Restoration Age can work only because Goriot's two children happen to be girls. Upon their marriage, in obedience to the rules of the état civil, they had to take their husbands' last names. This bureaucratic, yet politically significant, detail allows the two women to feign not being Goriot's daughters. When Balzac named individuals, he followed the rules functioning in the nation state's archive, comprising those which caused the dissolution of a woman's identity into her husband's. He carried out, in the symbolic mode, operations that thousands of clerks were executing in registry offices throughout the country. While it made perfect sense for a realist writer to abide by his age's norms in a seemingly irrelevant question such as the legal name of a character, I would like to stress that through this compliance he also aided in enforcing those rules. In other words, his literary work helped to solidify, reify, normalize, disseminate, and reproduce in the domestic/leisure sphere of fiction and reading, the rules of the "contemporary discourse of power." Not differently from an employee in the nation state's archive, he was instrumental in producing a certain reality in the form of a particular identity for people. Since this reality matched the one that the contemporary discourse of power was molding, Balzac's works appear realist in a way unknown to novels written in different ages.

In addition to the establishment of the register of births, marriages, and deaths, the introduction of the passport and the fashioning of a reliable method for identifying criminals represent the other two pillars in the modern state's project of creating a reliable, bureaucratically ascertained identity for all of its residents. A passport, and any "ID" for that matter, "corresponds to an entire series of files chronicling movements, economic transactions, familial ties, illnesses, and much else besides—the power/knowledge grid in which individuals are processed and constituted as administrative subjects of states."[23] Since 1814, officials in charge of preparing passports were the first to use the *signalement*, the methodic recording of "name, age, hair, forehead, eyebrow, eyes, nose, mouth, beard, chin, face, skin color, and particular signs."[24] Anybody who is familiar with *La Comédie humaine* can understand that the *signalement* was the archival base for Balzac's descriptions of his characters.

The government-run archive of identification cards and the realist novel shared the epistemic core of their operations: both were the product of a practice in which writing served the visual. Until the introduction of photography for identification purposes in the 1870s, writing was the only medium for transferring onto paper the details that attentive eyes were catching in the world.[25] Balzac wrote his novels in an age in which thousands of public officials, all working in different capacities for the archive as judges, clerks, policemen, jailers, and employees of the état civil, strived to find the proper language for putting on paper what their eyes were recording of defendants, suspects, inmates, or common citizens in need of ID papers.[26] And the same questioning gaze assists the novelist and the official working for the archive. As meticulous beholders of details, both the writer and the bureaucrat apprehend objects by assembling particulars that result from visual observations. Just as Balzac's eye constructs his characters' personalities by checking bodily features, clothes, and characteristics of the environment, so the nation state's official ascertains citizens' identities, innocence or guilt, and nationality by visually inspecting their physical traits, manners, dress, and personal documents. Indeed, when Balzac portrayed himself as the secretary of French society and claimed to be in competition with the register of births, marriages, and deaths, he did not speak in a metaphoric way. As he was creating a taxonomy for classifying human types—the pictures and the galleries that in the "Avant-propos" stand for the single novels and the various parts comprising *La Comédie humaine*—he was actually taking part in the nation state's endeavor to make industrial society's citizen an intelligible subject. Balzac's operation is suggestive of the way Fielding turns *Tom Jones* into a historical record upon knowing of the Jacobite rebellion. Just as Fielding does not disguise his novel as an authentic historical document, but structures *Tom Jones* in a way that allows the novel to function as a historical record, so Balzac does not purport to write legal or bureaucratic papers, but composes texts that carry out those documents' very duties.

In *La Comédie humaine,* while the archive represents the foundation of all the narratives, there are novels in which the boundaries between the archival base and the overlaying fictional world become particularly porous. When this occurs, the archival practices that aid in building the diegesis, defining characters' identities, and generating plot turns become visible. Placed in a strategic position at the beginning of *Scènes de la vie de province*, *Ursule Mirouët* (1841) is an excellent example of a novel in which records determine characters' successes and failures.[27]

Ursule Mirouët is one of the many Balzacian narratives that deal with an inheritance. Throughout *La Comédie humaine*, Balzac shows a keen interest in issues such as identity, paternity, genealogy, and legitimation, which all are involved in the transmission of wealth across generations. As tradition ceased to count as proof, in coincidence with the demise of the ancien régime, all these matters began to be decided only by way of archival records, such as wills, identity papers, or purchase contracts. In *Ursule Mirouët*, the inheritance is that of Denis Minoret, a retired doctor who returns to his hometown of Nemours along with a ten-month-old baby, his niece and goddaughter Ursule. Given the doctor's successful career (he was Napoleon's physician), people in Nemours, in particular his heirs, suspect him to have amassed a substantial fortune. Despite his distaste for his greedy relatives, the doctor intends to respect their rights as his legal heirs. He splits, however, his fortune into two parts: he leaves to his relatives the capital accumulated prior to his coming to Nemours and bequeaths Ursule with his savings thereafter. Here, two opposite rights are in competition. Minoret's relatives can claim their uncle's patrimony because of their uninterrupted genealogical connection with him, while her godfather's love entitles Ursule to the inheritance. Unfortunately, the girl's position is weakened by her father's illegitimate birth that interrupts the continuity of her relation to Minoret. Two men of law, Nemours' notary, M. Crémière-Dionis, and Judge Bongrand discuss the legal details of the inheritance. Both back their counseling with proper references to court verdicts and the law of the country, the Napoleonic Civil Code published on March 21, 1804. By situating the story within a juridical framework, these learned expositions demonstrate how legal issues generate events and plot in the novel; and the law is the second pillar, in addition to the état civil, of the postrevolutionary France's archive.[28]

As invariably occurs in Balzac, in *Ursule Mirouët* the law establishes the context within which characters must develop their stories. In so doing, rather than simply echoing its age's legal discourse, the realist novel reinforces it. Realist fiction upholds the law, so much so that when it seems to support the breaking of the code, as was the case with adultery in Flaubert's *Madame Bovary*, the realist novel goes on trial. In *Ursule Mirouët*, Balzac takes great care to build a legal case around the issue of the girl's legitimacy. Ursule's illegitimate birth taints her position in society and casts a shadow on her right to inherit from her godfather: she is "la fille d'un bâtard, une fille prise par charité, ramassée sur la place" [a bastard's daughter, a girl taken for charity, picked up on the street].[29] Despite this stigma, the letter of the law does not prevent Ursule from becoming Doctor Minoret's legitimate heir. Though the contemporary civil code aims to grant only married couples the legal right to procreate, and consequently prevents grandparents from bequeathing any wealth to children born out of wedlock, this norm has nothing to do with Minoret's relation to Ursule, as the doctor is the girl's uncle.[30] However, for both counsels, the notary Crémière-Dionis and Judge Bongrand, the fact that the girl descends from an illegitimate father is the issue. While the notary states that a will in favor of Ursule should be successfully impugned on the ground of her illegitimate ascendancy, the judge believes that the "spirit of the law" rejects "*superfétations illégitimes*" from the family: this frame of mind could support a lawsuit and a lengthy litigation against the girl's right to inherit from her uncle.

In this context, in order to bequeath Ursule his wealth, Doctor Minoret hides three bearer bonds worth one million francs in a book from his library and writes a will in which he leaves the three certificates to Savinien, the girl's fiancé.[31] This testament is a supplementary precaution: Minoret wants to make sure that a legal document backs his donation to the girl. But this also means that in the archival age following the establishment of the état civil and the promulgation of the Napoleonic Code individuals are defined by records. What Ursule is, a legitimate heir and not a *thief*, as Minoret's relatives call her, must be written on legal paper.[32]

When the doctor dies, his nephew, Minoret-Levrault, steals

and destroys the will along with a letter containing the directions for finding the bonds. Robbed of her inheritance, and thrown out of her godfather's house, Ursule then lives in poverty. What leads to the restoration of the young lady's rights is a curious mix of supernatural events and archival practices. Almost two years after his death, Doctor Minoret's ghost appears to the sleeping Ursule and shows her the stolen letter, the book hiding the bearer bonds, and Minoret-Levrault in the act of committing the theft. Struck by Ursule's dream, Judge Bongrand inspects the book shown by Minoret's ghost: on the inside cover, scribbled in between two other numbers, one preceded by an M and the other by a U, he finds three numbers. The latter must refer to the stolen bearer bonds, he thinks, while the numbers preceded by a letter should correspond to two interest-bearing state certificates registered respectively to (M)inoret and (U)rsule. After checking that the inventory number of the girl's certificate matches the one scribbled in the book, he discovers in the public notary office that the digits preceded by an M correspond to the certificate listed under Minoret's name: his hypothesis that the three remaining numbers refer to the doctor's three bearer bonds is indirectly validated. Bongrand, has now only to submit his theory to the king's prosecutor who rapidly demonstrates Minoret-Levrault's guilt by obtaining his wife's confession. After the restoration of Ursule's legitimate rights—conducted in such a professional manner that showcases Balzac's mastery of archival know-how—the story can happily conclude with the girl's marriage. The plot of a major realist novel such as *Ursule Mirouët* relies on a basic archival operation, verifying the inventory number of a record.

What is remarkable in *Ursule Mirouët* is the convergence of all the story lines onto the scene of the archival investigation carried out by Judge Bongrand at the end of the story. The destiny of the novel's main characters hinges on Bongrand finding the right record in the archive, a discovery that in turn leads to the production of another document, the registration of Minoret-Levrault's wife's confession. Ursule's reward, in the form of wealth and a happy marriage, and Minoret-Levrault's punishment, i.e., his son's death and his wife's insanity, immediately follow the novel's turning point. In linking these events to the discovery of a crime, the theft of the bearer bonds, Balzac seeks to show how God's justice intervenes in this world. This faith in a supernatural power is expressed by Father Chaperon's cry—"Le doigt de Dieu est dans ceci" [Here there is God's finger]—upon the revelation of the imminent restoration of Ursule's rights.[33] However, in *Ursule Mirouët*, even supernatural elements are subordinated to the archival regime that ruled French society in the age of the état civil and the Napoleonic Code. Paranormal phenomena—magnetism, mesmerism, and apparitions of ghosts—constitute a crucial theme in *Ursule Mirouët*. One scene in particular proves fundamental: while in Paris, Minoret encounters a somnambulist who can see what is happening in his house in Nemours at that moment, an experience that prompts the atheist doctor to accept the existence of spiritual life and convert to Catholicism. In the narrative economy of the novel, it may seem that this episode simply foreshadows the doctor's apparition to Ursule toward the end of the story. Albeit important for the development of the character Minoret, the episode of the somnambulist must be narrated for another reason: it creates the epistemic premise for the doctor's apparition to his niece. Since supernatural phenomena occur, ghosts can come from the afterworld and help the living with their worldly business. As Ursule says, "Si cela [the somnambulist's vision] est . . . mes visions sont possibles" [If that is true then my visions are possible].[34] Given the fact that the ultimate consequence of Minoret's apparitions is Judge Bongrand's archival investigation, in *Ursule Mirouët*, even the supernatural works for the archive. In his last apparition, the doctor shows Ursule "une rangée de chiffres qui scintillèrent sur la muraille comme s'ils eussent été ecrits avec du feu" [a line of digits that shine on the wall as if they had been written with fire]; they are clearly the inventory numbers of the girls' bearer bonds.[35] In the age of the état civil, ghosts, too, practice the archive.

Balzac, the nostalgic of the ancien régime, the age in which humans and things were situated in their natural places, writes a novel that celebrates the epic of bureaucracy, of the anonymous force ruling upon the state born out of the ashes of the absolute monarchy. Under the aegis of the bureaucrat, everything has found its site again, only this time in the archive's shelves: humans and things can no longer find their position in the divine order of nature, but in the prosaic arrangement of the archive. As Peter Brooks has argued, "Balzac portrays a world in which representation is on everyone's mind—where self-representation is a central project—but where the signs used to represent are highly instable."[36] Signs fluctuate because a system of values based on the possession of land and titles of nobility has given way to an unstable one based on circulation. Following the French Revolution, individuals cannot be identified on the basis of their origins; they are defined by the things that surround them. To further complicate this situation, certain individuals' ability to mimic roles and behaviors determines an insane disorder: social hierarchy is disturbed "by the circulation of false images and deceptive signs."[37] In this context, the repositories of the police and the Bank of France, the état civil, and the Napoleonic Code, all the archives that *La Comédie humaine* either explicitly mentions or refers to, are desperately needed. As the natural and the godly no longer hold our world, and our situation within the world, in place, these archives are the only structures that can hold together society by countering the continuous slippage of identities, the impossibility to fix humans and things in firm positions.

La Comédie humaine aims at the same goals of the larger nineteenth-century archive: tying each individual living in society to his or her proper location. Balzac's plan of representing French society by narrating the stories of four thousand characters bespeaks the kind of totality that he had in mind. His plan of mapping out life in France after the revolution was archival in two senses: it systematically linked people to places and shaped a system of punishments and rewards that was modeled after the law. By ending with either gains or losses in social status and money, Balzac's stories show how human lives achieve their ultimate meaning. In so doing, they issue verdicts in the purest legal sense, by matching acts and consequences. Through his narratives, Balzac submits characters to the process that Foucault called "exam": constituting the individual as "a comparative system that makes it possible to measure global phenomena, describe groups, characterize collective events, as well as estimate how individual deviations from the norm relate to each other and spread through a 'population.'"[38]

Legal discourse is in and of itself archival because it not only generates, stores, and interprets records, but also creates general registers of human actions in their relation to a system of punishments. The law establishes univocal connections between the different positions a human being can assume—for example as an owner, thief, adulterer, or copyright holder—and their legal consequences: it matches these positions to the rights they enjoy in certain cases and the sanctions they deserve in others. As González Echevarría argues "legal discourse is the basic medium for the exchange of values, the metaphor of metaphors, the most archaic rule."[39] In particular, after the revolution, as the Napoleonic Civil Code turned the protection of property into its chief goal, the law focused on the legal situation of exactly those figures—the buyer, the creditor, the renter, or the heir—which crowd *La Comédie humaine* as fictional characters.[40] Balzac's stories invariably combine the greatest accuracy in describing the technicalities of the legal archive with an equal ability to foreground the actual content, in terms of the human lives involved, of the papers it stores. In so doing, *La Comédie humaine* provides a unique contribution to the archival discourse of its age by grasping the relations of power concealed in the creation and storage of records. The end result is an archive of unusual breadth that keeps not only records generated through correct procedures, but also those created by way of patent mistakes or wrongdoing. This is the case of *Le Colonel Chabert* (1844), a short novel that tells the story of an archival nightmare: an individual who is dead in one record series and alive in another. Chabert, a colonel in Napoleon's army and a count of the Napoleonic empire, is seriously wounded in the battle of Eylau and buried alive in the battlefield along with other fatalities. He manages to get out of the common grave and return to France after an eight-year-long ordeal in German prisons and hospitals.[41] Once in Paris, he discovers that his wife has remarried and refuses to see him. He then decides to seek legal advice, which leads him to Lawyer Derville.

Derville stands for the author.[42] A workaholic who makes the most of his evening hours, like Balzac, the lawyer dominates the novel's narrative materials: he listens to Chabert's and his wife's stories in the beginning, while he narrates the colonel's adventures to his friend Godeschal at the end. His skills are the same as a novelist's: an innate capacity to penetrate people's psychology, an inflexible work ethic, and the ability to conceive projects large enough to encompass individual destinies. What is more, by running his office as a perfectly organized bureaucratic machine, Derville hints at the working methods applied to the writing of fiction in the age of the paper archive. The physical layout of the lawyer's workplace—the copyists' studio/archive and the attached lawyer's room where he examines dossiers and conceives plans—is suggestive of the two phases of novelistic writing, i.e., the systematic gathering of records and their assembling in coherent narratives. *Le Colonel Chabert* begins with a slow motion representation of Derville's clerks copying a document, and then zooms in "un énorme casier qui garnissait le mur du haut en bas, et dont chaque compartiment était bourré de liasses d'où pendaient un nombre infini d'étiquettes et de bouts de fils rouge" [an enormous filing cabinet covering the entire wall from top to bottom whose compartments were stuffed with bundles of paper from which there dangled countless tags and wisps of red thread].[43] Exactly as Zviga Vartov does in *The Man with the Movie Camera*, when he shows his wife tagging, retrieving, and storing the reels for the film, Balzac displays the archival foundation of the cultural form he is practicing. The accurately tagged papers that Derville's filing cabinet stores make possible his speeches in the courts of law: creative language relies on bureaucratic know-how. The description of Derville's office carries out the same functions as Manzoni's copying from an old manuscript in *I promessi sposi*: both provide the archival novel with a moment of self-reflection over the material process that has generated the text. In a crucial step for the development of the genre, the description of Derville's rooms and the account of his clerks at work shift the focus of the novel's self-reflection onto the institution, the technology, and the practice that allow manuscripts to survive the passing of time and achieve the status of proof.

The document Derville's clerks are copying when Chabert enters the office is Louis XVIII's decree for restoring the nobles' rights over the properties they lost during the French Revolution and the Napoleonic Empire. As this decree refers to the charter the king promulgated in 1814 upon his return to power, it provides the novel with its legal frame, the Bourbon restoration and its attempt to erase the memory of the revolutionary era.[44] What is more, since Count Ferraud, the second husband of the colonel's wife, lost his land during the revolution, Louis XVIII's decree foreshadows one of the novel's key themes, the passing of property from the empire's nobility to Bourbon nobility. The royal decree provides the narrative with its documentary foundation, as the edict against the bravoes guilty of threatening parish priests does in *I promessi sposi*. While Derville's filing cabinet stands for the novel's technological base, Louis XVIII's decree constitutes its thematic foundation, with the archive being the discourse that makes both possible.

Chabert's hopes to recover his name and position in society hinge on his lawyer's ability to have the nation-state's archive validate the records that attest his identity. Chabert is a man made of paper whose development as a novelistic character relies on the outcome of archival operations. As a citizen of a bureaucratized state, the colonel is aware of the fact that only records can aid him to retrieve his lost identity. Appropriately, when he tells his story to Derville, Chabert marks the crucial moments of his ordeal as recorded events: his heroic sacrifice in the battle of Eylau is registered in the historical record, the surgeon who saved his life had the circumstances of Chabert's rescue recorded on a legal deed, and a German notary certified the colonel's declaration of identity.[45] While the last two documents supports Chabert's claim to his name, a formidable series of three records seems to deny him any hope: the certificate of his death (prepared according to the norms of military law), that of his wife's second marriage, and the birth certificate of the two children the woman had with her second husband. As Chabert desperately cries, he is buried "sous des actes, sous des faits, sous la société toute entière!" [beneath records, facts, the entire society!][46]

As the counsel of both Chabert and his wife, Derville attempts to reconcile the two series of records—the notarized papers proving the truth of the colonel's survival in Eylau on the one hand, and the legal acts that recognize his wife's right to receive his inheritance and marry again on the other—that support the incompatible claims of his two clients. He knows too well the relation of power hidden behind the formalistic surface of legal papers and immediately understands that, albeit indisputable according to justice and humanity, Chabert's claim to his name, wife, and fortune has dim chances of winning a trial. His adversaries, his wife and Count Ferraud, are "deux personnes puissantes qui pourront influencer les tribunaux" [two powerful persons who will be able to influence the courts].[47] Derville works out the problem by suggesting his clients to nullify two records, the certificate of Chabert's death, on the one hand, and that of his marriage, on the other. The former nullification allows the colonel to reclaim his identity, while the latter guarantees his wife against the invalidation of her second marriage. After eliminating the two conflicting records, Derville can create a new document, a legal deed that states Chabert's renunciation of all his wealth in exchange for a life annuity and the legal recognition of his name. As Derville tries to rebuild his client's identity by assembling a coherent series of records, his plan is consistent with the nation-state's practice of identifying citizens by situating them in networks of documents. Chabert's rescue from the deadly battlefield in Eylau is destined to remain an opaque event unless its record is included among a series of professionally stored papers.

Derville conducts his mediation by shuttling between the two separate rooms where he has confined the contenders. But his prudent diplomacy goes to pieces during his negotiation with Countess Ferraud, when Chabert barges into the room and unleashes his rage upon the greedy woman. As Cathy Caruth argues, the direct confrontation "rather than producing the recognition arranged by the legal papers, precisely produces the refusal of recognition that the settlement was supposed to correct."[48] The sudden appearance of the real thing, the colonel in the flesh, disrupts Derville's attempt to reestablish his paper identity. The enraged Chabert sets in motion a sequence of events that will end with Countess Ferraud's complete success and his own defeat. Chabert pays for the error of interrupting the compilation of the record, Derville's legal deed, which would have given him the possibility to end his life in a dignified way: archival discourse does not allow direct experience of external reality to replace the record as a cognitive tool. The novel registers this breaking down in the archive's operation by sidelining Derville, the head archivist, after the failure of his mediation. Without Derville's help, his two clients carry out a new attempt to reconcile their interests that results in Chabert's relinquishment of his name and wealth.

Derville and Chabert meet two more times, first in a courthouse where the colonel is tried as a vagabond and then in a poorhouse in Bicêtre after more than twenty years. Here, the colonel answers the lawyer's greeting by denying his own name: "Pas Chabert! Pas Chabert! je me nomme Hyacinthe . . . Je ne suis plus un homme, je suis le numero 164, septième sale" [Not Chabert! Not Chabert! my name is Hyacinthe, I am no longer a man, I am number 164, room seven].[49] After Derville's failure to anchor Chabert's identity to indisputable legal records, the colonel has been deprived of not only his name, but also the very right to have an identity. In juxtaposing the colonel's last name, which is indispensable in a country that has adopted the identification policies of the modern nation state, to his given name Hyacinthe, and suggesting that the latter provides only a weak form of identity, Balzac is again enforcing the law of a country obsessed with its citizens' bureaucratic identity. In absence of the record of his name, Chabert does not really exist: having survived physical death in the battlefield cannot reverse his bureaucratic death. Carrying a number—164, room 7—properly conveys his situation as a nonperson whose files have been sent to a high density storage, to an area of the archive where numbers tag records waiting for destruction.[50]

After Chabert's last appearance, the novel ends with Derville's decision to quit his profession and move to the countryside. He says to his friend Godeschal that his decision is motivated by his disgust for the human misery he is forced to meet as a lawyer, but it is the spectacle of Chabert's loss of identity that triggers his rejection. The archive expert, the lawyer/novelist, gives up the task of representing what cannot take the form of a record; Derville understands that he "can only approach but never fully capture the sight of the figure before him."[51] As Chabert's tumultuous life ends up with his civil death, in the state of quiet that represents living beings' ultimate goal as Freud reminds us, he has lived an antiarchival experience. The death drive that guides Chabert's adventure can be recognized when it takes the form of Eros, the colonel's love for his wife, but does not leave traces of its operations: Chabert enters life as a nameless and recordless child, a foundling in a foster house, only to become a number confined to the extreme periphery of the archive in his old age. Because the archive cannot locate Chabert's provenance and record his life, the novelist, in the person of Derville, must step back and stop narrating.

The archival ordeal generated by Chabert's unexpected return from Eylau ends with the victory of the most powerful side, the colonel's wife. Power and political interests defeat a merely formal conception of authenticity and truth, which would have supported Chabert's rights. His wife's marriage with the powerful Count Ferraud, a legitimist who never rallied around Napoleon, epitomizes old nobility's return to dominance during the Bourbon Restoration. Chabert's story gives a new sense to the expression "total archive" when referred to *La Comédie humaine.* Balzac's work not only stores the records of the archive's aporias, it also foresees archival errors. It preventively creates areas of nonlife, compensation rooms of sorts, such as the poorhouse in Bicêtre, where people whose identity falls outside of the reach of the état civil can drag on their existences. *La Comédie humaine* becomes a self-correcting archive that reserves a place on the shelves even for the absence of records, for the absolutely powerless, the Chaberts of the world who lack the right to possess a name. As the literary partner of nineteenth-century archival discourse, *La Comédie humaine* represents the moment of the greatest coincidence between the ends and means of the novel and the archive's. However, the Balzacian paradigm, a.k.a. realism, enjoys a short-lived success. Less than forty years later, with the writing of Flaubert's *Bouvard et Pécuchet*, this marvelously consistent assemblage of fictional realism and the practice of the état civil will show irreparable cracks.

5
Bouvard et Pécuchet by Gustave Flaubert: The Brilliant Stupidity of the Archive

GUSTAVE FLAUBERT WAS THE FIRST WRITER OF ARCHIVAL NOVELS to compose a work where two actual clerks are the heroes. He did so in his last and unfinished novel, *Bouvard et Pécuchet*, the story of two office workers who retire and move from Paris to Chavignolles, where they spend their abundant free time investigating nineteenth-century science. Endowed with insatiable curiosity in spite of being intellectually limited, Bouvard and Pécuchet storm through every branch of science, from agriculture to pedagogy, encountering history, chemistry, literature, and the rest of human knowledge along the way.[1] As no solid truth emerges from their epistemological quest, Bouvard and Pécuchet end up copying a disparate range of materials, from the notes of their investigations to random old papers bought by weight from a paper mill.

Paradoxically, turning two clerks into the heroes of an archival novel determines its implosion. *Bouvard et Pécuchet* brings the paradigm of legitimation to a close by showing that the archive's most precious epistemic asset, i.e., its ability to vouch for the authenticity of its records, actually depends on its ties with political and economic power. *Bouvard et Pécuchet* can achieve this result exactly because its heroes are two bureaucrats. This allows the novel to corrode archival discourse from the inside by bringing two key practices in the archive, copying and transferring records, to the their extreme consequences. Readers of *Bouvard et Pécuchet* experience the archive as radical disorder: once copied and shuffled from one location to another, records turn into unhinged verbal fragments that are destitute of sense. But transferring documents is exactly the method that allows the paradigm of legitimation to function. Archival novels achieve legitimacy by storing records that are taken from their original situation and transferred onto the fictional page. What's more, moving records is the ultimate archival practice, as records do not originate in the archive, but are sent there from the office once they are no longer in regular use: dislocation is the archive's foundational act.[2] *Bouvard et Pécuchet* shows that dislocation determines a decisive loss of meaning if the archive is isolated from the social elites that represent the ultimate signifier for the records it stores. By separating the archive from its signifying agents and highlighting its ultimate entropy, Flaubert points to the direction that archival novels written within the paradigm of challenge will follow in the twentieth century.

As cited by Auguste Sabatier, Flaubert described his novel as "une commode dont les chapitres sont les tiroirs" [a chest whose chapters are the drawers].[3] While the static metaphor speaks of a story where time does not move, the dresser is suggestive of other furniture, the file cabinets in the offices where the two bureaucrats spend their working lives; the textual structure of *Bouvard et Pécuchet* mirrors its heroes' lifelong job, placing files and folders on shelves. It is because of its content that the novel has to be arranged as a chest: "ces tiroirs sont encore trop nombreux, mais ce défaut est celui de mon sujet ; j'ai essayé de le masquer, non de le supprimer ; ce serait supprimer l'œuvre elle-même" [These drawers are still too many, but this flaw depends on the subject matter of the novel. I have attempted to mask, not to suppress it. If I did so, I would suppress the very work.][4] What is, then, this subject matter, and what are the materials that compel the novel to assume its particular structure?

Flaubert did not finish *Bouvard et Pécuchet*, as death caught him when he was still working on the tenth chapter, the last of the projected first part. He left abundant documentation, in the form of scenarios, notes, and plans, that allow for the reconstruction of the rest of his work, I argue here, with satisfactory approximation. Nonetheless, a scholarly discussion of *Bouvard et Pécuchet* must wrestle with the incomplete nature of the text: if we limit our attention to the finished, but never published, manuscript, we hastily eliminate half of the novel from necessary analysis and debate. From Flaubert's correspondence, we know that he considered both volumes as two indissoluble halves of one single novel, which loses its meaning if read in the mutilated form that prevails in modern editions.[5] On the other hand, any attempt to expand the analysis of *Bouvard et Pécuchet* to Flaubert's plans for the second volume must recognize that their ultimate form as a published text cannot even be surmised. All in all, dealing with the work in its entirety, including the notes for the second volume, appears to be the more fruitful critical method. This approach defines *Bouvard et Pécuchet* as all the materials we possess now: a file comprised of finished and unfinished texts, a novel-in-progress that asks readers to construct their own version of the narrative in a more active manner than a finished text would require. In other words, this approach directly implicates readers in the construction of *Bouvard et Pécuchet*'s narrative. It also demands that readers entertain a careful dialogue with the author, whose voice, as expressed through letters and comments, can be of invaluable help. After all, we enter his workshop when we read a work he left incomplete.[6]

From Flaubert's notes and letters we know that *Bouvard et Pécuchet*'s two volumes would have performed different roles. When he initially conceived the novel, the first ten chapters were designed to function as the preface to the second part.[7] The story of Bouvard and Pécuchet's attempt to master their age's knowledge would have laid the foundation for *Leur Copie*, a dossier comprising all the notes the two clerks take during their epistemic adventure, as well as other disparate materials.[8] According to Claudine Gothot-Mersch's hypothesis, the *Copie* should have included sixteen different series of records: 1) Notes from Previously Read Authors; 2) Old Papers Bought by Weight from a Paper Mill; 3) Specimen of All the Styles; 4) Parallels: Crimes of People and Kings; Good Deeds and Crimes of Religion; 5) Beauty; 6) Contradictory Statements and Judgments; 7) History; 8) Scientific Ideas; 9) Literary Criticism; 10) Judgments and Prophecies; 11) Philosophy, Religion, and Ethics; 12) Adulation of the Low Classes; 13) The Manuscripts of Marescot's Clerk; 14) The Marquise's Album; 15) The Dictionary of Accepted Ideas; 16) The Catalogue of Chic Ideas.[9]

The novel's two parts were to assume different forms, since the preface would have combined narrative prose and records, while the *Copie* would have minimized the narrative component.[10] Although the internal organization of the *Copie* can only be the object of speculation, one fact remains certain: it would have taken the form of a dossier of quotations. Flaubert himself confirms this hypothesis by calling the *Dictionnaire des idées reçues,* the first nucleus of the *Copie,* a book that will not include one word of his own.[11] Twenty-eight years later, this time referring to the entire second part, Flaubert wrote: "J'irai à Paris pour le second volume qui ne me demandera pas plus de six mois. Ils est fait aux trois quarts et ne sera presque composé que de citations" [I will go to Paris for the second volume that will not take more than six months. It is three-quarters of the way done and it will be almost completely composed of quotations].[12] Four other letters, written between 1878 and 1879, confirm that the second volume, which "se fait de soi-même" [is written by itself] will be completed in six months.[13] As a book of quotations requiring no more than six months of work, the second part of *Bouvard et Pécuchet* would clearly have been the result of Flaubert's own readings in preparation for the novel. In short, Flaubert would have turned the notes he took during his research into the work's second part. This book would have narrated how Bouvard and Pécuchet copied the notes they had collected during their thirty-year-long pursuit of knowledge. As Flaubert's files become Bouvard and Pécuchet's dossier, the novel carries out its own archivization.

Two of Flaubert's several statements concerning his work are particularly insightful for the present analysis. The first appeared in an 1872 letter, in which Flaubert described *Bouvard et Pécuchet* as "l'histoire de ces deux bonshommes qui copient une espèce d'encylopédie critique en farce" [the story of those two fellows who copy a sort of critical encyclopedia in the form of a farce].[14] Two years later, he declared: "Si je réussis [in writing *Bouvard et Pécuchet*], ce sera, sérieusement, le COMBLE DE L'ART" [If I succeed it will be, seriously, the HEIGHT OF ART].[15] Once reconciled, Flaubert's statements describe *Bouvard et Pécuchet* as a spatially structured novel (the chest of drawers) that attains the greatest artistic achievements through a critique of the encyclopedia: a unique form and a bold epistemic goal combine in reaching a remarkable aesthetic result. Since Bouvard and Pécuchet carry out this operation as copyists, a question comes up: is copying the instrument for simply transcribing or also criticizing the encyclopedia? Put differently, does *Bouvard et Pécuchet* become a critical encyclopedia because it is copied?

In Flaubert's definition of the novel as "a critical encyclopedia in the form of a farce," human knowledge is the object of both critical analysis and comic representation. When related to a text, as in a "critical edition" of a book, the adjective "critical" signifies a scientific examination of the historical, cultural, and linguistic background of a written artifact. In Flaubert's words, comic displacement combines with the rational approach required in a critical examination in order to bring about the critique of the Encyclopedia. The etymology of *farce* suggests the kind of comic treatment the Encyclopedia undergoes in *Bouvard et Pécuchet:* the term derives from the Latin verb *farcire:* to fill, to stuff.[16] The repository that Bouvard and Pécuchet stuff with notions is the novel that is titled after them. As they fill the text with statements copied from their age's encyclopedia, the comic displacement consists in the oddity of submitting such an achievement of human genius to the treatment that folders and files require. As Flaubert has the encyclopedia (human reason's highest accomplishment in his age) wear the clothes of a bureaucratic register, he brings two presumably disparate worlds—the world of bureaucracy and the world of intellectual pursuit—together, in a literary carnival of sort.

Bouvard and Pécuchet do not possess the intellectual strengths that carrying out the critical examination of the encyclopedia would require. While the two clerks' stupidity compounds the carnivalesque atmosphere of the story, it is their being trained as copyists that makes the critical examination of knowledge technically possible. For years, Bouvard and Pécuchet have filled up registers and commercial books with their handwriting; they are accustomed to retrieving, storing, and copying statements. As bureaucrats, they believe that writing a statement on paper makes it authoritative. Thus, exactly as they have done with records throughout their working days, the two clerks cut, copy, and store scientific statements. Contrary to their expectations, once submitted to this treatment, these propositions lose their value and become absurd; they undergo a drastic decontextualization, a radical shift from one kind of order to another. They move from the encyclopedia, where notions are enchained according to a preexisting plan, to the archive, where records are arranged according to a principle, their provenance, that resides in the records themselves. Within this process, the transcription of a statement does not make it serious, as the two heroes believe, but rather transforms it into a ridiculously decontextualized assertion. The two copyists' comedy originates in this conflict between the plans they concoct and the results they obtain.

By writing as bureaucrats, Bouvard and Pécuchet do not aim at persuading any reader to accept their message, be it aesthetic, scientific, or political; they can combine together excerpts taken from their age's texts without being carried away by these texts' rhetoric.[17] They attempt to reach the core content of scientific statements, only to discover that, once the rhetorical layers are stripped away, what is left is either plain nonsense or a repetition of previous propositions. As Joëlle Gleize argues, for Flaubert's two heroes reading becomes an operation that "consists in fragmenting and taking out details."[18] As they transform these pieces into lists, Bouvard and Pécuchet employ writing in its primeval function, the preparation of inventories and tables for archival purposes.[19] For example, their intense reading of texts regarding human psyche produces this collage:

> Dans la faculté de connaître, se trouve l'aperception rationelle, où l'on trouve deux mouvements principaux et quatre degrés.
> L'Abstraction peut offrir des écueils aux intelligences bizarres.
> La mémoire fait correspondre avec le passé comme la prévoyance avec l'avenir.
> L'imagination est plutôt une faculté particulière, *sui generis*.
> (306)

> Rational perception is found in the faculty of knowing, wherein one discovers two principal activities and four degrees.
> Abstraction can hold out snares to perverse minds.
> Memory permits communication with the past as prevision with the future.
> Imagination is rather a particular faculty, *sui generis*.

Philosophical speculation becomes a bureaucratic memo whose function is "to leave bare by bringing closer, to criticize indirectly, silently, through the sole montage of the 'words' cited."[20] The list of philosophical propositions that I have just quoted exposes nineteenth-century psychology as an inconsistent discipline, to say the least.[21] Random daydreaming rather than coherent reasoning seems to produce the sentences on abstraction, memory, and imagination comprising Bouvard and Pécuchet's inventory. Out of the enormous mass of texts that the two clerks examine, very few propositions survive the loss of their rhetorical connections. In the hands of Bouvard and Pécuchet, copying, the transformation of knowledge into records, becomes a formidable instrument for the critical reading of the nineteenth-century encyclopedia. By silencing rhetoric, copying generates a productive kind of nonsense, so to speak: it helps in preventing readers from showing unmotivated agreement with propositions that are unable to convey any persuasive arguments at all once isolated from their linguistic context.

Bouvard and Pécuchet's achievements have momentous implications for the epistemic status of the narrative in *Bouvard et Pécuchet* and in the larger culture of the modern age. The two clerks' inquiry proves that scientific statements make sense only if they are parts of an overarching arrangement. In particular, in nineteenth-century science, meaning came from top down, from the encyclopedia as totality: "The encyclopedia represents the pretension to unify that which remains irremediably distinct, to fix a totality that continuously crumbles in order to recreate itself in different forms."[22] Compilers mastering all the connections tying together scientific disciplines organize encyclopedias: the *a priori* of encyclopedic discourse is that knowledge possesses order. This arrangement can originate in the historical evolution of humankind toward increasingly sophisticated knowledge, as in D'Alembert's *Discours préliminaire* (1751), or can depend on a hierarchy that attributes only to certain disciplines the status of true sciences, as in Coleridge's *Encyclopedia Metropolitana* (1818). By grasping the total order of knowledge, encyclopedists can divide science into separate entries and then arrange them according to the method they believe to be the most convenient. The alphabetical order represents only a practical layout that can function because deep, rational links integrate the various scientific disciplines into a harmonious system. Encyclopedic discourse considers science from the standpoint of an observer ideally placed at the end of human knowledge's historical progress, as Hegel stated: "The last philosophy in time is the result of all the previous philosophies and must comprise all their principles: hence it is—if it is a true philosophy, of course—the most developed, rich, and concrete."[23] By positioning itself at the summit of humankind's ascension toward a rational apprehension of the world, the panoramic discourse of encyclopedia embraces knowledge in its entirety.[24]

Contrary to the immanent order of nineteenth-century science, Bouvard and Pécuchet's movements from one discipline to another "do not seem, as a whole, to be submitted to logic, neither do they rigorously develop on the basis of probability."[25] At times, the two clerks use common sense; they shift, for example, from anatomy to physiology or from geology to mineralogy. However, they quite often simply follow random curiosity, as when they become interested in anatomy upon seeing a picture of a flayed man, or in cosmology out of their boredom with minerals. They display no consideration for the hierarchy among the various sciences that scholars such as D'Alembert, Coleridge, and Comte considered essential in encyclopedic discourse.[26] Flaubert's scenario for the twelfth chapter of *Bouvard et Pécuchet*, the last of the novel, ends with these words: "Il faut que la page s'emplisse, que [le monument] se complète—égalité de tout, du bien et du mal, du beau et du laid. de [sic] l'insignifiant et du caractéristique. Il n'y a de vrai que les phénomènes" [The page must be filled, (the monument) must be completed—everything, be it good and evil, beautiful and ugly, meaningless and remarkable, is the same. The only truth is the phenomenon].[27]

Here Flaubert joins his two heroes in considering the medium more than the message. What matters is that a piece of knowledge is recorded on paper. For Bouvard, Pécuchet, and Flaubert, since writing equalizes statements, as Roland Barthes will argue a century later, all stored records look alike independent of their contents.[28] It is the location where they are stored—the page that must be filled—that identifies these records. At the end of the two copyists' epistemic adventure, what looks foolish is the encyclopedic project, the pretense that arranging science according to a rational, comprehensive plan will inevitably bring about the apprehension of reality in its entirety: "La science est faite suivant les données fournies par un coin de l'étendue. Peut-être ne convient-elle pas à tout le reste qu'on ignore, qui est beaucoup plus grand, et qu'on ne peut découvrir" [Science is built on the data given by a corner of the whole field. Perhaps it does not agree with the remainder that remains unknown, which is much bigger and impossible to discover] (138).

As they reduce nineteenth-century science and its encyclopedia to a game of recording and positioning, Bouvard and Pécuchet sabotage their age's key instrument for arranging the objects of worldly reality in a meaningful way. Encyclopedias provide their users with taxonomies for ordering things and relating names to things. Therefore, when Bouvard and Pécuchet turn their encyclopedia (the one they received from nineteenth-century positivism) into a repository of recorded statements they plunged into a messy reality devoid of any structure. In a development that has significant consequences for the very possibility of writing a realist novel, words become separate from things, and Bouvard and Pécuchet experience an increasing difficulty to define objects. At the beginning of the novel, naming does not appear to be a problem. When Bouvard and Pécuchet meet for the first time, they read each other's names written on the inside of their respective hats. In an apparent fusion between word and object, the name functions as a tag that never abandons its referent. Later in the novel, when the two clerks tour the garden of their country house for the first time, "Ils avaient plaisir à nommer tout haut les legumes" [they felt the pleasure of naming loudly the vegetables] (72). This Edenic state of language vanishes when the practice of the archive exposes the cracks in the encyclopedic order. As nineteenth-century taxonomies fuzz out, objects become difficult to pinpoint, and naming amounts to guessing. When the two copyists become interested in meteorology and begin observing clouds, "Ils contemplaient ceux qui ressemblent à des îles, ceux qu'on prendrait pour des montagnes de neige—tâchant de distinguer les nimbus des cirrus, les stratus des cumulus ; les formes changeaient avant qu'ils eussent trouvé les noms" [they contemplated those which look like islands, those which could be mistaken for snowy mountains—as they were attempting to distinguish nimbi from cirri, strati from cumuli; the shapes changed before they could find their names] (88). The two heroes' enthusiastic faith in words' ability to match things meets the mocking refutation of reality. In Bouvard and Pécuchet's quest, irony originates in their incapacity to recognize that "language is incapable of grasping the nature of things."[29] As Bouvard and Pécuchet proceed investigating the articulation between language and reality, the hazardous nature of naming becomes clear. In the world they discover, names are movable, as though the hats on which they wrote their names could move by themselves from one person's head to another.

In Flaubert's years, the encyclopedia was the master-narrative, an inevitable reference for all the particular stories that were told in that age. At the core of the encyclopedia's logic, there lies the idea of progress: knowledge develops from infancy to maturity, while single disciplines occupy their positions in a hierarchy that assigns the most developed sciences the top of the pyramid of human achievements. In his *Philosophie première* (1830–42), the encyclopedia of positivism, Auguste Comte argued that human knowledge in its entirety, as well as each of its various branches, developed through three stages: theological, metaphysical, and positive. Science reached the third phase in the nineteenth century, when the human mind achieved its maturity along with the ability to focus on the effective laws of phenomena. The very idea of the encyclopedia is inseparable from that of progress, a concept that eighteenth and nineteenth-century encyclopedists expressed in narrative form by recounting how science advanced from the Middle Ages to modernity, as D'Alembert does in the second part of his *Discours préliminaire.*

In *Bouvard et Pécuchet,* when the two clerks' systematic copying leads the encyclopedia to crumble, all of the underlying narratives follow suit: they are all stories of how knowledge progresses. The two heroes' attempts to shape narratives out of science, religion, and history, fail miserably. After reading Cuvier's *Discours sur les révolutions du globe,* Bouvard and Pécuchet put together a story regarding the formation of the earth, from the emersion of the continents to the appearance of mammoths: "C'était comme une féerie en plusieurs acts, ayant l'homme pour apothéose" [It was like a fairy-tale in several acts having the human being as its apotheosis] (143). After further readings and several practical experiences with geology, however, Bouvard and Pécuchet come to the conclusion that Cuvier's science "était sapée. La Création n'avait plus la même discipline ; et leur respect pour ce grand homme diminua" [was undermined. Creation did not have the same discipline any longer; thus, their respect for the great man shrunk] (154).[30] As science cannot narrate the progress of life on earth, history fails to recount the human adventure on it. Roman history, for example, is a nest of contradictions: "Tite-Live attribue la fondation de Roma à Romulus. Salluste en fait honneur aux Troyens d'Énée. Coriolan mourut en exil selon Fabius Pictor, par les stratagèmes d'Attius Tullus, si l'on croit Denys. Sénèque affirme qu'Horatius Coclès s'en retourna victorieux, et Dion, qu'il fut blessé à la jambe. Et La Mothe le Vayer émet des doutes pareils, relativement aux autres peuples." [Livy attributes the foundation of Rome to Romulus. Sallust honors Aeneas' Trojans. Coriolanus dies in exile according to Fabius Pictor and because of Attius Tullus' tricks if one believes Dionysus. Seneca maintains that Horace Cocles came back the winner, while Dion argues that he was wounded in his leg. And La Mothe le Vayer conveys similar doubts regarding other peoples] (189). Finally, the Bible displays the same contradictions plaguing secular narratives: "L'Exode nous apprende que pendant quarante ans on fit des sacrifices dans le desert; on n'en fit aucun suivant Amos et Jérémie. . . . Dans le Deutéronome, Moïse voit le Seigneur face à face ; d'après l'Exode, jamais il ne l'a put voir" [*Exodus* teaches us that sacrifices were celebrated for forty years in the desert; *Amos* and *Jeremiah* never mention them. . . . In *Deuteronomy*, Moses saw God in person; according to Exodus he never did] (349).

In *Bouvard et Pécuchet*, the narrative malaise that plagues the master-story of the encyclopedia and afflicts all the tales of progress, science, and history takes the form of a plot crisis. This is an extraordinary feat indeed in an age that witnessed "the emergence of narrative plot as a dominant mode of ordering and explanation."[31] In Flaubert's view, plot was nothing more than a pretext, a necessary price to pay in order to lure readers into reading his book: "J'ai enfin terminé le premier chapitre et préparé le second, qui comprendra la Chimie, la Médecine et la Géologie, tout cela devant tenir en 30 pages! et avec des personnages secondaires, car il faut un semblant d'action, une espèce d'histoire continue pour que la chose n'ait pas l'air d'une dissertation philosophique" [I have finally finished the first chapter and prepared the second, which will include chemistry, medicine, and geology, let's say thirty pages as a whole! But I have added secondary characters since the book needs some sort of action, something like a continuous story in order not to sound too similar to a philosophical dissertation].[32] Reducing plot to a "sort of action" situates *Bouvard et Pécuchet* outside of the tradition of realism. In the first two chapters, Flaubert presents the reader with all the traditional elements of a vintage realist novel à la Balzac: an unexpected inheritance benefiting an illegitimate son, the sudden acquisition of "*Quinze mille livres de rente!*" and two guileless Parisians living in a country village among unfriendly local folks. Economic problems seem to be one of the novel's main concerns as the two clerks display their inanity as farmers and businessmen. The money-related issues that appear so important at the beginning recede into the background as the two heroes set out on their cognitive journey: wealth ceases to be a problem when Bouvard sells his farms in exchange for a life annuity in chapter 9. For the two heroes, this means both acknowledging their failure as entrepreneurs and receiving a serious economic blow: they have managed to halve their income and lose their capital. In Balzac, a setback of these proportions would have taken correspondent narrative implications as a signal of the heroes' defeat in the competition of life. This does not occur in *Bouvard et Pécuchet*, where the two clerks continue their epistemic quest unmoved by the sinking of their finances: the novel is clearly departing from the realist paradigm, a fact that the narrative time attests by slowing down almost to a standstill.

Since René Descharmes's study in 1921, the timeline of *Bouvard et Pécuchet* has caught the attention of Flaubert scholars.[33] Although the events of the novel cover at least three decades, time does not affect the characters.[34] Despite being forty-seven at the beginning of the novel and in their late seventies toward the end, Bouvard and Pécuchet do not show any signs of aging. They do not lose their hair, nor do they suffer from any age-related disease. Along with all the other characters, the two clerks seem to live in an eternal present that prevents the novel from moving along a temporal axis: "the novel simulates progression and uses *time* as a décor."[35] Just as they seem immune to aging, Bouvard and Pécuchet resist evolution. They undergo an astounding sequence of epistemic failures, from agronomy to pedagogy, all the while remaining faithful to their obsessive pursuit of knowledge. Despite reaching old age, the two copyists do not become wiser: to the contrary, they embark in new cognitive adventures with the same youthful spirit they displayed more than two decades earlier. In their compulsion to repeat, they are followed by the novel's supporting figures who continue to play their fixed roles and reiterate the same clichés. Bouvard, Pécuchet, and all the townsfolk in Chavignolles lack the very quality that defines novelistic characters in nineteenth-century fiction, the ability to change.

If the crumbling of the encyclopedic order deprives realism of its cognitive horizon, i.e., the certainty that reality is knowable, it is a peculiar approach to the archive that ultimately prevents a Balzacian kind of narrative from jelling up in *Bouvard et Pécuchet*. In fact, if Bouvard and Pécuchet's investigation into nineteenth-century science is conducted by way of archival operations, such as the creation of records, why can these documents not help in generating a narrative, as occurs in Manzoni and Balzac? Because they are prepared by powerless bureaucrats is the answer. By playing the archive against the encyclopedia, Flaubert situates archival discourse at the opposition, so to speak, of the elites who enjoy the monopoly of power/knowledge. The novel represents this peculiar relation between the two heroes' archive and social power through Bouvard and Pécuchet's choice of friends and foes. Social leaders in Chavignolles—the Count of Faverge, Abbot Jeufroy, Mayor Foureau, and Doctor Vaucorbeil—grow increasingly suspicious of the two clerks' irreverent attitude toward religion, science, traditional ethics, and social hierarchies. Despite their comfortable lifestyle, Bouvard, an illegitimate child, and Pécuchet are two outcasts. A nonconventional family by all means, the two clerks possess a flair for connecting with people living on the margins of society: Gorgu, a drifter turned revolutionary; Mélie, a foundling; Marcel, a deformed vagabond; as well as Victor and Victorine, the children of a convict. As troublemakers, Bouvard and Pécuchet have three run-ins with the law—two arrests and a trial ending with a fine—and are threatened with confinement in an asylum at the end of the unpublished section of the book.

Bouvard and Pécuchet must be two subversives since their task is to criticize social stupidity, *bêtise,* or the reduction of language to a limited set of unchallenged and incessantly repeated propositions. As the two morons they are, they become the only ones who can take on this widespread conformism. From Flaubert's vantage point, to attack *bêtise* from above, so to speak, by attempting to demonstrate its intellectual fallacies would have resulted in a supreme act of stupidity, since he believed that those affected by social idiocy could not be persuaded of being wrong. *Bêtise* can be conquered only from the inside, by applying to its destruction its own weapons; it must be allowed to be itself so as to display all its grotesque nonsense. Under this perspective, Bouvard and Pécuchet are the right persons for the job of rooting clichés out of discourse because, and not in spite, of their stupidity. Their limited intellectual skills allow them to do only operations that they have learned through passive repetitions, such as the routine of transcribing, reusing, and summarizing texts that has been their life as clerks for thirty years. From this habit, they have learned that statements are too often made of other statements.

In nineteenth-century fiction, the copyist's subversion of language takes two forms: the simple refusal to write any longer, as Melville's Bartleby suddenly does, and Flaubert's clerks' obsession with copying, as occurs with the compulsive recycling of texts that brings about the writing of the *Copie*. In the second part of Flaubert's novel, Bouvard and Pécuchet assemble a subversive archive: it aims to criticize language as a tool for perpetuating the dominant form of power/knowledge in society. Like Bartleby, Bouvard and Pécuchet decline to cooperate, but their refusal takes the form of an autistic archive that cuts itself out of the world instead of collaborating with the ruling elites. In short, after playing the archive against the encyclopedia, Flaubert plays the archive against itself. He does so by entrusting the archive to two pariahs and showing that, in those conditions, it simply becomes a recycling machine lacking any hold on the external world. That grip, the final link between words and objects, depends on processes unfolding in the living fabric of society where matching records and individuals is an operation of power carried out by dominant social groups. In Bouvard's and Pécuchet's archive, what is missing is the laywer Derville, the Paris police, and the bank of France, all the authorities who hold together the archive in the age of realism and make sure it functions toward the identification of individuals.

The *Copie* is an archive that operates in a vacuum of social relations, as in a laboratory where the lack of contamination allows for studying phenomena in their purest form. It proves that an archive severed from power can neither identify individuals, nor refer to authentic records as the source of its authority. Situated in an age where paper is available in a previously unknown quantity and the reproduction of texts is on the verge of a technological leap, the *Copie* is the realm of endless duplication.[36] It reflects the historical passage that has occurred in the domain of material production with the advent of industrial society, "in which manufactured objects produced in series multiply themselves in a way that makes it impossible relating copies to an original."[37] The *Copie* is the Derridian "irrepressible desire to return to the origin" that gives up in defeat, the *mal d'archive* channeled into compulsive repetition.[38] The crisis of authority and that of originality are actually two sides of the same coin.[39] As the archive sabotages authoritarian knowledge, it loses its privileged access to original documents and allows the copy to substitute for the authentic document. In this context, both Manzoni's and Balzac's paradigms, namely the narrative based on proven facts recorded in faithful documents and the novel that apprehends individuals through their localization, go to pieces in *Bouvard et Pécuchet*.[40] Flaubert's work brings to conclusion the experience of the archival novel as a cognitive tool in the age of realism. At the same time, by criticizing the relation tying the archive to power, it paves the way for a new paradigm of archival fiction. Based on the acknowledgement of the linguistic nature of the archive, this model will inform archival fiction in the last decades of the twentieth century; it will rely on the paradoxical outcome of *Bouvard et Pécuchet,* the fact that the archive is shaken but somewhat unharmed by the double loss of authenticity and authority. The dossier where Bouvard and Pécuchet's epistemic efforts end up is an archive of stunning modernity: by storing "Old Papers Bought by Weight from a Paper Mill" and inserting trash in the work of art, the *Copie,* which is the second part of a novel, becomes the forerunner of the twentieth-century avant-garde's practices. All in all, Flaubert's work remains the greatest archival novel of the nineteenth century, a unique piece of fiction that slowly dissolves narrative into the arranging of records.

In a sense, there are no other solutions. Bouvard and Pécuchet's epistemic adventures demonstrate how, in addition to the encyclopedia and the realist novel, even the library and the museum do not qualify as viable instruments for making sense of our experience of the world. The library is the immanent foundation of Bouvard and Pécuchet's quest for science: just as the two clerks are insatiable consumers of volumes, so the novel folds scores of books into its fabric. The quotations stored in *Bouvard et Pécuchet* originate in the enormous repository of volumes that the proliferation of printed paper has made available.[41] However, whenever libraries are represented in *Bouvard et Pécuchet* their depiction conflicts with the idea of organized knowledge. In Pécuchet's personal bookshelves, books are stored in a rather chaotic fashion: "dans les coins se trouvaient pêle-mêle plusieurs volumes de l'Encyclopédie Roret, le *Manuel du magnétiseur,* un Fénelon, d'autres bouquins,—avec des tas de paperasses, deux noix de coco, diverses médailles, un bonnet turc" [in the corners were scattered a number of volumes of the Roret Encyclopedia, the *Mesmerite's Handbook,* a Fénelon, and other old tomes, as well as a pile of dirty papers, two coconuts, various medallions, a Turkish fez] (56). Later on in the story, the two clerks simply amass their books in a room of their country house along with the volumes left by the previous owner. Despite the prodigious amount of texts they read, their arrangement never worries Bouvard and Pécuchet: they buy, borrow, and read books according to the need of the moment. Once turned into notes, these books are never mentioned again as if they had simply disappeared. Significantly, when Bouvard and Pécuchet visit the National Library, they are interested in knowing only the number of the books stored, not their titles or contents. To the two heroes, the library is nothing but a holding bay, a storeroom for books whose knowledge has been exhausted. Since its ability to classify and order books never becomes a novelistic theme in *Bouvard et Pécuchet*, the library never functions as a metaphor for the systematic arrangement of knowledge.

In *Bouvard et Pécuchet*, the same disorder that turns libraries into messy depositories of books plagues museums. Although Bouvard and Pécuchet begin their flirtation with academic science by visiting museums while they still live in Paris, their visits do not unfold according to any logic or guiding questions, but rather in response to their ever-shifting sense of curiosity. In anticipation of their future investigations, they move randomly from art to natural science, from technology to history. Once in Chavignolle, as a result of their passion for archaeology, Bouvard and Pécuchet turn their house into a private museum. It contains a pile of heterogeneous objects—an alleged Gallo-Roman sarcophagus, a statue of Saint Peter, old books, and of course Pecuchet's two coconuts, to name just a few—and ends up looking more like the back shop of a junk dealer than a professionally organized museum. Years later, their ancient passion for antiquities will turn into irritation at all the objects that clutter up their house. The two clerks' rejection of the museum points to the same predicament that plagues the encyclopedia in Flaubert's novel. As Eugenio Donato argues, "the set of objects the Museum displays is sustained by the fiction that they somehow constitute a coherent representational universe."[42] The museum aims to convey totality through metonymy. While an item displayed in the museum functions as a fragment standing for an entire object, the narratives that order these items speak of the larger story of the "non-linguistic universe."[43] In *Bouvard et Pécuchet*, the museum loses its representational value as the two clerks unveil the arbitrary nature of all the narratives seeking to explain natural, as well as human, history. When the encyclopedic order collapses, just as the library's arrangement of linguistic signs loses consistency, so the museum's narratives appear arbitrary. In becoming a farce, the encyclopedia drags down with it the other totalizing systems of the age.[44] Once all nineteenth-century totalizing discourses, the encyclopedia, the library, and the museum, become unavailable, the archive is the only option left. But why so? Why is the archive the only cultural form to survive the exposition of its own shortcomings in *Bouvard et Pécuchet?* The fact is that Bouvard and Pécuchet's archive paradoxically benefits from severing its relations to authority and renouncing its ambition to store the records of foundational acts of power and knowledge. What it is left after this double rescission is the chest of drawer, the repository that does not know other rules than those of provenance and positioning and points to the agent who places and takes objects out of it more vividly than the encyclopedia, the realist novel, the library, or the museum. It is exactly because it has lost its metaphysical foundations that this archive can stand tall as the only remaining totality in *Bouvard et Pécuchet*. The repository that survives the collapse of all the nineteenth-century systems for holding together culture is a dossier of signs referring to signs, an archive that flaunts itself as a self-contained, nonmetaphysical, discourse. As *La Copie* stores records that recycle records, *Bouvard et Pécuchet* finally achieves its goal. Only a novel that eliminates the most tenacious of all clichés, the belief in the referential power of language, can reach *Le Comble de l'art*, the eradication of platitudes from human communication.

6
La Vie mode d'emploi by Georges Perec: The Archive as a Game

AMONG THE NOVELISTS I CONSIDER IN THIS BOOK, ONLY GEORGES Perec was formally trained as an archivist. From 1961 to 1978, he was employed as a documentalist in one of the laboratories belonging to France's National Center for Scientific Research (CNRS), where he had to "organize the information contained in the unit's research library so that people could get out of it anything that might concern their current work."[1] To this purpose, he arranged a paper database of index cards, instead of the digitalized records and search engines that would become available in the computer age.[2] In 1965, the laboratory's archive comprised a total of one hundred thousand cards, "every one of them typed up, coded, and holepunched by Georges Perec."[3] His experience working for CNRS turned out to be helpful to Perec the writer engaged in the composition of *La Vie mode d'emploi*, as archival practices are a key constituent of the text's structure. What is more, *La Vie mode d'emploi* combines the ability to weave archival scholarship into its textual fabric with the highest degree of fictionality. The allegiance to truth that Perec's novel displays when it encodes archival theory in the text coexists with the purest joy of narrating utterly fictional stories: clearly, the archival novel has come a long way since Defoe's first experiment with the genre. By means of this particular mix of facts and fiction, *La Vie mode d'emploi* can show the reader how the archive malfunctions rather than discussing its shortcomings as if they were a merely theoretical problem. As a consequence, Perec's novel conjugates the paradigm of challenge in a way that situates the reader squarely at the center of an archival experience in the age of the archive's decomposition. Here the obvious reference becomes Flaubert's *Bouvard et Pécuchet,* another archival novel that foregrounds its fictional nature, all the while being true to the reality of the archival practices it narrates. In a text so firmly grounded in archival praxis, the novel's fictional capacity translates into a captivating, and at the same time dispassionate, depiction of the bureaucratic archive mired in its epistemic crisis. *La Vie mode d'emploi* assesses the functioning of this archive in the context of both its technological and material constraints, as well as with respect to the information overload that floods its repositories in the twentieth century. As Sven Spieker has argued, "when an archive has to collect everything, because every object may become useful in the future, it will soon succumb to entropy and chaos"; translate this sober statement into fiction and you have *La Vie mode d'emploi.*[4]

The complete title of Georges Perec's novel reads *La Vie mode d'emploi: romans,* thus suggesting a complex text that assembles several autonomous stories within one work. This coexistence of the one and the many challenges a key precept in literary theory since Aristotle's *Poetics:* the idea that one plot ($\mu\tilde{\upsilon}\theta o\varsigma$) must connect the contents of a fictional work, be it a tragedy, as in Classical Greece, or a novel, as in the modern age.[5] In *La Vie mode d'emploi,* the archive substitutes for the plot in the task of tying the novel's disparate elements into a coherent whole. Within this archival approach to the text's organization, the key structuring device is a one hundred square, ten by ten grid representing the vertical plan of an apartment building situated at 11 Rue Simon-Crubellier, Paris: each square corresponds to a different location—rooms, cellars, staircases, entrance hall, etc—in the house and, with one exception, to a chapter in the novel.[6] Perec arranged *La Vie mode d'emploi* by way of the knight-tour—a chess conundrum whereby a knight must land on all the squares of the chessboard without touching the same square twice.[7] With this purpose in mind, he turned his ten by ten grid into an oversized chessboard whose columns and rows he numbered from one to ten, going from left to right and from top to bottom respectively. On this grid, an imaginary knight that starts at square six, six, chapter 1, executes its tour; since each square corresponds to a location on the map of the building, the knight also connects all the rooms in the house. Because the subject matter of each chapter relates to the locale identified by the corresponding square in the grid, the map of the building as traversed by the knight also determines the order of the novel's content.

The epistemic principle that informs this arrangement is the same functioning in the modern, post-French Revolution archive: understanding an individual means to refer him/her/it to a physical location or, better, to the bureaucratic expression of this location. Just as a record is identified by the office that generated it, and people's identities are determined by the documents that prove their birthplaces and addresses, so Perecs' *romans* are defined by the location in the apartment building where they originate. Appropriately, each chapter's title comprises a Roman digit indicating its position in the novel's arrangement, the proper name of the person living in the corresponding locale, and an Arabic digit designating the room in multi-roomed apartments.[8] Balzac's *Le Père Goriot* represents the obvious literary reference for the building-like arrangement of *La Vie mode d'emploi*. Although both novels apply the archival principle of "apprehension through localization" to the representation of their characters, they function within distinct epistemic paradigms. Balzac had absolute faith in the modern archive's cognitive procedures—supporting truth by way of original, professionally stored documents and arranging records in a way that invariably leads to finding the sought for piece of information—as his admiration for the repositories of the police and the bank of France demonstrates. He operated within the French state's archival project, in osmosis, so to speak, with the état civil, whose tools he largely applied to the composition of *La Comédie humaine*. Perec builds, instead, a self-sufficient repository that relies on a set of norms he creates ad hoc. He arranges his novel by way of game rules and mathematical laws whose epistemic thrust lies outside archival theory. In so doing, he rules out that coincidence of purposes between the novel's and the nation state's archival projects that represents the cognitive cornerstone of *La Comédie humaine*.

In sketching the layout of *La Vie mode d'emploi*, Perec was inspired by the poetics of the OuLiPo—Ouvroir de Littérature Potentielle—a group of avant-garde writers, artists, and mathematicians that he had joined in March 1967. Among the OuLiPo's principles, the idea that formal constraints are more helpful to the writer's creativity than mere inspiration had the greatest influence on Perec's writing. Plays on words, combinations of letters, and mathematical theorems are the types of constraints that guide authors in generating texts.[9] As for *La Vie mode d'emploi*, Perec's posthumously published work *Cahier des charges de "La Vie mode d'emploi"* (1993) contains both his self-generated rules for the composition of the novel and the forty-two lists (each comprising ten elements) from which he took its contents.[10] Perec put these lists to work by drawing a 42 x 10 grid: on the horizontal rows, he used forty of them, which divided into ten groups of four each. Thus, on each vertical column, he could arrange ten sets of four elements, with each element belonging to a different list.[11] Perec's lists functioned as the source materials needed for the creation of his novelistic world, as one item from each of them, whose titles vary from "Citations" to "Animaux" and from "Meubles" to "Sentiments," had to appear in each chapter of *La Vie mode d'emploi*.[12] Perec relied on a mathematical system, an algorithm of permutation called "pseudo-quenine d'ordre 10," to identify on the grid the element from each list that had to be copied into each chapter of the novel.[13] Two of these lists, called *"manque"* [gap] and *"faux"* [wrong], disturb the methodical functioning of the system. They do not comprise identifiable items, but numbers from one to ten corresponding to the ten sets of four elements. When the pseudo-quenine selects a number from either *"manque"* or *"faux,"* this number identifies one of these sets: in the case of *"manque"* one element is not inserted, while in the case of *"faux"* another is substituted by one taken from another list.[14] This mathematical process for connecting his lists to the novel's chapters functions as an automatic, and at the same time unpredictable, device for transferring reality into a text.[15] It also conveys Perec's ambivalent attitude toward rational methods for managing information, which translates into his maniacal interest in fine-tuning these systems to perfection, only to sabotage them through the insertion of imperceptible, but fatal, flaws.

Ultimately, because one of the formulas Perec uses to write *La Vie mode d'emploi* involves transcribing items from lists into his novel, he relies, in part, on copying as a necessary tool for novelistic writing. These lists, in turn, are nothing but rolls for calling the names of objects belonging to empirical and cultural reality. Thus, a mechanical system akin to those used in computer generated film scripts, where writers can choose from a limited amount of plots, is fundamental to the genesis of *La Vie mode d'emploi*. In both cases, an archive allows the process to function: a repository of lists in Perec's novel and a digital database of plots in film script software. By establishing a detailed set of rules for writing his novel as early as 1972, Perec was able to work at the composition of *La Vie mode d'emploi* as a bureaucrat could have done it: "he could keep a folder for each chapter, accumulate things to put in it, and distribute elements appropriately by means of his diabolical multiplex jumble device."[16]

Without the author's help, no reader could discover the norms that Perec applied to the composition of *La Vie mode d'emploi*. Perec himself cautiously distilled the secrets of his composition for the public. In spring 1978, during a Oulipian debate on the opportunity for writers to reveal the constraints used in their works to a larger audience, he explained the rules he had applied to the writing of *La Vie mode d'emploi* in an ambiguous manner that made it possible for his listeners to have only a partial understanding of their functioning.[17] What the text itself reveals, however, matters more than its author's public statements. In this respect, it is highly significant that *La Vie mode d'emploi* foregrounds its links to bureaucratic writing and not the mathematical constraints that Oulipian poetics advocates. I am referring to the indexical apparatus that takes up 60 of the text's 640 pages (in the 1978 Hachette edition) at the end of *La Vie mode d'emploi*.[18] The first of these annexes is a sketchy map of the building, the grid whose squares are identified by either the residents' names or generic terms such as "stairs," "elevator machinery," or "store room." This outline of the novel's spatial structure is followed by an alphabetical index of all the entities that receive a name in the *La Vie mode d'emploi*: literary, cinematographic, and pictorial works; geographical places, historical events, fictional and historical figures, and the novel's characters. As each entry includes the page numbers of the corresponding passage in the novel, readers can conveniently consult the book through the index.[19] They can also approach the novel without following the sequence of its pages from the first to the last that the numerated book suggests.

The next annex is a detailed chronology listing the dates of all the main events of the novel from 1833 to 1975. Then, an "alphabetic checklist" displays the titles of the 107 stories narrated in *La Vie mode d'emploi,* along with the chapter number where they can be found.[20] After a postscript comprising the names of thirty authors cited in *La Vie mode d'emploi,* the indexical apparatus ends with a traditional table of contents. The appendices of *La Vie mode d'emploi* are reminiscent of the archive's finding aids, such as inventories (succinct descriptions of the items belonging to the various record series), calendars (chronologically ordered tables of contents), and indexes (systematically arranged lists of the contents of files, records, or groups of records).[21] The finding aids at the end of *La Vie mode d'emploi* help in turning the reading of the novel into an archival experience. As Perec's *romans* are told in installments, each of which correspond to a different room of the building, readers wanting to reconstruct a complete story must use one of the finding aids and move back and forth through the book. One might argue that any novel of some complexity asks its reader a similar approach, although without providing them with specific and detailed indexes as in *La Vie mode d'emploi.* Again, what matters is how the text directs the apprehension of its contents. Because the book equips readers with specific archival instruments for reconstructing its disjointed narrative units, what would have been a typical narrative experience in a traditional novel becomes a foray into the archive in *La Vie mode d'emploi.*

For readers of *La Vie mode d'emploi,* the indexes are a valuable, at times indispensable, tool for turning the segments of the text into meaningful narrative sequences. In certain passages of the novel, Perec regulates the flow of information going from the text to readers in a way that requires the latter to use the indexical apparatus in order to make sense of the story. In chapter 31, for instance, when readers learn that "a detective from Rethel was put in charge of the investigation on the double murder at Chaumont-Porcien," they come across a place name, that the novel mentions in passing 130 pages earlier. Only later in the chapter, when they encounter the name of Vera Beaumont, the mother of one of the victims, they can find the archival clue for retrieving the chapter that narrated the discovery of the double killing. They should now look up the index of characters, find Beaumont (Vera, born Orlova), and go back to page 40 where chapter 6 begins. Here, they can read how Vera Beaumont's daughter, Elizabeth, along with her husband, was murdered at Chaumont-Porcien in September 1959. After learning of this murder, impatient readers can use the finding aids to move forward in the text so as to anticipate the solution of the homicide in Chaumont-Porcien. In this case, they can look up, in the annexes, the clue leading to chapter 31, where the mystery of the two killings is solved. The Barthesian "hermeneutic code" for deciphering narrative enigmas functions only for readers perusing the text as if it were an archival dossier.[22] The indexical apparatus requires readers to perform certain archival operations, such as researching and retrieving data, which shape their experience of the text as much as the traditionally narrative elements of the novel (plot, characters, or style) can do. More important here, for my argument, is the role of Perec's finding aids in foregrounding the archival foundation of *La Vie mode d'emploi*: they point out the bureaucratic substratum of the novel. The archival procedures that the text requires readers to perform mirror the clerical job the author carried out when he organized the preparatory work for the novel as if he were running an administrative office.

At the linguistic level, the flat and impersonal jargon of bureaucrats dominates the prose, as if to suggest that Perec maintained a clerk's mindset while writing the novel. In *La Vie mode d'emploi*'s frequent descriptive statements, Perec mobilizes all the resources of the French language in order to prevent the enunciating subject of the text from being identified as a person: the recurrent presence of either impersonal pronouns, such as "*ça*," "*cela*," and "*on*," the deictic expression "*il y a*," the use of passive forms, and the simple elimination of the verb. All these techniques aim at making sure that the agency in charge of the descriptions in *La Vie mode d'emploi* be always anonymous. Through this strategy, Perec flaunts his willingness to break from the modernist principle of turning descriptive passages into analyses of the cognitive operations of a perceiving subject. As the following citations demonstrate, "the perceptual activity of the character contemplating" that sets apart the classic of description during modernism, Marcel Proust's *À la recherche du temps perdu*, never informs *La Vie mode d'emploi*:[23]

> Au second, chez les Altamont, on prépare la traditionnelle réception annuelle. *Il y aura* un buffet dans chacune des cinq pièces en façade de l'appartement. Dans celle ci ... les tapis *ont été roulés*, mettant en évidence un précieux parquet cloisonné. Presque tous les meubles *ont été enlevés* ; *il ne reste* que huit chaises en bois laqué, au dossier décoré de scènes évoquant la guerre des Boxers.
> *Il n'y a* aucun tableau sur les murs car les murs et les portes sont eux-mêmes décor : *il sont revêtus.* [my emphasis][24]

> On the second floor, at the Altamonts', preparations are underway for the traditional annual reception. There will be a buffet in each of the five rooms of the flat facing the street. In this room ... the carpets have been rolled up, revealing a valuable cloisonné floor. Almost all the furniture has been removed; they have left only eight chairs, made of lacquered wood with scenes from the Boxer Uprising painted on the backs.
> There are no paintings on the walls, because the walls and doors are themselves the decor: they have been hung.[25]

In an even more radical passage, the fourteen line long description of Doctor Dinteville's office, Perec simply creates a catalog of the objects crowding the room:

> Le cabinet du Docteur Dinteville : une table d'examen, un bureau métallique, presque nu, avec seulement un téléphone, une lampe articulée, un bloc d'ordonnances, un stylo d'acier mat dans la rainure d'un encrier de marbre ... et sur tout le mur de droite des panneaux de métal brillant dissimulant divers appareillages médicaux et les placards où le médecin range ses instruments, ses dossiers et ses produits pharmaceutiques. (76)

> Dr Dinteville's consulting room: an examining couch, a metal desk, almost bare, with only a telephone, an anglepoise lamp, a prescription pad, a matt-finished steel pen in the groove of a mar-

ble inkstand . . . and along the whole right hand wall, shining metal panels concealing various pieces of medical apparatus and the cupboards where the doctor keeps his instruments, his records, and his pharmaceutical stores.[26]

Passages such as the description of Dinteville's office, which includes the representation of the Doctor's archive, à la Balzac in *Le Colonel Chabert*, are quintessential *La Vie mode d'emploi*: they employ the style of memos jotted down by clerks who do not have time for stylistic and grammatical rules.

Perec's bureaucratic approach to the composition of his work also explains another distinctive feature of *La Vie mode d'emploi*, the frequent insertion of copies into the novel. Duplicates of heterogeneous texts, in particular of materials deprived of any literary value, such as advertisements, obituaries, crosswords, commercial catalogs, letters, and bibliographies, continue to surface throughout *La Vie mode d'emploi*.[27] For instance, the story of Madame Moreau, the CEO of a company that produces household tools, swiftly becomes the transcription of her firm's catalog. The first entry of this inventory reads as follows:

> NÉCESSAIRE À PAPIER PEINT : mallette plastique comprenant 1 double mètre pliant, 1 paire de ciseaux, 1 roulette, 1 marteau, 1 règle métallique 2 m, 1 tournevis contrôleur de courant, 1 émargeur, 1 couteau, 1 brosse, 1 fil à plomb, 1 paire tenailles, 1 couteau de peintre, 1 sabre. Long. 45, larg. 30, haut. 8 cm. Poids 2,5 kg. Garantie totale 1 an. (101)

> WALLPAPERING KIT. Includes 6' folding yardstick; scissors; roller; hammer; 6' metal rule; electrician's screwdriver; trimmers; knife; brush; plumbing; pliers; paint knife; handle; all in a portable plastic case, lgth. 2', wdth. 4', hgt. 4". Weight 6lbs. Fully guaranteed 1yr.[28]

At times, Perec inserts facsimiles—business cards, restaurant menus, a chess problem with the relative diagram, a family tree, posters, and several signboards—directly into the text. By duplicating everything he can lay his hands on, he reminds us of Bouvard and Pécuchet's copying from old papers bought by weight from a paper mill: both Perec and Flaubert's two clerks point to the copyist as the novelist's necessary, at times embarrassing, partner.

The imprint of bureaucratic writing is also evident in the lists of objects, persons, and events that crowd the pages of *La Vie mode d'emploi*. In all, forty-nine major catalogs dealing with any aspect of reality appear in Perec's novel.[29] They remind us of the archive's daily routine: archivists compose lists in order to keep track of the items the archive stores, establish initial classifications of records, and draft indexes or calendars. Historically, lists are as old as archives and writing; as Jack Goody has argued, "administrative lists dominate the uses of writing in ancient Mesopotamia. They can take a whole variety of forms, receipts of tribute, itemisation of war booty on the income side, distribution of rations, payments to officials, among the expenditures."[30] By packing his novel with inventories, Perec fosters a spatial apprehension of reality that only written language can make possible. Goody's examples show that early chirographic cultures were able to make verbalized material "immediately retrievable through its spatial organization. Lists arrange names of related items in the same physical, visual space."[31] The compilation of inventories acts upon the same principle that inspires the spatial structure of *La Vie mode d'emploi:* the world becomes intelligible only when spatial coordinates help in understanding it.

Since the publication of *Les Choses* (1965), the apprehension of reality as an inventory of items characterizes nearly all Perec's texts.[32] In these works, one encounters "the continuous happiness of enumerating or simply naming all the traces that a society continuously produces and rejects."[33] By preferring this bureaucratic style, Perec disenfranchises the more encyclopedic systems of realist writers. Balzac, for example, in the foreword to *La Comédie humaine,* states that he wants to climb from the archaeology of "social furniture" to the analysis of the relationship tying society to principles of truth and beauty.[34] By shunning this ascendance from particulars to universals, Perec chooses instead to record the traces left by social furniture, to perform a clerical job that begins by writing down the lists of society's debris.

At the thematic level, descriptions of archives, as well as accounts of archival research and archivists' adventures, constitute a crucial component of the novelistic world in *La Vie mode d'emploi*. Among the several archival stories that

Perec narrates, the life of Grégoire Simpson assumes a unique importance. As a part-time assistant sublibrarian in the Astrat Collection, Simpson has to transform articles regarding opera performances into permanent files [*Dossiers en place*] to be stored in an apposite archive (289). When his position expires for budgetary reasons, he spends months in complete inactivity and then disappears among rumors of a possible suicide.[35] Simpson is a doppelganger for the author of *La Vie mode d'emploi*. In addition to carrying out operations similar to those the archivist Perec performed in the lab of CNRS, Simpson shares with him an unequivocal habit: when he smokes, he holds the cigarette between his middle and ring fingers (294). We know from *Tentative d'épuisement d'un lieu parisien* (1975) that this was exactly Perec's manner of smoking: "il tient sa cigarette de la même façon que moi (entre le médius et l'annulaire): c'est la première fois que je retrouve chez un autre cette habitude" [he holds the cigarette in the same way as I do (between the middle and the ring fingers): it is the first time I notice this habit in another person].[36]

Through his identification with Grégoire Simpson, Perec clearly makes a point of presenting himself, the writer, as an archivist and, consequently, associating the composition of a novel to the arrangement of an archive. This association appears consistent with the fact that the privileged vehicle for accessing the past in *La Vie mode d'emploi* is the archive and not natural memory. As Claude Burgelin convincingly argues, Perec, as a patent "anti-Proust," utterly mistrusts memory.[37] He reproduces innumerable documents, letters, records, notes, and memos, but pays scarce attention to human beings' effort to remember: recording information on paper is the only way for preserving the remnants of the past in *La Vie mode d'emploi*. Perec delivers his harshest criticism of natural memory through the story of Valène, a painter who aims at the same goal he is pursuing as a novelist: to portray all the residents at 11 Rue Simon-Crubellier on one canvas (87–90). Even though he can remember everything that has happened in the building, as its doyen and resident artist, he fails in his project.[38] The canvas he leaves in his room before dying is practically blank, except for a few charcoal lines sketching the map of the apartment house (580). Natural memory can leave behind only the faintest traces of the past, while the copying, storing, and arranging of records carried out by Perec-the-archivist creates a book.

While Valène, the living memory of the apartment house, does not accomplish any useful task, archivists frame the memories of human history by establishing structures that enable people to access their past.[39] *La Vie mode d'emploi* fictionalizes the archivist's crucial role in society by narrating several stories in which characters embark on investigations in archives and/or build repositories of records. In chapter 22, James Sherwood discovers a veritable archive of documents relating to the relics of Jesus Christ's passion abandoned in an old trunk (116). In chapter 46, Monsieur Jérôme peruses historical records for five years in order to make a card index of the Spanish clergy. He writes 7,462 biographies of clergymen that he arranges under twenty-seven headings (254). In chapter 60, Cinoc builds an index card database of the words that the evolution of language has made obsolete (346). In chapter 62, Wehsal searches the archives of the federal government in Washington D.C. in order to discover the secret for making synthetic petrol (360). In chapter 66, Madame Marcia keeps a well-arranged archive of the customers of her antique shop (382). In chapter 80, the Spanish archivist Juan Mariana de Zaccaria retrieves an ancient document concerning the first name imposed on the New World toward the end of the fifteenth-century (455). In chapter 83, two kleptomaniacs, Berthe and Maximilien Danglars, record in a notebook all the thefts they commit (475). In chapter 88, Véronique Altamont stores the documents of her family's secrets in apposite folders (517). In chapter 91, Marcelin Échard creates a massive repository of documents that should prove how Adolf Hitler survived the end of WWII (535). In chapter 96, in order to publish a critical edition of a seventeenth-century medical treatise, Doctor Dinteville spends four years doing research in archives and libraries (555).

Even though all the abovementioned stories provide readers with in-depth descriptions of the archive's modus operandi and goals, the most important archival story in *La Vie mode d'emploi* concerns another painter, Percival Bartlebooth. An Englishman of immense wealth, he decides to dedicate his life to a single, albeit meaningless, project. He plans to paint five hundred watercolors of seaports around the world and have them turned into jigsaw puzzles that he will store and solve. Then, after having the puzzles turned into the original sheets of painted paper, he will have them dipped in a detergent solution that will erase all their lines and colors. In the end, no trace will remain of a project that will have taken up the greater part of its author's life, from 1925 to 1975. Bartlebooth's story functions both as the structural backbone of the novel, through its links to several other characters' adventures, and its metaphor, by narrating an attempt to establish an arbitrary order on a limited piece of reality.

Like Melville's hero, Bartleby the Scrivener, from whom Bartlebooth receives the first part of his name, Perec's painter is also a copyist, though his medium differs: pictures in lieu of words.[40] In his dreams, by painting five hundreds watercolors he should become an artist. However, as a painter totally devoid of creativity, he can only make five hundred brute copies of reality and call them paintings.[41] He is the truest archivist in *La Vie mode d'emploi* because he carries out all the practices involved with the archive: creating/copying, storing, and destroying records. By narrating how Bartlebooth desposes of his own archive—the five hundred watercolors he plans to obliterate one by one—Perec proves to be familiar with the tendency to self-destruction that is historically associated with archival discourse. A routine task in our daily lives—having to systematically throw away useless papers in order to keep our files in order—constitutes a standard procedure for running bureaucratic archives. The main worry of modern public administrations is not the preservation, but the elimination of records: "The National Archives of the United States, for example, now retains less than two percent of the records produced by the government."[42] By saving 12 percent of Bartlebooth's records (sixty-two puzzles are still intact at the Englishman's death), Perec designs an archive whose practices are considerably less destructive than those carried out by modern states.[43]

Jacques Derrida ascribes the archive's tendency to self-destruction, its precarious balance between recording and forgetting, to the existence of an antiarchival principle, the "*archiviolithique*," that lies at the core of the archival endeavor, as though what we really want when we create records is to destroy them.[44] Derrida's *archiviolithique* stems from the archive's longing for the origin, the ἀρχή, i.e., the first principle on which political authority, law, and civilization itself rest. As the origin can exist only before the practice of recording begins (we create records because we need substitutes for something we miss: the origin), if the archive could register the primeval beginning it would deny its very raison d'être. By ultimately aspiring to reach a state where no record can exist, the archive hosts the principle of its own destruction. It is no wonder that Derrida can talk of the death drive as the force that is hiding behind the archival endeavor. The archive's aim at an origin in which its very existence is denied parallels the desire for the primeval quiet that precedes the turmoil of organic life, which Freud attributes to all living beings.

In order to destroy his watercolor/puzzles Bartlebooth must also elaborate an efficient method for storing them, thus putting the archive at the service of its own effacement. By describing the search for the original quiet, the great nothing, *through* archivization, Bartlebooth's story foregrounds the death drive as a core component of archival discourse. It narrates the schizophrenia of the archive, the fact that the institution bound to the storing of records gets rid of almost all the documents it receives in consignment from society. Bartlebooth is a compulsive archivist, the epitome of the obsession to accumulate (and destroy) records that affects several characters in *La Vie mode d'emploi*. In a Derridian mode, it is the search for the origin that sets this cycle of construction and destruction in motion. In his five hundred paintings, Bartlebooth depicts only seaports, *ports de mer* in French. As Burgelin argues, since *mer* as sea and *mère* as mother are homophones in French, Bartlebooth's project amounts to a compulsive search for the very epitome of the origin, the lost maternal harbor.[45]

Apart from the compulsive type, another class of archivists operates in *La Vie mode d'emploi;* their defining trait is their outright trust in the archive's ability to bring about perfect order. Perec's utopian archivists look for a type of totality that cannot be found in the empiric world. They ask the archive to store complete and reliable documentation about the portion of reality that lies at the center of their interests. In their repositories, records refer to objects in an unequivocal manner, by establishing a straightforward, one to one relationship with them: there cannot be an object without a record and a record without an object. Since the same absolute consistency must characterize the internal functioning of the system, these archives operate as infallible machines for retrieving records. Archival utopias ignore the loss and falsification of documents that characterize the operations of the archive in the real world, as well as the self-destructive longing for the origin that defines compulsive archivists' experience of the archive. In *La Vie mode d'emploi*, utopian archivists' attempts to achieve totality and perfect order combine with the eerie futility of their interests. There appears to be an absolute disproportion between the professionalism and determination of characters such as Wehsal and Echard and the meaningless documents they collect regarding the secret formula for producing synthetic petrol or Hitler's survival after the Second World War.

The story of Monsieur Jérôme's index card database of the Spanish clergy may be considered the epitome of the utopian archivists' experiences in *La Vie mode d'emploi*. No credible motivation brings about the search for totality that characterizes this archive: an "aged scholar" casually met on a train commissions Monsieur Jérôme to realize this archival project for a compensation of 150 francs a month. The 7,462 biographies of seventeenth-century Spanish churchmen divided into the twenty-seven headings that Monsieur Jérôme classifies bear witness to the thoroughness of his archive. He unveils the utopian streak of this endeavor when he proudly notices that "par une coïncidence, admirable ajoutait-il en ricanant, 27 est précisément, dans la classification décimale universelle—plus connue sous le nom de C.D.U.—, le chiffre réservé à l'histoire générale de l'Église chrétienne" (255) [by a marvellous coincidence, he would add with a grin, 27 is precisely the number, in the universal decimal classification system—better known as Dewey Decimal—for the general history of the Christian Church].[46] As the archive of the Spanish clergy functions in sync with the universal arrangement of knowledge, totality achieves a new, epistemic meaning. The marvelous consistency between the catalog of churchmen's biographies and the universal decimal classifications system ensures that methodological rigor has informed Monsieur Jérôme's project. In a context where the particular connects to the universal through the language of numbers, as in hermetic doctrines, and the actual repository is the empirical materialization of the ideal archive, nothing can escape the utopian archivist's dream of perfect classification.

After the aged scholar's death and innumerable vain attempts to have prestigious academic institutions interested in his work, Monsieur Jérôme burns his catalog in the courtyard of the Sorbonne. A similar fate rewards Wehsal's and Echard's archival enterprises. The former's dossier is thrown in the wastebasket (361), while the latter's monumental research produces sixty-odd copies of a complete bibliography on Hitler's death that end up rotting in the basement among filing cards, file paper, notebooks, and other junk (535). Despite their attempts to construct perfect archives, utopian archivists encounter the same fate as their compulsive colleagues, i.e., the destruction of their dossiers. In *La Vie mode d'emploi*, the archive asks his practitioners to make tremendous efforts by luring them with the hope of fixing our untidy world—but this arrangement appears to be a short-lived illusion that in any moment can degenerate into a heap of garbage:

> Caves. La cave des Rorschachs.... On y trouve des restes de rouleaux de papier peint dont les motifs semi-abstraits évoquent des poissons, des pots de peinture de toutes teintes et tailles, quelques dizaines de classeurs gris intitulés ARCHIVES, résidus de telle ou telle fonction officielle à la Direction des Programmes de Télévision. (389)

> Cellars. The Rorschachs' cellar.... On them are to be found remnants of wallpaper with vaguely fish-like semiabstract patterns, paint pots of all sizes and shades, a few dozen grey boxfiles labelled ARCHIVES, the residue of some official function or other at TV Programme Control.[47]

The archival leftovers created by Perec's characters stay in the basement until somebody, the very author of *La Vie mode d'emploi* comes to collect them. Although he remains skeptical about the archive's ability to neatly arrange our messy experiences of the world, Perec believes that the archive can leave behind a legacy of still usable remnants. This represents a minimal, but significant, result given the void surrounding human experience in *La Vie mode d'emploi*. Perec is interested in the trace of the bureaucracy, in the records of recording, or in assembling archives of archives. By having all the repositories of documents in the novel achieve such poor results, Perec demonstrates that he knows all to well about the problems that hinder the storing, classifying, and interpreting of records.[48] What matters is that he can put this knowledge at the service of a productive program: while compulsive and utopian archivists fail, the novelist/clerk Perec succeeds. The only archive-based project that achieves its goal in *La Vie mode d'emploi* is Perec's writing of the archival novel by way of his forty-two lists. This operation manages to establish some order on a well-defined section of reality because it aims at a limited set of goals and utilizes a self-contained methodology. It pursues a moderate agenda and follows principles that its very author has tailored to these limited goals. While the novel eschews the search for totality, it also harbors a sane mistrust in the archive's ability to prove truth by exhibiting original documents and to organize records in a rational, effective manner.

Perec succeeds in shaping *La Vie mode d'emploi* as a repository of records by approaching the archive as a game. Rather than adopting the epistemology of the archive for cognitive purposes, he plays with it. For example, in *La Vie mode d'emploi*, the principle of "apprehension through localization" does not assume the same epistemic value that it takes in *La Comédie humaine*. In Balzac's works, the act of defining persons through their connection to their habitat is a praxis that nineteenth-century knowledge supports as a methodologically sound manner to understand reality. Instead, in *La Vie mode d'emploi*, the relation between an individual and his/her territory functions in a context in which characters are assigned a site on the basis of ad hoc laws—Perec's constraints based on the rules of a game, continuous plays on words, and mathematical theorems. While these conventions give the archival novel a marvelous consistency, one should point out that this is the relative coherence of games, where you may decide that ten players cannot use their hands and one can, as in soccer, simply because this allows for playing more interesting contests. By contrast, the Balzacian archive applies principles that are meant to be intrinsically natural and rational, such as the idea that the environment molds people's identities. For the novel and the état civil alike, it is a matter of finding the proper instruments, i.e., records, for documenting the relationship between people and their surroundings, but that relationship is already there as it has always been: it is part of the fabric of the world. As he proves that positing a relation between archival theory and outer reality is a metaphysical proposition and that the only archive that functions is self-validating, Perec moves from realism to postmodernism, from the paradigm of legitimation to that of challenge. And yet, what he creates remains an archive: it depends on arbitrary rules, which, nevertheless, are instrumental in safekeeping a great deal of valuable knowledge in the form of documents, objects, and narratives. Among these stored items, the glimpse of an effective, albeit elusive, order appears. By passing on to future generations this concretion of precariously arranged traces, *La Vie mode d'emploi*, once more, belongs to archival discourse. As he criticizes the archive through the archive itself, Perec demonstrates the weakness of archival discourse along with its historical necessity.

7
Libra by Don DeLillo: The Archival Novel in the Autumn of the Paper Archive

EARLY IN *LIBRA*, DON DELILLO'S NOVEL THAT NARRATES THE ASSASsination of President Kennedy, readers come across a character, Nicholas Branch, who retrieves information by entering a date on his computer. As a retired intelligence analyst who is writing the secret story of the assassination, Branch carries out the same operation as DeLillo the novelist. Given this analogy, the first scene with Branch at the keyboard is once again reminiscent of the intention behind the description of the lawyer Derville and his clerks working in his office in Balzac's *Le Colonel Chabert*. In both cases, the novel displays its archival foundation. In *Libra*, this means demonstrating how one should handle data in the messy archive of Late Modernity: by way of databases and search engines, as Branch does. The appearance of the digital database aids in framing the reader's experience of the text, as well as highlights the technological context for arranging records in *Libra*. In a novel that narrates an event of enormous historical significance such as the Kennedy assassination, the digital database speaks of a new epoch in the history of archivization. *Libra* carries the archival novel into the age in which its epistemic partner, the paper archive, has reached the threshold of its technological obsolescence. Clearly moved by the same concerns as Georges Perec in *La Vie mode d'emploi*, DeLillo strives to create a novel that might combine historical accuracy with a critique of the prevailing methods for keeping those records on which historicity is based. In the history of the archival novel, *Libra* applies the paradigm of challenge to an extreme situation, when what is at stake is not so much a critique of the archive as the very possibility of shaping a truthful narrative within the technological boundaries that delimit archivization in the paper age. Appropriately, DeLillo's novel executes a strategy for surviving the archive's entropy that is the opposite of the one implemented in Balzac's *Comédie humaine,* the text that epitomizes the coincidence between the novel's and the bureaucratic archive's epistemologies. As it emphasizes limitation against totality and chance against determinism, *Libra* outlines a design to replace the archive rather than relying on it. It does so by both foregrounding archivists' inability to arrange their archives and proposing a manner for shaping narratives out of archival documentation that can function even when the archive falls prey to radical disorder.

At the time of the writing of *Libra,* two opposite principles, contingency and conspiracy, informed the extant narratives of the assassination.[1] Theories based on contingency maintained that a lone gunman, Lee Harvey Oswald, was the sole person responsible for the president's death: as a Marxist and a pro-Castro activist, Oswald killed President Kennedy in retaliation for the US government's hostile policy toward Communist Cuba. On a personal level, as a deranged individual who had repeatedly failed in his private life, Oswald hated John Kennedy and everything he represented: success, popularity, and power. Since Oswald's crime originated in a mix of ideological zealotry and personal troubles, it neither followed any rational and predictable plan, nor required an investigation into a possible conspiracy: the assassination began and ended with Lee Harvey Oswald. Narratives based on the hypothesis of a conspiracy followed an opposite pattern. They insisted that the CIA, the White House, and the top brass in the military had joined anti-Castro hard liners and the mob in a plot to kill the president. After the assassination, the conspirators masterminded the institutional cover-up of their plan, the systematic elimination of witnesses, as well as the disruption of all the investigations into their plot. In narratives inspired by the idea of a conspiracy, Lee Oswald was a mere decoy, a scapegoat that the real killers of President Kennedy had offered to public opinion.

Contingency and conspiracy theories found distinct supporters in the cultural and political arena. While the establishment (the United States government, the military, academia, and the mainstream media) endorsed narratives based on contingency, an army of freelance researchers, grassroots organizations, and alternative media supported histories inspired by conspiracy. The report presented by "The President's Commission on the Assassination of President Kennedy" on September 24, 1964, a.k.a. the *Warren Commission Report* from the chairman of the commission, Chief Justice Earl Warren, represented the institutional truth on the assassination. As for the conspiracy theories from the opposite camp, no narrative could achieve a prestige comparable to that of the *Warren Commission Report*. Instead, it was the sheer number of studies critical of the government's version of the assassination published in the span of more than two decades that conveyed the idea of an alternative history of Kennedy's death.[2] Although triggered by different motivations, both the supporters of contingency theories and their opponents shared an equal mistrust in the archive. Those who believed in the institutional accounts of President Kennedy's death were suspicious of any new record that could undermine the official version of the assassination. They would have liked to seal the files on the killing forever, thus shutting out what they perceived as an unpredictable component of the archive. For the believers in conspiracy theories, instead, government-run repositories were by definition prone to the manipulation and destruction of truthful records. Only investigators independent from the secret powers that rule over society could discover the truth hidden among the files of the Kennedy assassination. Ultimately, in conspiracy theories, it is the authority in charge of the investigation that enjoys the power of turning the archive into either a trustworthy or a deceitful institution.

In the late 1980s, the gargantuan Dallas archive (the collection of police records, intelligence memos, institutional reports, and independent stories written on the assassination) seemed to hit an epistemic wall.[3] While its official constituent continued to produce the same immutable truth, its unauthorized component could generate only unchanging stories of plots against democracy. Only an act of cognitive imagination could enable a writer to shape a meaningful story out of the worn-out documentation on the killing of the president. This is what DeLillo did as he composed *Libra* by keeping his distance from both contingency and conspiracy theories. Without postulating the existence of an almighty power hidden in an obscure area of the government, he imagined a scheme that originated in the mid management of the CIA and counted on accomplices in the administration and in organized crime. In particular, by describing the assassination as the result of a chain of accidents, DeLillo differentiated himself from paranoid readings of recent American history. *Libra* traces an anti-Kennedy plot initially meant to fire shots at the president without hitting or killing him. Chance, however, inexorably derails the plotters' original plans. At the end of the day, hazard—in the form of: an unreliable gunman, Lee Oswald, certain conspirators' personal hatred for the president, the itinerary chosen for Kennedy's visit to Dallas, and good weather—determines the outcome of the conspiracy. Letting things unfold on their own, rather than controlling every detail of the intrigue, is the cipher of the machination that kills JFK in *Libra*. The plot starts when a disgruntled CIA agent, Win Everett, forced out of active service after the Bay of Pigs fiasco, decides to stir up anti-Cuban sentiment in the United States by organizing a failed attempt on President Kennedy's life. By planting evidence that ties the assassins to the Cuban Intelligence Directorate, Everett plans to cause an anti-Castro backlash and gain support for a military strike against Communist Cuba. After recruiting three veterans of the Bay of Pigs invasion, Frank Vásquez, Wayne Elko, and Raymo, Everett and his coconspirators, Larry Parmenter and T. J. Mackey, get in touch with a pro-Castro activist, Lee Harvey Oswald. As a former defector to the USSR, Oswald appears to be a perfect patsy, one who can easily shift the suspects from the real assassins to a communist machination. As T. J. Mackey deliberately omits to tell the hit men to miss their target, the plot inexorably proceeds toward its deadly conclusion. On November 22, 1963, while Oswald just wounds Kennedy, Raymo kills the president by shooting from behind a fence on top of the grassy knoll bordering Elm Street.

As the following "Author's Note" at the end of the novel spells out, a peculiar relationship between the archive and the fictional text underpins DeLillo's narrative of the assassination.

This is a work of imagination. While drawing from the historical record, I've made no attempt to furnish factual answers to any questions raised by the assassination.

Any novel about a major unresolved event would aspire to fill some of the blank spaces in the known record. To do this, I've altered and embellished reality, extended real people into imagined space and time, invented incidents, dialogues, and characters. Among these invented characters are all officers of intelligence agencies and all organized crime figures, except for those who are part of the book's background.

In a case in which rumors, facts, suspicions, official subterfuge, conflicting sets of evidence and a dozen labyrinthine theories all mingle, sometimes indistinguishably, it may seem to come that a work of fiction is one more gloom in a chronicle of unknowing.

But because this book makes no claim to literal truth, because it is only itself, apart and complete, readers may find refuge here—a way of thinking about the assassination without being constrained by half-facts or overwhelmed by possibilities, by the tide of speculation that widens with the years.[4]

The immediate goal of DeLillo's note is to shield *Libra* from the heated debate on John Kennedy's death, including its possible legal ramifications, by reiterating the novel's fictional status, playing down its ambition to establish the historical truth, and carefully pointing out the imaginary nature of the intelligence officers that it represents. To this purpose, the first two paragraphs of the note places the novel on the sideline of the archive, in a parasitic position where the novelist has simply to cherry-pick the records that best fit his project. This defensive goal achieved, the note assesses the deplorable situation of the Dallas archive and flaunts DeLillo's plan of turning *Libra* into a viable alternative to the extant narratives on the assassination.

Initially, it may appear that replacing the missing links in the record on the assassination as a series of data points, facts, details, and somewhat shadowy clues is the method for emending the documentation on Kennedy's death that *Libra*'s author advocates. The Dallas archive, however, is mired in such chaos (conflicting sets of evidence, official subterfuge, labyrinthine theories) that bridging the gaps in its collections of documents becomes an impossible feat. Indeed, when the archive deteriorates into a messy storeroom where facts are undistinguishable from rumors and suspicion, how can a researcher detect which records are missing? Blank spaces are evident in well-ordered series, not in chaotic collections in which the relations among records appear misleading and obscure. In this context, a novelist aiming at emending the historical record must first elaborate a strategy for imposing some order on the available archival material and only then can he or she attempt to complete the extant documentation through fictional methods. What sets *Libra* apart from the archival novels of its age is the fact that DeLillo, in his attempt to fix the Dallas archive, by which I mean to repair its inconsistencies and gaps, as well as to stabilize and fasten it into place so that it is no longer a slippery mess of information and suspicions of varying reliability, not only answers the specific questions arising from the Kennedy assassination, but also addresses the larger relationship between the novel and the archive in the epistemic context of postmodernism. In other words, DeLillo manages to write an archival novel that centers and relies on an archive whose integrity is soiled by omissions, contradictions, hypertrophy, and intrusions from powerful external agents. He can succeed in this endeavor by creating a refuge for readers left stranded by the postmodern archive's failure to provide its users with conclusive documentation about a given event. *Libra* answers this need for finality because it is a complete object, a haven from the chaos of external reality. Being such a refuge, a mission that the classic archive routinely performed, is a task that its postmodern counterpart executes with increasing difficulty.

DeLillo works the archive from within, by showing that this institution's shortcomings depend first and foremost on its own, historically determined, limits and only secondarily on power's abusive intrusion in its operations. The hypothesis of a secret authority that masterminds the storage and arrangement of records while, at the same time, concealing its operations from external investigations, relies on the archive's perfect functioning; only in this utopian case could the archive hide the proof of its own obedience to some hidden agency. But in *Libra*, rather than being a faultless machine, the archive is a decrepit organization that is crumbling because of its methodological contradictions. No external plot prevents the Dallas archive from storing documents that could help in discovering the truth about the president's death. In a context where archival practices based on the principle of provenance become increasingly ineffective, the archivists' consequent inability to keep their house in order turns the arrangement of records into a cumbersome and epistemically futile activity. The fictional instrument for assessing the archive's situation is Nicholas Branch, a character who plays a crucial role in *Libra* even though he makes only six short appearances in the novel.[5]

When the narration of the conspiracy begins, Nicholas Branch "sits in the book-filled room, the room of documents, the room of theories and dreams" (14). Apparently, he enjoys ideal working conditions. The CIA Curator that supervises his works satisfies any request of his: "when he needs something, a report or transcript, anything, any level of difficulty, he simply has to ask. The Curator is quick to respond, firm in his insistence on forwarding precisely the right document in an area of research marked by ambiguity and error, by political bias, systematic fantasy"(15). Branch can also analyze material "not seen by anyone outside the headquarters complex at Langley," such as the CIA's confidential files and the records of its internal investigations. Despite, or perhaps because of, this utopian availability of documents, Nicholas Branch's progress is painfully slow; after fifteen years working on his assignment, he has written very little of "actual finished prose" (59). His situation thus appears radically different from DeLillo's, the other writer who attempts to shape a narrative out of the Dallas archive. And yet, when Branch makes his first appearance in *Libra* the scenario seems to suggest his identification with the author. The analyst is shown in his office typing the date of the first meeting between the novel's three chief conspirators, Win Everett, Laurence Parmenter, and T. J. Mackey: "He enters a date on the home computer the Agency has provided for the sake of convenient tracking. April 17, 1963. The names appear at once, with backgrounds, connections, locations. The bright hot skies. The shady street of handsome old homes framed in native oak" (15). The cinematographic technique of fade-out and fade-in that helps readers make the transition from Branch's computer to the streets of Dalton also lures them into regarding Branch as the agent responsible for the narration of the following episode. If readers factor in that Branch is composing a story of the assassination through research in the archive, exactly as DeLillo does, the identification between the character and his author could not be more precise.

Providing the story of Win Everett's conspiracy with its archival foundation represents Branch's chief narrative task in *Libra*. The main instrument in this operation is his frequent quoting from the "roster of the dead," a list of "the names of witnesses, informers, investigators, people linked to Lee H. Oswald, people linked to Jack Ruby, all conveniently and suggestively dead" (57). Branch's roster is a shrewd combination of fiction and historical truth. It comprises nineteen individuals, from relatively famous characters like Jack Ruby or Sam Giancana to unknown anti-Castro activists such as Eladio del Valle or Antonio Veciana. Seven of these names belong to historical figures who are also cited in two crucial official documents on the assassination, the *Warren Commission Report* and the *Report of the Select Committee on Assassinations of the U.S. House of Representatives* (1979).[6] As the remaining twelve names, notably those of the three chief conspirators and the three gunmen, are not quoted in official documents stored in the National Archives, they should be considered as belonging to fictional characters.[7] In this calculated mix of true and false data, what matters is the procedure that Nicholas Branch implements. In the story he writes, he inserts the information on characters belonging to the roster of the dead in the form of records, as though they were items in a bureaucratic list. In so doing, he carries out the same function that the classic device of the "hidden and found manuscript" performs in nineteenth-century fiction: he points out the novel's relation to the archive, at the same time legitimizing the text as a truthful rendition of the past that is backed by records. Branch's initial identification with DeLillo is part of the same legitimizing strategy. By prompting readers to relate the author of *Libra* to the man of the archive, Nicholas Branch, DeLillo establishes a solid connection between the novel and the known record on the assassination. But in Branch's following appearances, as he becomes increasingly distant from the author, this identification blurs. This development occurs because Branch has to carry out another task in the novel, notably laying out the shortcomings of both the Dallas archive and the extant narratives of the assassination.

In addition to the different readerships they address (a secret elite of CIA's top officials for Branch versus the anonymous consumers of literary products for DeLillo), the chief difference between the two writers consists in the opposite outcomes of their efforts: while the CIA analyst does not even come close to finishing his project, the novelist completes his novel. That he will never see the end of his predicament is painfully clear to Branch: as his story progresses, the futility of his labor saps his morale and energies, and he becomes increasingly morose. The reason for his fiasco is certainly inscribed in the profile of his mission and the tricks the CIA plays with him. But above all Branch fails because of his epistemic situation. He is an old-fashioned archivist trapped in a repository that cannot be arranged by applying the basic tenet of classical archival theory, the principle of provenance.

Indeed, Nicholas Branch is a lost archivist: "He is in the fifteenth year of his labor and sometimes wonders if he is becoming bodiless. He knows he is getting old. There are times when he can't concentrate on the facts at hand and has to come back again and again to the page, the line, the fine-grained detail of a particular afternoon" (14). Records outgrow Nicholas Branch's ability to store them: "Paper is beginning to slide out of the room and across the doorway to the house proper. The closet is stuffed with material he has yet to read. He has to wedge new books into the shelves, force them in, insert them sideways, squeeze everything, keep everything" (378). Branch has merged so deeply into his archive that his own mind functions as archival software: "But he knows where everything is. From a stack of folders that reaches halfway up a wall, he smartly plucks the one he wants. . . . There is no formal system to help him track the material in the room. He uses hand and eye, color and shape and memory, the configuration of suggestive things that link an object to its contents" (15).

"The stuff keeps coming" is the refrain that continues to appear (three times, at pp. 59, 378, 441, in addition to "the data keeps coming" at p 301) in the descriptions of Branch's vain attempts to write the story of the assassination. Here, as

Branch's archive functions as a synecdoche for the larger Dallas archive, DeLillo is pointing out the latter's predicament. It is the Dallas archive that is jammed by the 125,000 pages of the FBI's papers on the assassination, the 26 accompanying volumes of testimony and exhibits of the *Warren Commission Report*, and the CIA's 144 volume file on Oswald. The list of records crowding the pages of these volumes speaks of a ravenous archive that is caught in true documentation frenzy: "Everything is here. Baptismal records, report cards, postcards, divorce petitions, canceled checks, daily timesheets, tax returns, property lists, postoperative x-rays, photos of knotted string, thousands of pages of testimony, of voices droning in hearing rooms in old courthouse buildings, an incredible haul of human utterance" (181). The Dallas archive stores oddities such as Jack Ruby's mother's dental chart, a microphotograph of three strands of Lee H. Oswald's pubic hair, and "a special FBI report that includes detailed descriptions of the *dreams* of eyewitnesses following the assassination of Kennedy and the murder of Oswald" (441). Nicholas Branch fails because the main instrument for his project, the paper archive based on the principle of provenance, has grown beyond its physiological and epistemic boundaries: while its physical structures crack, its conceptual categories can no longer help in arranging documents whose reciprocal relations are infinitely more complex than those tying records to a record series and the latter to its originating agency. This archive does not succeed in offering a single truth upheld by its documents, especially due to the constant influx of new records. The integration of the most recently acquired documents becomes a more and more unrealistic goal that exacerbates the chaos of the already-present materials and worsens the archive's conceptual inconsistencies. Instead of helping the public to know the truth of the assassination, the archive produces a quite opposite outcome: the spreading of the ideology of secrecy, the idea that truth can exist only in an extremely private form.

In his last appearance, toward the end of the novel, Branch mulls over the CIA's culture of secrecy. He "understands that the Agency is a closed system" that cannot share the information it possesses with other subjects. But he wonders why "they are withholding material from him"; after all, he is writing a history that is expected to circulate only among the top hierarchy of the CIA. Maybe, Branch asks himself, "the Agency is protecting something very much like its identity—protecting its own truth, its theology of secrets" (442). The transition from these thoughts to the ultimate understanding of his failure to write the story of the assassination is quick. At the end of his meditation, Branch realizes that "he can't get out [of his room/of his attempt to write]. The case will haunt him to the end. Of course, they've known it all along. That's why they built this room for him, the room of growing old, the room of history and dreams" (445).

The CIA has used Branch as a guinea pig. By monitoring his botched attempt to write the history of President Kennedy's murder, the agency tests its own archive's ability to function as a sealed system informed by a "theology of secrets." Branch falls into the trap because he implements those very methods that the CIA supports. Throughout his endeavor, he falls prey to the agency's obsession with obtaining complete information about the events it is investigating: "It is vital to his sense of responsibility that everything in his room warrants careful study. Everything belongs, everything adheres." (182). As a maniac of the archive, he believes that "there is nothing in the room he can discard as irrelevant or out-of-date. It all matters on one level or another. This is the room of lonely facts" (378). The archive's totality is the issue, here. The CIA is running a total archive that adheres to two principles: (1) it aims at creating records about any event that might fall under the agency's watch; (2) it considers that even the most trivial record deserves a place on its shelves. Totality has always been an item on the agenda of the modern archive's founders and keepers, an ambitious goal meant to reach, in its turn, toward the equally ambitious, if not impossible, outcome we might call archival utopia. During the revolution, the ambition of the French legislators to create an agency, the National Archives, that could store all the records produced within the nation's borders betrayed their longing for totality. One can apply the same argument to the archives of nineteenth-century law enforcement agencies as described by Balzac, whose goal was to gather complete documentation of all the acts of illegality committed in the entire society. The very principle of provenance, finally, the idea that records must inevitably lead to the offices that generated them, thus allowing their keepers to draw perfect maps of any administration within the reach of their operations, bespeaks of archivists' aspiration to capture the totality of record creating agencies' organizational arms. Nineteenth-century archival scholars expressed this longing for totality within the paradigm of organicism. They viewed both archives and record-creating agencies as living organisms whose parts harmoniously integrated each other: "A well ordered archival collection should present in the arrangement of its documents the external picture of the organic structure of the State, just as a good architect reveals in the façade the purpose and internal structure of a building."[8] For the archive, reproducing the inner organization of a living body, in which even the smallest parts are vital to the functioning of the whole, means grasping it as a totality that can and must be recorded in its entirety. The image of the archival collection as a mirror of the organic structure of the state reveals a utopian dream of the archive as a total repository that can document even the least significant detail of the administration whose records it stores.

In Late Modernity, technology has delivered the tools (typewriters, Xerox-machines, computers, printers) that might convince archivists to move within the reach of their dreams of totality. Indeed, creating and storing records have never been so easy. As Branch experiences, however, while the stuff keeps coming, the utopia of bureaucracy, the total archive where every event is recorded and every record is stored, sinks under the weight of its own folders. Totality, assembling complete documentation on a certain object, be it an event, a bureaucratic agency, or a governmental program, is a feasible goal only if the target of the archive's operations is a finite and reasonably organized entity. But when archivists come across an event like the assassination, which cannot be circumscribed within either temporal or spatial limits and keeps generating chaotic heaps of records, achieving totality becomes an impossible goal that can only produce neurotic behavior in its suitors. And an untamable proliferation of documentation is indeed what Nicholas Branch is supposed to shape into a story. In order to communicate the sense of Branch's predicament, DeLillo takes great care in conveying the image of an archive flooded by paper: "Paper is beginning to slide out of the room and across the doorway to the house proper. The floor is covered with books and papers" (378). As the same synecdochical relation connecting Branch's room to the Dallas archive ties the latter to the larger Paper Archive of late modernity, *Libra* takes on the issues that define archival discourse during postmodernism. The sickness that affects Branch's office is that of the paper archive in the age of its historical decline. The very material whose abundance was instrumental in the rise of governmental and private bureaucracies becomes the poison that prevents them from functioning. In the paper archive, the search for totality leads to paralysis and, ultimately, to the affirmation of a theology of secrecy. An archive that chokes under its own files becomes an opaque gathering of records, a deposit of unreadable documents, in other words the ideal location for hiding truth.

Along with the excess of documentation, an insane desire to gesture toward the original event lying at the source of a record series plagues the Dallas archive. Totality is again the issue, here. It is a new kind of totality, however, one that operates chronologically rather than spatially, that archivists pursue when they dream of arranging a record series that might hook to an event rather than a document. This is Derrida's very search for the ἀρχή unfolding in a postmodern context, the idea that technology might deliver the desired encounter with the origin by making writing obsolete. This aspiration to bypass written records in order to arrive at the original event is a defining trait of the Dallas archive. When he receives from the Curator "an actual warped bullet that has been fired for test purposes through the wrist of a seated cadaver" Branch thinks he is "on another level." He feels like he is operating "beyond documents" in a context in which his employers want him "to *touch* and *smell*" (299). This is the peculiar hubris that mars archival discourse ever since the availability of new storage media (photography, gramophone, film) infringed on the privileged position of writing as the chief archival medium: the idea that technology might make it possible to store the real thing, something that can be apprehended directly through our senses without the intellectual mediation of the record and, in particular, of the written document and its cumbersome reading protocol.

In the Dallas archive, the epitome of this attitude is the Zapruder film, the 8mm home movie shot by Abraham Zapruder, a Dallas dressmaker who witnessed the assassination. Since the publication, one week after the killing, of thirty-one frames taken from the Zapruder film in the magazine *Life*, the movie was hailed as the only "unimpeachable" witness on Kennedy's death.[9] However, when the Warren Commission utilized the Zapruder film, it turned the movie into a source of information for a staged reconstruction of the assassination: "Using another limousine and stand-ins, the crucial moments of the motorcade were reenacted based on the Zapruder imagery. A camera mounted behind the telescopic sight on the alleged murder rifle photographed the point of view from the sixth floor of the School Book Depositiory, Oswald's alleged line of vision, each frame intended to correlate with the position of the limousine as recorded in the Zapruder film." (38)[10] In short, when the Zapruder movie became forensic evidence, it helped in creating another film. The presumption that a visual record could grant easy access to the truth of the assassination proved to be fallacious. Rather than bringing the original event closer to investigators, the movie exhibited a tendency to reproduce itself, to generate other series of records that, with each iteration, moved farther away from the original event of Kennedy's death. Far from clarifying once and for all the mechanics of the assassination, the Zapruder film generated its own line of conflicting interpretations as it became the object of spirited discussions that dissected each of its frames in slow motion. The film inserted itself between the viewer and the killing of the president; it asserted its own existence, thus nudging aside that very event it was supposed to bring nearer to the observer.[11] Because of the ability of film, as media, to be "more real than reality," to paraphrase Kittler, the encoding of Kennedy's assassination became inseparable from representation, "from the films and still photographs and conclusions drawn from the reenactment."[12]

Rather than producing one more interpretation of the Zapruder film, as inevitably would have occurred if he had ventured into a description of the contents of the movie, *Libra* narrates the shooting of the film: "Someone with a movie camera stood on an abutment over there, aiming this way.... The movie camera running" (400). Through his handling of the

Zapruder film in *Libra*, DeLillo creates a filter that prevents the novel from being overflowed by the zillions of interpretations that the film content has produced; he also demonstrates his awareness of the ambiguous role of audiovisual records, which both point to and move away from the event they are meant to document. By situating the making of the film in the novel's diegesis, DeLillo reverses the epistemic position of the camera operator. Rather than recording an event, Abraham Zapruder is recorded as a part of it: *Libra*'s concern is not what happens in the movie, but the very act of its filming.

If the Kennedy assassination became the first truly postmodern event, this did not depend on some particular feature of Kennedy's death, but on the mode of its archivization.[13] In a postmodern discussion of the assassination, truth becomes a negotiable concept bound to the observer's point of view because the Dallas Archive has stored too many tricky records. The Zapruder movie, the footage of Oswald's death, the pristine bullet that should have hit both the president and Governor Connally, all these records become events on their own. They lie at the centers of autonomous archives and generate their own lines of debate, each time obfuscating the very facts they are supposed to clarify. DeLillo confronts the oversized and multicentered archive of postmodernism by rejecting totality in favor of an accurate selection of the few records that can be assembled into a meaningful story. In other words, his method is the opposite of Nicholas Branch's.

Indeed, in his botched attempt to write the history of the assassination, Branch commits the methodological error of pursuing the same goal of totality that has led the Dallas archive to paralysis: "It is vital to his [Nicholas Branch's] sense of responsible obsession that everything in his room warrants careful study. Everything belongs, everything adheres, the mutter of obscure witnesses, the photos of illegible documents and odd sad personal debris, things gathered up at a dying—old shoes, pajama tops, letters from Russia" (182). As he wants to explain every detail of the assassination and refuses to dispose of even the most trivial record, Branch is overreaching. By applying his method, should he ever compose his history he would produce a text similar to Borges's map, which represents a territory in a scale of 1:1.[14] As he strives to write a total narrative, he is playing in the hands of his bosses at the CIA, who prevent him from finishing his work by supplying every record that might even slightly relate to the assassination. The CIA officials drive Branch toward writing a story modeled after the *Warren Commission Report*, "the novel in which nothing is left out," in which the abundance of documentation cohabits with the inability to deliver a meaningful account of the assassination: "There is also the Warren Report, of course, with its twenty-six accompanying volumes of testimony and exhibits, its millions of words. Branch thinks this is the megaton novel James Joyce would have written if he'd moved to Iowa City and lived to be a hundred" (181).

Ever since the *Warren Commission Report* was published in September 1964, its critics blamed it as a cover-up document that made it all but impossible to unveil the truth on the assassination. Rather than following this paranoid approach, DeLillo finds faults with the commission's effort to collect all the extant evidence on Kennedy's death and to summarize it into one conclusive narrative. Treating the Warren Commission as an overreaching body that engaged itself in a heroic but senseless endeavor allows DeLillo to use the *Report* as a mine of records taken from an institutional archive. These records provide *Libra* with its "historical center," an essential attribute of the novel, as DeLillo stated in his interview with Anthony DeCurtis in 1988.[15] DeLillo achieves this goal by scattering fragments of the *Warren Commission Report* throughout the novel. It is like a kind of archival dust that he spreads all over *Libra* without privileging any particular section of the book. For DeLillo, it becomes crucial not so much to preserve the integrity of the single document as to convey the sense of the Dallas archive at large. Although shattered and dispersed throughout the novel, official records still function as the backbone of the narration. By lending *Libra* words, data, dates, and names, they create a network of references that firmly ties the novel to the official component of the Dallas archive. In this operation, DeLillo's chief goal it to catch the record*ness* that emanates from the assassination rather than exhibiting proofs regarding specific facts. *Libra* is interested in the Dallas archive as a whole, in its effort of documentation: the historical event that *Libra* narrates is first and foremost the building of the great archive of the assassination, the urge to partake in creating the historical record that thousands of documents, books, reports, and investigations convey.

Lee Oswald's life story represents an appropriate example of how the *Warren Commission Report* threads its way through *Libra*'s main narrative. Chapter 7 of the *Report*, "Lee Harvey Oswald: Background and Possible Motives," provides DeLillo with the records he needs for putting together a documented biography of his main character. This chapter also offers *Libra* the structure for Oswald's story, from his troubled youth to his attempt at the life of President Kennedy. As the two texts align the events in the same order, the main episodes of Oswald's life in the *Report* become chapters in *Libra*. On the linguistic level, as DeLillo inserts fragments of records into the fabric of his story, the language of the *Report* permeates the novel's descriptions and dialogues. Let us take, for example, the Warren Commission's assessment of the interviews between Oswald and the psychologists at a Youth House in New York City: "Lee confirmed some of those observations by saying that he felt almost as if there were a veil between him and other people through which they could not reach him, but that he preferred the veil to remain intact."[16] In *Libra* this remark becomes, "The social worker wrote, 'Questioning elicited the information that he feels almost as if there is a veil between him and other people through which they cannot reach him, but he prefers this veil to remain intact'" (12). Later in the *Report*, Irving Sokolow, a psychologist, observes that, "[Oswald's] Human Figure Drawings are empty, poor characterizations of persons approximately the same age as the subject. They reflect a considerable amount of impoverishment in the social and emotional areas."[17] A few lines below, the *Report* reads that, "Lee scored an IQ of 118 on the Wechsler Intelligence Scale for Children. According to Sokolow, this indicated a 'present intellectual functioning in the upper range of bright normal intelligence.'"[18] In *Libra*, these observations become: "He did Human Figure Drawings, which were judged impoverished. The psychologist found him to be in the upper range of Bright Normal Intelligence" (11). The pattern of transferring fragments of records from the official archive to a fictional context defines the relationship between the *Report* and *Libra*.[19] It is a strategy that can function because DeLillo, while disagreeing with the *Report*'s narrative of the assassination, cautiously avoids challenging the commission's good faith. The two legitimizing instruments in *Libra*, one fictional, Nicholas Branch, and the other archival, the *Report*, complement each other. While the novelistic character places fiction, i.e., the story of Win Everett's conspiracy, in an archival context, the official document injects archival materials into the novelistic text.

With typical postmodern ambiguity, *Libra* builds its historical verisimilitude through references to the very archive that it describes as a messy, unreliable repository of papers. While nineteenth-century archival novels competed/cooperated with nation-states' bureaucracies—Balzac's *concurrence avec l'état civil*—by implementing methods employed in government run archives, their postmodern epigones elaborate oppositional strategies for sorting out records and making sense of the archive. *Libra* discusses the interaction between the archive and fiction by presenting a negative example, i.e., the strategy that one should not implement, once again Nicholas Branch's wrong approach to the turning of records into readable narratives.[20] It is at the beginning of the novel that Branch elaborates on his task of writing the history of the assassination: "Let's call a meeting to analyze the blur. Let's devote our lives to understanding this moment, separating the elements of each crowded second. We will build theories that gleam like jade idols, intriguing systems of assumption, four-faced, graceful. *We will follow the bullet trajectories backwards* to the lives that occupy the shadows, actual men who moan in their dreams" (15) [my emphasis]. In an archive arranged according to the principles of classical archival theory (notably the principle of provenance), a straightforward path, such as the one that follows the bullet trajectories backward, might still appear as a sensible way to achieve truth. The very organization of this archive, with its inescapable connections from one record to another, and from a series to its originating agency, would make it possible to create chains of homogeneous documents and use them as backbones for narratives. However, in Nicholas Branch's archive, in which everything may lead to everything, this straightforward path to truth cannot function. It is not by following record series or retrieving new documents, as in the classical archival research that Manzoni, for instance, carried out in order to write *I promessi sposi*, that one can build a truthful narrative. As DeLillo stated in his 1988 interview, fiction can redeem Branch's despair vis-à-vis the data that are flooding his room by discovering "rhythms and symmetries" in the raw facts that are overwhelming the analyst.[21] Compared to the epistemic situation of realism, here the relationship between records and fiction is reversed: it is the novel that supports the archive by elaborating the instruments (rhythms and symmetries) that can help in structuring the archival collections.

Nicholas Branch's desperation originates in his being a Newtonian archivist who operates in an Einsteinian environment. His personal archive is a site where "everything belongs, everything adheres," a web of relations that interconnect records, embryos of narratives, and Branch himself as a researcher. Katherine Hayles's concept of "field," a heuristic model for describing the reality posited by post-Newtonian physics, can help us apprehend this archive. In a field model, the discrete entities on which Newtonian science focuses are inextricably tied: "a field view of reality pictures objects, events, and observer as belonging inextricably to the same field; the disposition of each, in this view, is influenced—sometimes dramatically, sometimes subtly, but in every instance—by the disposition of the others."[22] While interconnection and uncertainty rule over the field model, unidirectional causality, along with reality as an aggregate of discrete objects, defines the Newtonian world. Correspondingly, in the field model, knowledge proceeds by detecting patterns as the basic threshold for the appearance of the "real" and by seeing objects as "merely temporary manifestations" of particular patterns.[23] In a Newtonian world, instead, science advances by analyzing individualized objects and discovering the cause effect relationships linking one object to another.

An evident isomorphism, based on linear causality as the principle for explaining the relations among the discrete components, be they records or particles, that comprise their universes, ties the classical archive ruled by the principle of provenance to the physical world conceived by Newtonian science. But then Nicholas Branch is using Newtonian categories, the linear trajectories tying effects backward to causes, for understanding an archive that already belongs in an Einsteinian context.[24] In the Dallas archive, investigators should not focus on the single, discrete record, which invariably leads to an unnavigable maze of relationships, but on the meaningful patterns within which significant data appear. Postmodern archival theory has arrived to the same conclusion: in the words of Terry Cook, who quotes extensively from Hugh Taylor, "faced with incredible information overloads and technological transformations, they [archivists] need to concentrate less on 'dealing with individual documents and series' and more on 'the recognition of forms and patterns of knowledge which may be the only way by which we will transcend the morass of information and data into which we will otherwise fall.'"[25] In this context, detecting these patterns and grasping the mode of their solidarity is the preliminary step toward writing a credible story. By ignoring the cognitive value of patterns, Branch becomes the novelistic embodiment of a "climate of opinion," to borrow a term from Katherine Hayles, that considers Newtonian physics as the grammar of the universe rather than one of its possible readings.[26] To this fossilized epistemology, DeLillo opposes his dynamic interaction between the archive and fiction, whereby the latter decodes the former by detecting "rhythms and symmetries," or patterns by any means, in an archival repository shaped as a web rather than a grid.

A persuasive example of *Libra*'s strategy of building knowledge through the creation of patterns is represented by what occurs the day of the assassination, when Lee Harvey Oswald misses the first shot at the president. The gunman does so because his error is consistent with his pattern of failing whenever life has tested him: as a marine, as a defector to the Soviet Union, as a plotter against the life of General Walker, and as a husband.[27] Likewise, a conspiracy to kill JFK led by anti-Castro activists matches a pattern of plots to assassinate political adversaries that characterizes the activities of the most militant elements among Cuban exiles.[28] By following a trail of record patterns, *Libra* traverses the archive of JFK's assassination. Instead of fitting all the main pieces of the Dallas puzzle into his narrative, DeLillo designs a trajectory cutting through it. In so doing, his novel provides a narrative response to the questions rising from an archive that simultaneously suffers from an excess of documentation and the lack of crucial records, from secrecy and openness, from governmental control and anarchical unruliness.

The curve of probability that DeLillo draws by discovering patterns in the Dallas archive leaves out many more records than those it comprises. In an epistemic context in which the paper archive shaped by the French Reform and nineteenth-century archival theories has entered the age of its historical decline, DeLillo's strategy has no alternative. Once a cognitive tool that fit into a universe ordered by Newtonian physics, the archive now mirrors a world (our own by all means) turned into "an endless and unstructured collection of images, texts, and other records," as Lev Manovich has argued.[29] A wild world that only the database, we believe, can bring to domestication. Indeed, the Dallas archive that takes over Nicholas Branch's office already possesses certain traits of the database: it is an open-ended collection of data, lacks a central collection, and adopts the list as its only possible arranging instrument. By displaying these features, the Dallas archive exposes the crisis of its technical and conceptual foundation. As a repository of records that traditional archival theory and practice can no longer arrange, the Dallas archive occupies an ambiguous position halfway between the paper age and the digital era. With satisfying approximation, one could maintain that the Dallas archive possesses the boundlessness and shapelessness of the electronic database without utilizing, except for a few rare cases, the latter's digital search engines: it experiences the problem, but still grasps for a solution. Far from being just one more postmodern novel challenging the archive's epistemology, *Libra* occupies a key position in the history of the relation between archive and fiction. DeLillo's novel does not simply narrate an archival story or even allegorize the rules and goals of the archive, but rather turns a crucial chapter in the history of record arrangement, the shift from the paper archive to the digital database, into matter for novelistic representation. At the end of the day, it is up to the archive, the institution that guaranteed the novel's legitimacy at the dawn of modernity, to find the clues to its future development in the mirror of fiction.

Epilogue

IN THE CONTEXT OF EARLY MODERN ENGLAND, SOCIETY DISCOVered the cognitive value and the technical possibility of creating timely records of the fleeting moments that comprise our lives. A crucial product of that environment was the novel, a fresh cultural form that could narrate ordinary people's lived experiences with unknown immediacy, in particular the events belonging to their most private and often intimate, even secret, sphere. This interest in novelistic characters' privacy was related to "the novel's tendency toward the confessional and the exhibitionistic," as J. Paul Hunter has argued.[1] A key component of the discourse of the novel was the desire to make private life visible, to eliminate the barriers that sheltered the individual's most personal domain from the gaze of the crowd. To summarize, the eighteenth-century novel's project consisted in opening up the private sphere to public debate by recording reliable and timely narratives of individuals' experiences. As a genre, the archival novel represents one of the possible realizations of this project, one that relies on the bureaucratic archive as both a source for records of private lives and a guarantee of their reliability. Because of its history as a self-reflexive genre that has accompanied the entire development of novelistic discourse, the archival novel can provide evidence for a larger claim. It can aid in proving that some support from the archive, either as the public institution that stores official records or the private repository that aids in the composition of a fictional work, is needed for any text aiming at fulfilling the eighteenth-century novel's original project. Despite the Romantic emphasis on individual creation as the sole source of the literary work, the kind of approach to writing that Friedrich Kittler calls "the narcissism of creation," methods used in bureaucracy for storing, cataloging, and retrieving records have traditionally been applied to the writing of novels.[2] The research in archives, the copying of records, and the systematic arrangement of papers are prerequisite to the narrative surface (plot, characters, adventures, and dialogues) of the novel. Goethe's methodic "collecting and ordering his collections" of letters, documents, and notes, Manzoni's systematic note-taking from historical sources, and Perec's use of lists and ledgers for writing *La Vie mode d'emploi* are three examples of the novel's flirtation with bureaucratic practices in distinct historical and cultural situations.[3] Under this perspective, the archival novel is the genre that turns the novel's subterranean relation with the archive into the key feature of its own novelistic world; what is hidden in traditional novels instead emerges in the open in archival fiction.

Achieving the eighteenth-century novel's project requires, in the writer's workshop and/or in society at large, the adoption of cumbersome and time consuming procedures: writing memos, installing archival hardware, organizing the workplace as a bureaucratic office, spending time copying and storing records, and wasting an impressive amount of paper. The best case scenario is represented by an office like the lawyer Derville's in *Le Colonel Chabert*, where a solid chain of command and a clever management of space and time allow for a smooth running of the archive. But even in this rosy picture of life in the paper age, the bureaucratic archive cannot compete with the achievement of our contemporary digital technology. If one thinks again of the eighteenth-century novel as a project, then one must recognize that it has been ultimately fulfilled in our time, but through practices based on digital media. Indeed, it is hard to think of a better way of creating almost instantaneous records of private lives or of opening the individual's intimate sphere to the crowd's gaze than using Facebook, text messages, YouTube, Twitter, emails, and blogs. Which is to say that the digital database (all the above mentioned tools are interfaces of digital databases) has turned the lawyer Derville into an obsolete professional figure and the cultural form that is homogeneous to his practice, the novel (archival as well as traditional) into an outdated cognitive tool.

Derville's retirement does not mean the end of the novel. After all, five centuries after Gutenberg we continue to enjoy short stories, the narrative genre that was born out of orality.

Novels will continue to be written and read even though they will have to compete with communicative forms based on digital media. What is more, as a multisecular accumulation of narrative structures, formal instruments, and paradigms of communication, the novel possesses immense cultural capital, whose investment will certainly have an important effect on the development of digital narratives. It is not a case that, at least at the lexical level, the novel has begun to expand its operations to the digital environment: we now talk of hypertext novels, while the highly popular Japanese narratives written and read on cellular phones are called *keitai shosetsu*, or "cell-phone novels."[4] The lexical expansion of the term novel notwithstanding, because of the rise of the digital database and the obsolescence of the paper archive, the novel's documentary foundation is no longer in sync with the cutting edge technology for the management and the dissemination of knowledge. In other words, the novel has reached its technological old age. Nobody can foresee how long this age will last. Nor is it possible to know if a cultural form as important as the novel has been in the paper age will be created in the digital environment. We can just be thankful to H. F., Pécuchet, Bouvard, the lawyer Derville, Nicholas Branch, and all the bureaucrats who, as characters or writers, have been involved in fiction—especially for having made our knowledge of the novel deeper and our lives more enjoyable in the meantime.

Notes

Introduction

1. In my approach to the archival novel as a genre, I am clearly indebted to John Frow's definition of genres as interpretive structures that guide our readings of both cultural artifacts (texts, painting, films, articles of fashion) and the world said cultural artifacts discuss: "far from being merely 'stylistic' devices, genres create effects of reality and truth which are central to the different ways the world is understood in the writing of history or philosophy or science, or in painting, or in everyday talk." See *Genre*, 19.
2. Pearce-Moses, *Glossary of Archival Terminology*.
3. Foucault, *Archaeology of Knowledge*, 49.
4. Frow, *Genre*, 74–76.
5. Gustave Flaubert's *Bouvard et Pécuchet* (1881) represents the earliest case of an archival novel committed to calling into question the cognitive value of the archive's operations. Flaubert's modus operandi became prevalent in postmodern archival novels, such as Georges Perec's *La Vie mode d'emploi* or José Saramago's *Todos os Nomes* to name just two examples.
6. Frow, *Genre*, 75.
7. Dimock, "Genre as World System," 86.
8. Frow, *Genre*, 24.
9. Dimock, "Genre as World System," 86.
10. Frow, *Genre*, 25.
11. "The great archive at Simancas, begun by Charles V but finished by the King Bureaucrat Philip II, is the first and possibly the most voluminous of such storehouses [repositories of legal documents] in Europe." González Echevarría, *Myth and archive*, 29. I owe this historical perspective on the bureaucratic archive and its role in the construction of the European nation state to Terry Cook, who shared his deep understanding of the archive with me in a few insightful emails.

Chapter 1. Prehistory

1. Congreve, *Incognita*, 32. While Geoffrey Day judges Congreve's definition of romances and novels as "a neat distinction," Ioan Williams maintains that "the 'Novel' to which Congreve refers is the short *nouvelle*,

turning on an intrigue or love situation." See Day, *From Fiction*, 2, and Williams, *Novel and Romance*, 6. Despite Williams's criticism, it seems to me that Congreve's definition maintains its value for us in that it delineates with absolute precision the regime of truth under which a narrative form must operate in order to compete with the romance. In other words, what matters is that Congreve had in mind a modern taxonomy in which a box was available for a narrative that aimed at a truthful representation of common individuals' everyday life.

2. Day, *From Fiction*, 22.
3. Hunter, *Before Novels*, 22.
4. Day, *From Fiction*, 15.
5. Ibid., 50–57.
6. "They [Richardson and Fielding] did not even canonise the changed nature of their fiction by a change in nomenclature—our usage of the term 'novel' was not fully established until the end of the eighteenth century." Watt, *Rise of the Novel*, 10.
7. McKeon, *Origins of the English Novel*, 20.
8. Ibid.
9. Ibid.
10. Ibid., 119.
11. For Ian Watt, the novel's epistemological problem is that "of the correspondence between the literary work and the reality which it imitates," an issue that the novel solves by adopting procedures that match those that are followed "whenever the relation to reality of any report of an event is being investigated." See *Rise of the Novel*, 11. As the obvious reference is to what occurs in the courts of law, a novel behaves like a jury that "wants to know 'all the particulars' of a given case," 31.
12. McKeon, *Origins of the English Novel*, 120.
13. Hunter, *Before Novels*, 172.
14. Ibid., 310.
15. "H. F., the supposed author of the *Journal*, can be identified with Defoe's uncle, Henry Foe, with complete certainty." Bastian, "Defoe's *Journal*," 158.
16. Defoe, *Journal of the Plague Year*, 3. Subsequent references appear parenthetically in the text.
17. The title pages of the two works are slightly different: "The Life and Surprising Adventures of Robinson Crusoe" are "written by himself," while "The Fortunes and Misfortunes of the Famous Moll Flanders" are "written from her own memorandums." See Defoe, *Robinson Crusoe*, 1; *Moll Flanders*, 1.
18. See Rambuss, "'Complicated Distress,'" 118. Lennard J. Davis argues that Defoe situated his works in an ambiguous territory between facts and fiction because he was operating within a news/novel discourse that was still to break into the distinct subdiscourses of the novel and journalism. *Factual Fictions*, 155.
19. Ellis, "Defoe's *Journal*," 77, 78.
20. Mayer, "Reception of *A Journal*," 534.
21. Bastian, "Defoe's *Journal*," 173.

22. Mayer, "Reception of *A Journal*," 537.

23. "Despite general agreement in our time that the *Journal* is a highly problematic novel, but a novel nonetheless, the history-fiction concretization is alive and well and the history concretization still survives, albeit just barely." Ibid., 544.

24. Lukács, *Historical Novel*, 19. See also Bastian: "To a large extent H.F. was a convenient mask, from behind which comes the voice of Defoe himself." "Defoe's *Journal*," 165. By reducing H. F. to the mouthpiece for a writer living almost sixty years after the plague, Bastian confirms the discrepancy between the narrator of the *Journal* and the historical environment where the novel is set.

25. Davis attributes the urge to creating a record to the entire corpus of Defoe's fiction: "There is not enough 'art' about them [Defoe's works], no dazzling plots, not much in the way of form—just a kind of dogged attention to the cumulative details, to getting the story down on record." *Factual Fictions*, 155.

26. Rambuss, "'Complicated Distress,'" 123.

27. Despite the *Journal*'s concern with record making, Defoe did not believe that print was in and of itself a purveyor of truth. As Paula McDowell argues, in the Journal "no form of communication, whether print, manuscript, or oral, is exempt from the 'Invention of Men'—undermining any clear distinction or hierarchy among them such as H. F. elsewhere tries to make." "Defoe and the Contagion," 89.

28. Ricœur, *La Mémoire, l'histoire, l'oubli*, 209.

29. McDowell, "Defoe and the Contagion," 87.

30. Ibid., 104.

31. The redaction of memorandums is quoted in the *Journal* at pages 32, 65, and 193. On page 153, Defoe uses the term "minutes" in place of memorandums. Manuel Schonhorn has made a persuasive case for H. F.'s awareness of the temporal gap separating the time of his memorandums and that of the final redaction of the *Journal*: "the supposed author of the Journal is fully aware of the physical changes which have occurred in London between the time of his 'original' memorandums and his later ordering of them for his published narrative." See "Defoe's *Journal*," 391. By almost always choosing topographical landmarks (eighty-three out of almost ninety) that existed at the time of the Plague and were still in place in 1720, Defoe makes a deliberate effort to give his eighteenth-century readers the image of a city they can recognize in spite of the narrative taking place in 1665 London.

32. Brooks, *Reading for the Plot*, 5.

33. *A Journal of the Plague Year* "is a fiction, a non-fiction fiction like Truman Capote's *In Cold Blood* (1965), but still a fiction." Ellis, "Defoe's *Journal*," 79.

34. In addition to being an archivist, H. F. is a witness. I am using the term in the sense it takes in Giorgio Agamben's meditation where a witness is a voice who speaks on behalf of those who cannot. See *Quel che resta di Auschwitz*, 31–36 and 147. Archival novels often seem to emerge from an ethical duty to narrate the unspeakable core of historical tragedies, as is

the case with *I promessi sposi, Il sorriso dell'ignoto marinaio, Libra, La chimera,* and *El cantor de tango.*

35. By viewing H. F. as an archivist one can attribute a new meaning to John J. Richetti's claim that H. F. "is an intensified and almost abstract version of the ordering self that we have seen in Defoe's other narratives." See *Defoe's Narratives,* 234. Records are the mediation between H.F. as an ordering self and the chaotic world that surrounds him.

36. Frank H. Ellis has meticulously noticed the sloppiness of the *Journal*'s language, which he identifies as the reason for the book's failure to conquer the reading public. He points out the "echolalic repetition of a nameless class of repetition-indicators" that soils Defoe's prose. See "Defoe's *Journal,*" 77.

37. Celati, *Finzioni occidentali,* 38. Unless otherwise noticed, all the translations in this book are mine.

38. Ibid., 42.

39. Hunter, *Before Novels,* 52.

40. In the eighteenth century, Sterne's *Tristram Shandy* (1759–67) represents the most egregious case of a novel that makes a frequent use of paste-ins. Paste-ins are affixed on the following pages of the *Journal:* 6, 7, 30, 32, 43, 79, 82, 93, 96, 122, 123, 142, 148, 149, 161, and 193 (the phoenix at the end of the text).

41. In addition to the "Bills of Mortality," the other crucial official record inserted in the *Journal* is the "Order Conceived and Published by the Lord Mayor of the City of London, concerning the Infection of the Plague 1665." It is copied verbatim in the text from page 36 to 43.

42. McDowell, "Defoe and the Contagion," 88.

43. Rambuss, "'Complicated Distress,'" 126; Richetti, *Defoe's Narratives,* 298.

44. Mayer, "Reception of *A Journal,*" 546.

Chapter 2. Legitimation and Challenge

1. Davis, *Factual Fictions,* 193.
2. Fielding, *Tom Jones,* 326.
3. Ibid.
4. Day, *From Fiction,* 85–99.
5. Davis, *Factual Fictions,* 201.
6. Ibid., 202.
7. Fielding, *Tom Jones,* 300.
8. Davis, *Factual Fictions,* 204.
9. Fielding, *Tom Jones,* 387.
10. "Paradoxically, by virtue of the admission of fictionality, Fielding can now incorporate news without really causing ambivalence in the reader." See Davis, *Factual Fictions,* 206.
11. See Casanova, *Archivistica,* 387; Posner, "Some Aspects," 25; Schellenberg, *Modern Archives,* 4.
12. Posner, "Some Aspects," 25.

13. The law of the seventh of Messidor II prescribed "to destroy all the documents recording the feudal rights as well as the painful privileges the people hate." See Casanova, *Archivistica*, 389. To this purpose, for ten years, the newly established *Bureau du triage des titles* sifted through the old records in order to select documents to destroy. Furthermore, by canceling tradition as a legitimate instrument for asserting rights on land, the French reform of the archive got rid of all the feudal privileges that up to then had coexisted side by side with bourgeois property. After the French Revolution, only written documents could entitle people to exploit natural resources.

14. Horsman, "Taming the Elephant," 53.

15. See Posner, "Max Lehmann," 37. As for the ultimate formulation of the "Principle of Provenance," it occurred in Germany with the Privy State Archives' Regulations of July 1, 1881.

16. In this book, I use the term, "document" as a synonym of "record." Archival theory employs stricter categories than mine: in Richard Pearce-Moses's *Glossary of Archival Terminology*, document means record only when the latter "connotes an official document, especially the final version of one created in the routine course of business."

17. See Gränström, "Janus Syndrome," 14; Horsman, "Taming the Elephant," 56–60; Casanova, *Archivistica*, 392.

18. Spieker, *Big Archive*, 18.

19. In the humanities, historians were the first scholars to grasp the epistemological significance of the archival paradigm. Leopold von Ranke (1795–1886) fostered the advent of a new generation of professional historians who considered the hard evidence of the record as the ultimate test for the validity of their interpretive hypotheses: "I see the time approaching when we shall base modern history no longer on the reports even of contemporary historians, except insofar as they were in possession of personal and immediate knowledge of facts; and still less, on works yet more remote from the source; but rather on the narratives of eyewitnesses, and on genuine and original documents." See *The Secret of World History*, 72. At the foundation of academic, scientific history, there lay the idea that one truth did indeed exist, could be attained, and rested on evidence provided by archives. Historiography exited the literary field where it had belonged since Aristotle and sought admission in the realm of science. A new appreciation of the document, now correctly perceived as an archival record rather than a historical text, as Fielding had instead believed, made this epistemic leap possible.

20. Noiriel, "L'identification des citoyens," 3.

21. The first secular register of births, marriages, and deaths, the *état civil*, was established by the Legislative Assembly on September 20, 1792. Previously, as dictated by the royal decree of Villers-Cotterêts in 1539, parish registers had recorded people's births, marriages, and deaths. Ibid.

22. Balzac, *La Comédie humaine*, 2:123.

23. Foucault, *Power/Knowledge*, 125.

24. Foucault, *Surveiller et punir*, 226.

25. Ibid., 223.

26. Ibid., 222.
27. Ibid.
28. See Sekula, "Body and the Archive," 18. In 1882, Bertillon became the first director of the "Service de l'identité judiciaire," an agency initially created inside the Paris Police and then extended to the rest of France. Noiriel, *La Tyrannie du national*, 163.
29. Matsuda, *Memory of the Modern*, 135.
30. Ibid., 136.
31. Noiriel, *La Tyrannie du national*, 162. In Bertillon's system, photographs were used to facilitate a "systematic classification that allowed for a rapid retrieval of the signifying elements"; these photographs, all of the same size and in the same pose, in profile, did not speak the language of realistic mimesis. They were formal signs, detached from the body's concrete physicality: the *individu policier* was a symbolic being, 163.
32. Fingerprinting was introduced for the first time in the district of Hooghly, in Bengal, by the British Commissioner Sir William Herschel in 1880. See Ginzburg, "Morelli, Freud, Sherlock Holmes," 27.
33. Jenkinson, *Manual of Archive Administration*, 131.
34. Schellenberg, *Modern Archives*, 16.
35. Jenkinson, *Manual of Archive Administration*, 21.
36. Stille, *Future of the Past*, 303.
37. Ibid., 304.
38. Ham, "Archival Strategies," 208.
39. As González Echevarría argues, in Latin American archival fiction, "the Archive is shown to be also a form of mythic discourse, not removed from the literary but a part of it." *Myth and Archive*, 153.
40. In *Go Down Moses*, the key episode occurs when Ike MCaslin, the novel's hero, reconstructs the history of his ancestors by reading the ledgers stored in his family's plantation commissary. Thus, in a radical separation from the paradigm of legitimation, Faulkner places a new emphasis on reading as the indispensible mediation between the record and the narrative. As *Go Down, Moses* offers readers not records but Ike's reading of them, which foregrounds their textuality, the archive's ability to support truth slides away. Indeed, reading the ledgers, a practice that is radically different from searching an archive in order to retrieve a document, as occurs in Balzac's and Manzoni's novels, turns the record into a text open to unlimited interpretations. During postmodernism, novelists operating within the paradigm of challenge will capitalize on this intuition by relating the archive's various truths to the specific position of power occupied by different groups (defined by class, gender, and/or ethnicity) in society.
41. MacNeil, *Trusting Records*, 21.
42. See also González Echevarría: "So arch [which stem from the Greek ἀρχή], as in monarch, denotes power to rule, but also the beginning, that which is chief, eminent, greatest, principal; it denotes primitive, original." *Myth and Archive*, 32.
43. Cook, "Fashionable Nonsense," 25.
44. Zelenyj, "Archivy Ad Portas," 66.
45. Ibid.

46. Cook, "Mind over Matter," 39.

47. Linda Hutcheon argues that postmodern historical metafictions can problematize the writing of history by pointing out the textual nature of archival records: "if the archive is composed of texts, it is open to all kinds of use and abuse." See *Politics of Postmodernism*, 80. I believe, however, that the discourse of the archive is much more complex and cannot be invalidated by simply claiming the textuality of archival documents. Gathering, selecting, ordering, and destroying records are essential components of the archive, all operations that define the nature and the meaning of records. If the critique of the archive focuses only on the textual quality of its documents, than the bulk of its practices remains untouched and safe from criticism.

48. Cook, "Fashionable Nonsense," 30.

49. Ibid., 31.

50. The archive's allegiance to political power represents a key theme in Augusto Roa Bastos's *Yo el Supremo* (1974), the account of Paraguay's history from the Spanish colonization to the first four decades of the nineteenth century. This book appears as the very epitome of the archival novel: in the "Nota final del compilador," the author maintains that his work, which he calls a *compilación*, does not comprise a single word that he has not copied from either oral or written sources. What is more, the diegetic agent responsible for creating and/or arranging most of the records that the novel stores is José Gaspar Rodríguez de Francia, dictator of Paraguay from 1814 to 1840. In *Yo el Supremo*, records are generated by an authority that *dictates* them through a political and archival act of power. As their factual truth does not matter at all, their ultimate meaning will always be the confirmation of the dictator's absolute rule.

51. Kundera, *L'art du roman*, 20.

52. For the idea that both archives and novels hoard knowledge see, Roberto González Echevarría, *Myth and Archive*, 32.

53. Taylor, "Collective Memory," 121.

54. For the concept that one of the defining traits of being human is participating in the transmission of cultural legacies from the dead to the unborn by way of the living, I am clearly indebted to Robert Harrison's *Dominion of the Dead*.

55. Davis, *Resisting Novels*, 24.

Chapter 3. *I promessi sposi*

Portions of this chapter previously appeared in *MLN* 121, no. 1 (2006): 187–206. I am grateful to the editors for their kind permission to reproduce the material here.

1. Academic history began with the establishment of the first chairs in history at the University of Berlin (1810) and at Sorbonne (1812). See Anderson, *Imagined Communities*, 194.

2. Among modern editions, *I promessi sposi (1840). Storia della colonna infame*, book 2 in Alessandro Manzoni's *I promessi sposi*, edited by

Salvatore Silvano Nigro and published by Mondadori in 2002, appears to be the most faithful to the original. Consistent with Nigro's argument that only by recreating the original relation between words and illustrations can a modern edition recapture the spirit of Manzoni's text, this edition reproduces Francesco Gonin's drawings that illustrated Manzoni's works. Thus, it consists in a facsimile of the 1840 edition of *I promessi sposi/Storia della colonna infame*.

3. In 1823, Manzoni finished a first, untitled version of his novel. This text, commonly known as *Fermo e Lucia*, is mentioned in a letter sent by Ermes Visconti to Gaetano Cattaneo on April 2, 1822. The title "I promessi sposi," which comes up in Manzoni's papers for the first time in 1824, appears in the first published version of the novel, which came out from 1825 to 1827. As for *Storia della colonna infame*, this text was originally meant to be a chapter of *Fermo e Lucia*. Subsequently, Manzoni changed his mind and decided to deal with *Storia della colonna infame* in an apposite "appendix" at the end of the novel. Unpublished in the early 1820s, the work is again mentioned in the first edition of *I promessi sposi* (1827). This time, in Manzoni's words, the appendix has become "un altro scritto" [a new written text], thus implying its greater autonomy from the novel. However, even this new written text was not published. See Manzoni, *I romanzi*, 1: XLIII; 1:CXVIII-CXX; 1:695; 2, bk. 2:XXI; and 2, bk.1:664.

4. Pupino, *Il vero solo è bello*, 19.

5. Pearce-Moses, *Glossary of Archival Terminology*.

6. Manzoni, *Lettere*, 1:254. Cesare Arieti, the editor of Manzoni's correspondence, suggests the first months of 1821 as the most probable time for the writing of this letter, which its author did not date, 1:831.

7. Manzoni, *Scritti letterari*, 298.

8. Nigro, *La tabacchiera*, 60.

9. The other character the anonymous author has met is a notary who, early in the morning following the uprising of November 11, 1628, arrests Renzo. Manzoni describes the notary as *un furbo matricolato* (a true trickster) who seemed to have befriended the anonymous author. Here Manzoni not only describes a professional of the archive, such as a notary, as an unreliable person, but also hints at the association of this trickster with the original writer of *I promessi sposi*. Literature positions itself at a close distance to the archive, in an ambiguous area where the recording and forging of documents coexist side by side. See Codebò, "Scomodi compagni," 191–96. On the same issue, Francesco Bruni argues that a third character, a passerby who comes across Renzo in Milan, might have met the anonymous writer. There are no textual elements, however, that can prove this hypothesis. See Bruni, "Manzoni, l'anonimo, la storia," 202.

10. Spang, "Apuntes para una definición," 69.

11. In a letter to Victor Cousin on April 30, 1821, Ermes Visconti writes: "Manzoni has been busy reading Scott. He was struck by the possibility of utilizing historical habits and historical events for writing novels. He does not want to repeat Scott's mistake as Scott changes the historical truth whenever he thinks that this may be convenient." In Manzoni's thought, being faithful to records trumps the need to tell intriguing stories. Manzoni, *Lettere*, 1:825.

12. Vigny, *Cinq-Mars*, 25.

13. Melchiorre Gioia's *Sul commercio dei commestibili e caro prezzo del vitto* (1802), which quotes the edict against threatening priests in order to prevent the celebration of marriages, appears as the most probable source of the first episode of *I promessi sposi*. Repossi and Stella, "Commentary," 701.

14. Manzoni, *I promessi sposi (1840)*, 53. Subsequent references appear parenthetically in the text.

15. In a letter written in spring 1821 when he was laying the ground for his novel, Manzoni asked Gaetano Cattaneo to look for the edicts published between 1626 and 1633, which were missing in the *gridario* (catalog of edicts) already in his hands. The edict of October 15, 1627, belongs to this catalog. Manzoni, *Lettere*, 1:236.

16. In a review of *I promessi sposi* that appeared in "Ueber Kunst und Alterthum," in 1827, Adolf Friedrich Streckfüss summarized the criticism on Manzoni's novel that Goethe had expressed in private conversations with Eckermann. See Manzoni, *I promessi sposi (1840)*, XXVII. Goethe had blamed the second part of *I promessi sposi* for the unordered inclusion of historical data. In Goethe's argument, the writing of a historical novel amounts to a negotiation between fiction and history, i.e., between an invented story in the making and an already shaped narrative of the past. As Manzoni views history as a never-ending dialogue with the historical record, Goethe's point becomes moot. By placing the examination of records at the center of historiography, Manzoni appears in sync with the academic history that was achieving scientific status just in the years of the writing of *I promessi sposi*. Goethe's criticism prompted Manzoni to begin his theoretical reflection on the historical novel that will later on develop into *Del romanzo storico*.

17. As in Seymour Menton's definition, one of the traits of the "New Historical Novel" is "metafiction or the narrator's comments on the creative process." See *La nueva novela histórica*, 43.

18. I am referring to novels such as *Yo el supremo*, *Il sorriso dell'ignoto marinaio*, *La chimera*, and *Santa Evita*.

19. Nigro, *La tabacchiera*, 70. The formula "carta, penna e calamaio" (paper, pen, and inkwell) is repeated four times in the novel. In chapter 8, Don Abbondio takes "paper, pen, and inkwell" in order to write a receipt acknowledging the payment of an old debt by a parishioner. Paper, pen, and inkwell appear again when the innkeeper of the Full Moon vainly attempts to record Renzo's name before hosting him for the night. In the same episode, the three words resurface when a disguised policeman, Ambrogio Fusella, discusses a made-up plan for assigning every family a just ration of bread. The same formula comes out one last time when the novel describes the tools available to scholars in the public library Cardinal Federigo Borromeo founded. It must be noted that in *I promessi sposi* Manzoni portrays even himself with the pen in hand, thus acknowledging writing a novel as an exercise of power. See Manzoni, *I promessi sposi (1840)*, 143, 277, 283, 419, and 493.

20. As Ezio Raimondi notices, Renzo has one mission: searching for jus-

tice. It is part of Manzoni's ironic approach to life that a justice seeker ends up with his name recorded as a fugitive in the judicial archive. In his quest, almost inevitably, Renzo encounters lawyers, cops, notaries, all characters who have a professional relation with the archive. See *Il romanzo senza idillio*, 175–80.

21. *I promessi sposi* dedicates important pages to the representation of another type of relation between the archive and power, the one tying cultural warehouses to sociopolitical authority. The person who puts together the largest library, which is the biggest archive of the texts of his culture, is also the most powerful character in the novel. This person is Cardinal Federigo Borromeo, the founder of the Ambrosian Library, which stores about thirty thousand printed volumes and fourteen thousand manuscripts.

22. Caputo, "La '*Colonna infame*,'" 342.

23. "Piazza and Mora were under compulsion to write an historical novel, but one unmoored from the least responsibility to reality." Gladfelder, "Seeing Black," 78.

24. Manzoni possessed inaccurate information on Gabriele Verri, Pietro's father. Verri senior never served as the president of the senate, a position he coveted for his entire life. Repossi and Stella, "Commentary," 1165.

25. Brothman, "Declining Derrida," 79.

26. Ibid., 80.

27. Jenkinson, *Manual of Archive Administration*, 11.

28. "It is clear that Manzoni believes in the existence of a truth independent of any discursive or political formation; yet equally clear in the history he actually writes that what counts for truth in this matrix of forces is socially determined." Gladfelder, "Seeing Black," 76.

Chapter 4. La Comédie humaine

1. Moretti, *Atlas of the European Novel*, 17.
2. Balzac, *La Comédie humaine*, 1:11.
3. Garval, "Balzac's *La Comédie humaine*," 30.
4. Ibid., 34.
5. Ibid.
6. Balzac, *La Comédie humaine*, 1:530.
7. Foucault, *Surveiller et punir*, 234.
8. Balzac, *La Comédie humaine*, 6:726.
9. Ibid., 2:636.
10. Balzac, *Œuvres diverses*, 3:203. In "Le Notaire," Balzac describes the notary as an official who enjoys the privilege to enter people's secret archives, 3:204. He clearly shares his role and tasks with the novelist, which should explain why he becomes such a common character in *La Comédie humaine*.
11. Balzac, *La Comédie humaine*, 7:761.
12. In Paul Ricœur's thought, the *mise en intrigue* is the translation of

the Aristotelian μῦθος, the process whereby an author ties discrete events into one unifying system. *Temps et récit*, 69.

13. MacNeil, "Trusting Records," 39.

14. "Document" is a key term in the lexicon of realism. It means both the record that attests the truth of a literary text, as Manzoni theorized, and the text itself in realist authors such as Émile Zola and Giovanni Verga. As late as in 1918, a writer outside of the realist experience, Federigo Tozzi, still defined his short stories as "documents of human and social reality." See *Pagine critiche*, 191. It is worth observing that *documento* in Italian and Portuguese also means piece of identification.

15. On mimesis, I agree with Christopher Prendergast's idea that there is profound ambiguity in the mimetic order: "In one of its aspects, it is . . . part of the equipment of the Censor, whose repressive work inevitably generates a rebellious move . . . . In another of its aspects, however, it is that to which we assent, not so much because of its tyrannical exhortations or hegemonic authority, but simply because no coherent set of human practices can escape its aegis." *Order of Mimesis*, 8.

16. Ian Watt states that "the novel is surely distinguished from other genres and from previous forms of fictions by the amount of attention it habitually accords both to the individualisation of its characters and to the detailed presentation of their environment." *Rise of the Novel*, 17. By way of this sweeping generalization, Watt can support his argument that the novel is in essence realist, at least since Defoe. I disagree with this thesis, as I believe that realism is a historically determined mode that assumes specific characteristics depending on the socioeconomic context, the media, and the cultural environment, in which it takes effect. The foregrounding of localization as a way to apprehend the individual, a technique that begins to appear in Defoe, Richardson, and Fielding, assumes an almost cliché-like status in nineteenth-century novels, but fades away in the age of modernism.

17. After *Le Père Goriot*, several imitators of Balzac, such as Émile Zola in *Pot bouille* (1882), Michel Butor in *Passage de Milan* (1954), and George Perec in *La Vie mode d'emploi*, situated the characters of a novel in different rooms of the same building.

18. I am borrowing the notion of "New Regime" from the title of Isser Woloch's book; the term defines the "civic order," or "the framework, in other words, for the collective public life of the French people," that established itself in France from 1789 to the 1820s. See *New Regime*, 14.

19. Watt, *Rise of the Novel*, 20.

20. Anderson, *Imagined Communities*, 173.

21. Sekula, "Body and the Archive," 34.

22. Noiriel, "L'Identification des citoyens," 14.

23. Torpey, *Invention of the Passport*, 16.

24. Noiriel, *La Tyrannie du national*, 55.

25. There is no accord among scholars on the year in which photographs began to be used to identify criminals. In his analysis of search warrants in nineteenth-century Germany, Peter Becker proposes 1860 as the year in which police departments started the first criminal albums. See "Standard-

ized Gaze," 159. On the other hand, in her discussion of Bertillonage, Martine Kaluszynki maintains that "photography was in use in sections of the police prefecture in Paris as early as 1872." See "Republican Identity," 124. Susan Sontag, finally, argues that photographs were already used to identify the Communards in June 1871. See *On Photography*, 15.

26. In the age of identification through verbal description, writing served the visual, but worked for the archive. No system for gathering information on a large population of discrete individuals can deliver useful knowledge without an archive for arranging the collected data and making it available on demand. This is what police departments in Paris understood when they started to photograph criminals in the 1870s: after a while they were overwhelmed by piles of prints, sixty thousand in a few years. It was only when photographs were standardized and cataloged according to the physical characteristics of the individuals photographed that they became a useful identification tool. See Kaluszynki, "Republican Identity,"124.

27. Allan H. Pasco correctly argues that the plot structure of *Ursule Mirouët* functions as a model for the entire first half of *Scènes de la vie de province:* from *Ursule Mirouët* through *La Muse du department*, these novels "are organized around the repulsion of foreigners, of strangers, usually from Paris, in order to maintain an indigenous monopoly." See "Ursule through the Glass," 39.

28. Balzac was trained in the law. He worked as a clerk for two lawyers, Guillonet-Merville and Victor Passez, from 1816 to 1819, and passed the first law baccalaureate at the start of 1819 before giving up legal practice for literature. Robb, *Balzac*, 42–53.

29. Balzac, *La Comédie humaine*, 3:845.

30. In her commentary to *Ursule Mirouët*, Madaleine Ambrière-Fargeaud notices that Balzac has a weak case in suggesting that Minoret's will in favor of Ursule could be legally challenged. The law intended to prevent only parents from bequeathing their wealth to their illegitimate children. An uncle could leave his fortune to his niece, even if she was an illegitimate son's child, without encountering legal problems whatsoever. Ibid., 1589.

31. Consistent with the legal context framing Ursule Mirouët's story, Minoret hides his bearer bonds in a crucial text of legal discourse, the "Pandects," a digest of Roman laws compiled by order of the emperor Justinian I in the sixth century AD. See ibid., 916.

32. Ibid., 842.
33. Ibid., 981.
34. Ibid., 961.
35. Ibid., 970.
36. Brooks, *Realist Vision*, 33.
37. Prendergast, *Order of Mimesis*, 92.
38. Foucault, *Surveiller et punir*, 223.
39. González Echevarría, *Myth and Archive*, 174.
40. On the larger issue of the relation between law and literature, I am heavily indebted to Roberto González Echevarría's analysis of legal discourse as the matrix for the development of narrative prose in colonial Latin America. See ibid., 32–33, 43–92, and 174–78.

41. The battle of Eylau was fought in 1807, while Chabert arrives in Paris at the same time as the invading Russian army after Napoleon's defeat at Waterloo in 1815. Balzac, *La Comédie humaine*, 3:332.

42. By arguing that Derville is "the arch-narratee, and also figure of the novelist: he who listens to, and retells, all the secret, buried stories of society," Peter Brooks is more interested in Derville's ability to gather society's informal storytelling than in his being an expert in written legal documentation. Appropriately, in Brooks's analysis, Derville's position is akin to the analyst's in psychoanalytical therapy. See "Narrative Transaction," 109.

43. Balzac, *La Comédie humaine*, 3:314. Detailed representations of offices and clerks are common in *La Comédie humaine*. In particular, sees Lawyer Desroches's studio in *Un début dans la vie* and M. Rabourdin's office in the Ministry of Finance in *Les Employés*.

44. Caruth, "Claims of the Dead," 423.

45. Balzac, *La Comédie humaine*, 3:323, 327.

46. Ibid., 328.

47. Ibid., 341.

48. Caruth, "Claims of the Dead," 435.

49. Balzac, *La Comédie humaine*, 3:372.

50. "Chabert's is a bureaucratic tragedy; he is the exception, the man whose case is not covered by any given forms or formulae. Rejected from administrative categories, he sinks into the anonymous waste matter of the social machine." Good, "Le Colonel Chabert," 853.

51. Balzac, *La Comédie humaine*, 3:441.

CHAPTER 5. BOUVARD ET PÉCUCHET

1. Flaubert is the first to concede that his characters are two idiots: in a letter to his niece Caroline, in August 1874, he writes: "La bêtise de mes deux bonshommes m'envahit" [My two folks' stupidity overcomes me]. *Correspondance*, 7:189.

2. Consignment, the act that Derrida situates at the foundation of the archive, is a form of dislocation, or better yet represents the original act of dislocation. See *Mal d'archive*, 26.

3. Leclerc, *La Spirale et le monument*, 70.

4. Ibid.

5. Lalonde, "Une alliance anormale," 146. Geneviève Bollème argues that, "By establishing the pages of the 'Sottisier' according to the order of the manuscripts and presenting them as both a summary and a 'model,' I wanted to give all the readers the right, of which they have been unfairly deprived, to know *Bouvard et Pécuchet* as it should have been published." See Flaubert, *Le second volume*, 12.

6. In some ways, the incomplete and unpublished novel is a sort of accidental and quite genius literary coup—because it means that Flaubert's readers must do the kind of work his protagonists do, that is to say: comb through, organize, analyze, categorize documents, with the ultimate dis-

covery that the search does not turn up the answer or answers they are looking for. I owe this acute observation to Magdalena Edwards.

7. In his letter to Luis Bouilhet, on September 4, 1850, Flaubert writes: "Tu fais bien de songer au *Dictionnaire des idées reçues.* Ce livre *complètement fait* et précédé d'une bonne préface où l'on indiquerait comme quoi l'ouvrage a été fait" [It is good that you are thinking of the *Dictionnaire des idées reçues.* This book, which has been *completed*, should be preceded by a proper preface for stating how the work was made]. *Correspondance,* 2:237. Hence, the *Dictionnaire,* a compilation of accepted ideas, represents the first generative nucleus of *Bouvard et Pécuchet.* Flaubert discusses the preface to the *Dictionnaire* again in a letter to Louise Colet on December 17, 1852: "Une vieille idée m'est revenue, à savoir celle de mon *Dictionnaire des idées reçues* (sais-tu ce que c'est?). La préface surtout m'excite fort, et de la manière dont je la conçois (ce serait tout un livre), aucune loi ne pourrait me mordre quoique j'y attaquerais tout" [An old idea has come back to my mind, that is my *Dictionnaire des idées reçues* (you know what it is, don't you?). Above all, I am very excited about the preface. I imagine to write it (it would be an entire book) in a way that would not allow any law to strike me even though I bash everything]. *Correspondance,* 3:66.

8. Flaubert, *Bouvard et Pécuchet,* edited by Gothot-Mersch, 26. Subsequent references appear parenthetically in the text. Flaubert employs the expression *Leur Copie* in the last known scenario for the second volume of his novel, 442.

9. Ibid., 428–31.

10. The macrostructure of *Bouvard et Pécuchet* strikingly resembles that of *I promessi sposi/Storia della colonna infame,* with a mainly fictional first part followed by a chiefly documentary second part. I do not intend to suggest a direct intertextual connection between the two works. Rather, I would like to use Flaubert's description of *Bouvard et Pécuchet* as a template for a fresh reading of Manzoni, for a provocative approach that views *I promessi sposi* as the preface to *Storia della colonna infame.* This interpretation would reverse the traditional relationship between the two works and allow for a deeper assessment of Manzoni's twenty-year long meditation on truth and fiction.

11. Letter to Louise Colet, on December 17, 1852. Flaubert, *Correspondance,* 3:67.

12. Letter to Mme Roger des Genettes, on January 25, 1880. Ibid., 8:356.

13. Letter to Mme Roger des Genettes, on March 1878. Flaubert, *Correspondance: Supplément,* 4:62. Letter to Hippolyte Taine, on January 10, 1879, ibid., 147. Letter to Mme Brainne, on August 4, 1879, ibid., 255. Letter to Maxime du Camp, ibid., 273.

14. Letter to Edma Roger des Genettes on August 18, 1872. Flaubert, *Correspondance,* 6:402.

15. Letter to his niece Caroline on October, 15, 1874. Ibid., 7:213.

16. Ippolito, "Critique du positivisme," 62.

17. The second volume of *Bouvard et Pécuchet* contains a long section dealing with stylistic issues: it exposes the stupidity of seventeen different types of style, from scientific to revolutionary and from ecclesiastic to dra-

matic, to name just a few. Through this display of stylistic horror, Flaubert confirms his intention to expose the rhetorical nature of the greater part of contemporary knowledge. Flaubert, *Le second volume*, 37–186.

18. Gleize, *Le double miroir*, 182.
19. Ong, *Orality and Literacy*, 99.
20. Neefs, "Noter, classer, briser, montrer," 86. Jacques Neefs also maintains that while enumerations and catalogs are powerful instruments in all of Flaubert's works, they are particularly common in *Salammbô*, 69.
21. In French literature, the practice of lists finds two significant examples in Rabelais and Perec: "As the journey of the *Quart Livre*, *Bouvard et Pécuchet* implies the use of lists and the search for impossible knowledge." Ippolito, "Critique du positivisme," 63. In Rabelais's *Quart Livre*, chapters 30, 40, 59, and 64 almost entirely consist of lists. Furthermore, unlike the other four books of Rabelais's work, the *Quart Livre* is followed by a detailed dictionary of the most obscure terms it contains. Lists also represent a trademark of Georges Perec's prose in *La Vie mode d'emploi*.
22. Salsano, "Enciclopedia," 3.
23. Hegel, *Encyclopedia of Philosophical Sciences*, 21.
24. See D'Alembert's description of the historical development of science from the darkness of the Middle Ages to the enlightenment of the eighteenth century. *Discours préliminaire*, 75–126. Likewise, Comte positions positivism on top of human ascension toward true knowledge: "Today, to all the observers who know their century, it has become impossible ignoring that positive studies are the final goal of human intelligence." *Philosophie première*, 27.
25. Lalonde, "La somme et le récit," 76.
26. D'Alembert classifies sciences according to the object they study and, above all, the type of human faculty they employ: reason, memory, or imagination. From this classification stems the primary division of knowledge into Philosophy (reason), History (memory), and Fine Arts (imagination). Coleridge divides sciences into pure, mixed, and applied. The former stand on the highest level as they deal with ideas rather than practical concerns. Comte maintains that the encyclopedic order consists in the natural enchainment of sciences, which is made possible by connections tying physical phenomena. Hence, human knowledge achieves its internal order by following the innate order of nature.
27. Flaubert, *Le second volume*, 57.
28. Roland Barthes argues that *Bouvard et Pécuchet* is a text where nobody, not even the author, enjoys power over anybody else. It is writing that makes this achievement possible: "this is the function of writing: to make ridiculous, to destroy the power (the intimidation) of a language over another, to dismantle any meta-language as soon as it is constituted." *S/Z*, 96.
29. Donato, *Script of Decadence*, 13.
30. In *Bouvard et Pécuchet*, nineteenth-century positivism's inability to shape a plausible representation of the world is epitomized by the ideological parabola of those characters, such as professor Dumouchel or doctor Vaucorbeil, who function as mediators between the two clerks and academic knowledge. As Bouvard and Pécuchet's adventures go on, these dis-

tributors of knowledge appear more and more prone to transform their positivism into stubborn ideology, "in a type of scientism that transforms the scientific approach into spiritualism." See Deléage, "Acquisition et transmission," 102. For instance, upon observing Bouvard and Pécuchet's successful experiments with magnetism, doctor Vaucorbeil shouts: "Ne continuez plus! ce sont des amusements dangereux!" "[Stop! These are dangerous games!] (290). The town priest repeats the doctor's warning—two faiths side by side—by screaming: "Êtes-vous fou? sans ma permission! Des manœuvres défendues par l'Église!" [Are you crazy? Without my permission! Practices forbidden by the Church!]. Ibid.

31. Brooks, *Reading for the Plot*, 6.

32. Letter to Mme Roger des Genettes on April 15, 1875. Flaubert, *Correspondance*, 7:237.

33. Descharmes, *Autour de "Bouvard et Pécuchet,"* 66–84.

34. Descharmes reconstructs the chronology of *Bouvard et Pécuchet* through a detailed analysis of all the novel's events. He demonstrates that there is a gap of circa seven years between the chronology provided in the novel through historical dates, among other details, and the timeline deduced from the analysis of the novelistic events such as the birth of the child or the sequence of seasons. Descharmes interprets this difference as a sign of Flaubert's lack of concern for realism.

35. Kliebenstein, "L'encyclopédie minimale," 450.

36. Throughout the nineteenth century, following Nicholas-Louis Robert's invention of the paper-machine in 1799 and Friedrich Gottlob Keller's improvement of the treatment of wood pulp in 1840, the papermaking industry made decisive strides. See *History of Paper*, 76–89. Because of these technological breakthroughs, good quality paper was produced at a low cost and in apparently endless quantity. As for the duplication of text, Remington & Son developed the first mass producible "Type-Writer" in 1874. Kittler, *Gramophone, Film, Typewriter*, 187.

37. Leclerc, *La Spirale et le monument*, 109.

38. Ibid., 142.

39. The notions of authority and originality combine in the etymology of authenticity: the Greek term from which "authentic" derives, αὐθέντης, can be both a noun meaning "somebody who enjoys absolute power," and an adjective meaning "made by one's own hand." Conferring authenticity is a privilege enjoyed by an authority that is completely free from any external constraint.

40. In Pécuchet's words, Balzac does not write literature, but statistics and ethnography. From the clerk's subversive point of view, Balzac's macronovel loses all its structural connections and becomes a mere accumulation of data, just statistics. See Flaubert, *Bouvard et Pécuchet*, edited by Gothot-Mersch, 205.

41. Foucault, "La bibliothèque fantastique," 118. Foucault also notes that when Flaubert wrote *Bouvard et Pécuchet* he had already written a book made of citations, *La Tentation de Saint Antoine* (1874). In this work, however, all the fragments are taken from a single text, the Bible.

42. Donato, *Script of Decadence*, 64.

43. As Donato notes, once displayed in a museum, fragments lose their original meaning; the latter depended on the spatial and temporal context from which fragments were removed in order to become museum exhibits. Ultimately, in the museum, meaning originates in the spectator, rather than residing in the objects displayed. Ibid., 66.

44. *Bouvard et Pécuchet* criticizes another totalizing form, the dictionary. By means of "its limited format, its derisive aspect, and its inability to really represent the entire picture of stupidity," the *"Dictionnaire des idées reçues"* jokingly satirizes the dictionary as an instrument for classifying the facts of language. Lalonde, "Une alliance anormale," 152.

CHAPTER 6. LA VIE MODE D'EMPLOI

1. Bellos, *Georges Perec*, 252.
2. Laura Peperoni and Marina Zuccoli maintain that Doctor Dinteville's story (*La Vie mode d'emploi*, chapter 96) bespeaks Perec's professional understanding of the archivist's work. See "Georges Perec e l'invenzione bibliografica," 442. Likewise, Paul-Dominique Pomart argues that "The multiplication—up to derision—of minute and meticulous inventories, of exhaustive indexes and of any type of classification inevitably hints at the daily experience of archivists and librarians, who retrieve, analyze, describe, take out, or tag." See "Georges Perec et la documentation," 244.
3. Bellos, *Georges Perec*, 258.
4. Spieker, *Big Archive*, xiii.
5. Aristotle, *Poetics*, 1, 3.1.
6. As the novel comprises ninety-nine chapters, there must be a square that does not become the location for a chapter. Bernard Magné has demonstrated how the missing square coincides with the bottom left-hand corner of the grid, which corresponds to one of the basement rooms. *Perecollages*, 47–50.
7. See Bellos, *Georges Perec*, 514; Perec, *Cahier des charge*, 40–41.
8. When the featured locale is a common space that nobody lives in, that chapter is numbered and titled accordingly, for example "XXXVIII Lift Machinery" or "XXII Entrance Hall."
9. Chassay, *Le jeu des coïncidences*, 19–24.
10. In French, *cahier des charges* can mean both "a document stating terms and conditions of a legal contract" and "a document indicating the characteristics that a technical execution will require and the different stages of production to respect for its implementation." In both cases a *cahier de charges* is a legal document binding the parties in a contract to respect their obligations.
11. The remaining two lists, called "Couples," comprise pairs of elements, such as "Laurent and Hardy" or "Pride and Prejudice": these two lists do not obey the rules of "Gap" and "Wrong" that regulate the insertion of elements belonging to the other forty lists.
12. Perec, *Cahier des charges*, 22.
13. David Bellos notices that Perec was not always able to obey his own

rules: "He [Perec] kept a tally of how many of the forty-two constraints he had managed to use in each chapter—as far as Chapter 42, after which he gave up his accounting and just wrote on. Only eighteen of the first forty-two chapters respect all forty-two specifications, by Perec's reckoning." *Georges Perec*, 605.

14. "Gap" and "Wrong" are necessary for inserting a component of chance into the system of constraints that generates *La Vie mode d'emploi*. Perec calls this component "*clinamen*" (deviation), a term that in Lucretius's physics meant the atom's ability to spontaneously change its direction, thus breaking the mechanical chain of necessary causes that rules over the universe. Perec's *clinamen*, whereby a well-structured literary work accepts a principle contrary to its very rules, does not represent a novelty. In Boccaccio's *Decameron*, the character Dioneo, who, after the second day, narrates stories of his choice rather than expanding on the topic of the day, carries out a function similar to Perec's *clinamen*.

15. Bellos, *Georges Perec*, 363.

16. Ibid., 516. Perec unveiled his plans for *La Vie mode d'emploi* in the OuLiPo meeting of November 8, 1972.

17. Ibid., 593.

18. Although it does not belong to the appendix, chapter 51 appears to be another index: it displays a list of 179 stories that concern either the residents of the building or characters belonging to the various paintings, posters, or photographs that decorate the apartments.

19. *La Vie mode d'emploi* is organized as a medieval "*liber iurium*," i.e., a register where, in the twelfth and thirteenth centuries, Italian communes collated, in chronological order, copies of their most important documents. As heterogeneous records were taken from the shelves and copied on the pages of books by notaries, the *libri iurium* presented an innovation in the practice of the archive. At the end of the *libri iurium*, for the first time in history, there appeared indexes for helping readers to cross-reference documents dealing with the same subject. Behrmann, "Genoa and Lübeck," 18.

20. When closely scrutinized, the alphabetic checklist displays its ambiguous nature. Several stories on the list consist of minimal details, potential, rather than fully developed narratives, that are part of larger accounts or descriptions. "Histoire du bourrelier, de sa sœur, et de son beau-frère" [The Tale of the Saddler, His Sister, and His Brother in Law], for instance, originates in an invitation card that is lying on David Marcia's desk. As several of these potential accounts are nothing more than small narrative fragments, it may occur that a chapter includes two, at times three, tales. In short, in *La Vie mode d'emploi*, each of the finding aids guides readers to a specific approach to the novel. These approaches do not always agree with each other. The novel as dossier inserts into the most archival of its components, the finding aids, an element of uncertainty that obliquely criticizes the alleged consistency of archival theory.

21. See Muller, Feith, and Fruin, *Manual*, 165; Schellenberg, *Modern Archives*, 196.

22. Barthes, *S/Z*, 23. In *La Vie mode d'emploi*, finding aids become necessary instruments for providing the text with its *romanesque* component,

or "le goût des histoires et des péripéties" [the delight in stories and adventures] according to Perec. See Perec, *Penser/Classer*, 10. Readers can follow *romanesque* intrigues only with the help of final indexes.

23. See Genette, *Narrative Discourse*, 102.

24. Perec, *La Vie mode d'emploi*, 96. Subsequent references appear parenthetically in the text.

25. Perec, *Life*, 66.

26. Ibid., 49.

27. In Perec, *La Vie mode d'emploi*, the most significant occurrences of copying from other texts appear on the following pages: 26, 32, 35, 45, 76, 78, 97, 101, 110, 119, 120, 134, 146, 148, 156, 165, 182, 189 [this text is a letter that is copied within the text on page 182, which is another letter], 201, 210, 223, 228, 239, 244, 248, 274, 291, 303, 306, 307, 320, 322, 329, 336, 349, 363, 381, 384, 393, 395, 417, 434, 481, 492, 513, 518, 533, and 535.

28. Perec, *Life*, 70.

29. *La Vie mode d'emploi*'s forty-nine major lists appear on the following pages: 63, 80, 92, 93, 116, 129, 138, 140, 148, 151, 168, 193, 223, 281, 287, 298, 305, 338, 349, 379, 380, 386, 388, 389, 390, 391, 393, 395, 399, 406, 412, 415, 428, 482, 485, 488, 491, 495, 499, 512, 513, 532, 534, 535, 536, 541, 563, 575, and 577. Lists appear more often in the second half of the novel, as well as during the descriptions of the service rooms of the building, such as storerooms and stairs.

30. Goody, *Domestication of the Savage Mind*, 82.

31. Ong, *Orality and Literacy*, 124.

32. In *Les Choses*, his first published novel, Perec gives ample textual space to inventories of desired objects. In addition, lists represent crucial components of the following works: *Espèces d'espaces* (1974), *Tentative d'épuisement d'un lieu parisien* (1975), *Je me souviens* (1978), *Un cabinet d'amateur* (1979), *Penser/Classer* (1985), *L'infra-ordinaire* (1989), and *Voeux* (1989).

33. Burgelin, *Georges Perec*, 12. In "Les lieux d'une ruse," Perec ties his compulsion to jot down lists to a loss of memory that took place when he was undergoing psychoanalytic therapy. This amnesia prompted him to write a personal journal that was filled with this type of "objective" information: "l'heure de mon réveil, l'emploi de mon temps, mes déplacements, mes achats, le progrès—évalué en lignes ou en pages—de mon travail, les gens que j'avais rencontrés ou simplement aperçus, le détail du repas que j'avais fait le soir dans tel ou tel restaurant, mes lectures, les disques que j'avais écoutés, les films que j'avais vus, etc" [the time when I woke up, how I employed my time, my movements, my purchases, the progress—measured in terms of lines and words—of my work, the people I met or simply caught sight of, the details of the meal I had in the evening in this or that restaurant, my readings, the records I listened to, the films I watched, etc]. Perec, *Penser/Classer*, 69.

34. Balzac, *La Comédie humaine*, 1:11–12.

35. Grégoire Simpson's adventure represents the novelistic version of the theme outlined by Perec in *Un homme qui dort* (1967).

36. Perec, *Tentative d'épuisement d'un lieu parisien*, 30. The identifica-

tion between Simpson and Perec challenges Pomart's remark that "Perec never talked, wrote, or reported on his work as archivist." See Pomart, "Georges Perec et la documentation," 244. Indeed, Grégoire Simpson's story quite directly discusses Perec's experience as an archivist.

37. Burgelin, *Les Parties de dominos*, 73.

38. Only five other characters utilize their memory in *La Vie mode d'emploi*: León Marcia (219), Isabelle Gratiolet (332), the two friends Madame Moreau and Madame Trévins (409), and Lino Margay (424).

39. Chassay, *Le jeu des coïncidences*, 90.

40. The second half of Bartlebooth's name derives from Barnabooth, the hero in Valery Larbaud's *A. O. Barnabooth*.

41. Bernard Magné argues that, "whenever *La Vie mode d'emploi* deals with painting quite often it means writing." See "Lavis mode d'emploi," 239. Because it consists of copying, making collages, and framing, the type of painting represented by Perec becomes a metaphor for several operations, such as quoting, adding paste-ins, and compiling lists, that are performed in *La Vie mode d'emploi*.

42. Blouin, "History and Memory," 297.

43. Perec operates within the technical boundaries of the paper archive, while the situation discussed by Francis Blouin is situated in the digital age. By dramatically increasing the bureaucracy's ability to create records, the digital revolution has encouraged the destroying of documents. Paradoxically, the more we record, the less we record.

44. Derrida, *Mal d'archive*, 27.

45. Burgelin, *Les Parties de dominos*, 30. The search for the lost origin also motivates James Sherwood's, Véronique Altamont's, and Juan Mariana de Zaccaria's adventures in the archive. Two other characters, the archeologist Fernand de Beaumont and the anthropologist Maurice Appenzzell, waste their lives in the vain effort to find mythical original entities: the first capital of the Arab Kingdom of Spain for the former and the tribe of Sumatra's earliest inhabitants for the latter (26–29, 141–47). Both Beaumont and Appenzzell leave behind records of their research in the form of the archeologist's professionally organized notes and the anthropologist's notebooks.

46. Perec, *Life*, 204.

47. Ibid., 325.

48. I would like to point out that in the very archival section of his novel, the appendix, Perec subtly hints at the archive's deceptiveness: his indexes contradict themselves, thus presenting readers with misleading information. As an example of the archive's tricks, one can take the two entries in the alphabetical index of the stories, "Histoire de la cantatrice russe" [The Russian Singer's Tale] and "Histoire du petit Tunisien" [The Short Tunisian's Tale]. They do not correspond to chapters 5 and 58 respectively, as stated in the index, but to chapters 6 and 57.

Chapter 7. *Libra*

1. See, Willman, "Traversing the Fantasies," 407; "Art After Dealey Plaza," 622–25.

2. For a synthetic assessment of the rise of conspiracy theories during the 1970s, see Glen Thomas, "History, Biography, and Narrative," 107–8.

3. Art Simon maintains that 2300 articles and books were published between 1963 and 1979 on the subject of the assassination. *Dangerous Knowledge*, 7.

4. DeLillo, *Libra*, 458. Subsequent references appear parenthetically in the text. The author's note appears in this form at the end of the original Viking Penguin edition of *Libra* published in 1988. The paperback version of the novel, published by Penguin in 1991, presents a shortened version of the note that ends in line seven after "invented incidents, dialogues, and characters."

5. In *Libra*, Nicholas Branch appears on these pages: 14–16, 57–60, and 181–84; 298–302, 375–79, and 440–45.

6. The following is a list of the historical figures cited in Nicholas Branch's roster of the dead: Jack Ruby, George Mohrenschildt, David Ferrie, Guy Banister, John Roselli, Sam Giancana, and Antonio Veciana. Outside the roster of the dead, another historical character quoted by Branch is William Somersett, a police informer who discusses a plan to kill President Kennedy in Miami (376).

President Lyndon B. Johnson appointed the President's Commission on the Assassination of President Kennedy by Executive Order (E.O. 11130) on November 29, 1963. The commission's report consisted in a massive 300,000-word book accompanied by twenty-six volumes of evidence and testimony. The House of Representatives established the House Select Committee on Assassinations in 1976 to reopen the investigation into Kennedy's death. The committee, which also investigated the death of Dr. Martin Luther King, Jr., issued its report on March 29, 1979. Unlike the *Warren Commission Report*, it suggested that President Kennedy was probably assassinated as a result of a conspiracy.

7. These are the fictional characters: Win Everett, Carlos Príos Socarrás, Eladio del Valle, Laurence Parmenter, Ramón Benítez, Frank Vásquez, T. J. Mackey, Raymo, Carmine Latta, Wayne Elko, Bobby Dupard, and Brenda Sensibaugh.

8. Muller, Feith, and Fruin, *Manual*, 59.

9. Simon, *Dangerous Knowledge*, 42.

10. Ibid., 38

11. In DeLillo's *Underworld* (1997), a bootleg copy of the Zapruder film is shown during a private party in New York in 1974; by then, the movie has become a cultural product in its own right that can be shown for entertainment purposes.

12. Kittler, *Gramophone, Film, Typewriter*, 145. See Simon, *Dangerous Knowledge* 39. Timothy L. Parrish, who argues that DeLillo portrayed the assassination as an event performed before a waiting camera, maintains that, "the assassination itself is a home movie that becomes a film." See "Lesson of History," 19.

13. Carmichael, "Lee Harvey Oswald," 207.

14. Borges narrates the story of the map the size of the territory it represents in "Del rigor en la ciencia," which was published in the collection *El Hacedor* in 1960.

15. See De Curtis, "Outsider in This Society," 50.
16. President's Commission on the Assassination of President Kennedy, *Report*, 380.
17. Ibid., 381.
18. Ibid.
19. Skip Willman argues that although *Libra* "challenges the conclusion of the Warren Commission, the novel retains much of the Warren Commission's work." "Art after Dealey Plaza," 622.
20. John Johnston maintains that Branch "represents the failures of a strictly historical, empirically governed account, and its incapacity, when faced with the multiplicity of proliferating information generated by the event, even to represent it as a coherent totality, much less explain it." "Superlinear Fiction," 325.
21. De Curtis, "Outsider in this Society," 56.
22. Hayles, *Cosmic Web*, 10.
23. Ibid., 19.
24. According to Paul Civello, by attempting to write a story based on Zola's poetics, Branch demonstrates the epistemic flaws of his project. Zola's theory of the experimental novel shared the principle of linear causality with nineteenth-century positivism, which was Newtonian in its main tenets. As an epigone of Zola, Branch applies out-of-date instruments to a reality that should be approached through the "field concept" and the assumption that "Newtonian certainty and 'knowability' give way to uncertainty and indeterminacy." Civello, "Undoing the Naturalistic Novel," 35.
25. Cook, "What Is Past is Prologue," 35.
26. Hayles, *Cosmic Web*, 22.
27. Courtwright, "Why Oswald Missed," 89.
28. In his interview with Anthony De Curtis, DeLillo maintains that by tying the assassination to a plot of anti-Castro elements, he chose "the most obvious possibility." See De Curtis, "Outsider in this Society," 50.
29. Manovich, *Language of the New Media*, 219.

Epilogue

1. Hunter, *Before Novels*, 37.
2. Kittler, *Gramophone, Film, Typewriter*, 188.
3. Curtius, "Goethe as Administrator," 60; Toschi, *La sala rossa*, 112; Perec, *Cahier des charges*, 22.
4. *Keitai* is a combination of *kei*, "to carry," and *tai*, "kimono band," something that is easy to carry in the kimono band, that is a cell phone. *Shosetsu* is a combination of *sho*, "small," and *setsu*, "to explain," that is a small explanation, a novel. Hence *keitai shosetsu* is a novel to read on the cell phone. I am thankful to Michele Marra for patiently sharing his deep knowledge of Japanese semantics with me.

Works Cited

Primary Sources

Balzac, Honoré de. *La Comédie humaine*. Edited by Pierre-Georges Castex. 12 vols. Paris: Gallimard, Pléiade, 1976–81.

———. *Œuvres diverses*. Edited by Marcel Bouteron and Henri Longnon. 3 vols. Paris: Conard, 1910.

Boccaccio, Giovanni. *Decameron*. Milan: Mondadori, 2006.

Borges, Jorges Luis. "La biblioteca de Babel." In *Obras completas*, 4 vols., 1:465–71. Barcelona: Emecé, 1996.

———. "Del rigor en la ciencia." In *Obras completas*, 4 vols., 2:225. Barcelona: Emecé, 1996.

Capote, Truman. *In Cold Blood*. New York: Vintage, 1994.

Consolo, Vincenzo. *Il sorriso dell'ignoto marinaio*. Milan: Mondadori, 1997.

Da Cunha, Euclides. *Os Sertões*. São Paulo: Ática, 1998.

Defoe, Daniel. *A Journal of the Plague Year*. Edited by Paula R. Backscheider. New York: Norton, 1992.

———. *Moll Flanders*. New York: The Modern Library, 2002.

———. *Robinson Crusoe*. Oxford: Oxford University Press, 2007.

DeLillo, Don. *Libra*. New York: Viking Penguin, 1988.

———. *Underworld*. New York: Scribner, 1997.

Eco, Umberto. *Il nome della rosa*. Milan: Bompiani, 1980.

Eloy Martínez, Tomás. *El cantor de tango*. Buenos Aires: Planeta, 2004.

———. *Santa Evita*. Barcelona: Seix Barral, 1995.

Faulkner, William. *Go Down, Moses*. In *Faulkner: Novels, 1942–1954*, edited by Joseph Blotner and Noel Polk, 1–281. New York: The Library of America, 1994.

Fielding, Henry. *The History of Tom Jones*. London: Penguin, 1966.

Flaubert, Gustave. *Bouvard et Pécuchet*. Edited by Claudine Gothot-Mersch. Paris: Gallimard, 1979.

———. *Correspondance*. 9 vols. Paris: Conard, 1926–33.

———. *Correspondance: Supplément*. Edited by René Dumesnil, Jean Pommier, and Claude Digeon. 4 vols. Paris: Conard, 1954.

———. *Le second volume de "Bouvard et Pécuchet."* Edited by Geneviève Bollème. Paris: Denoël, 1966.

———. *La Tentation de Saint Antoine.* In *Œuvres,* edited by A. Thibaudet and R. Dumesnil, 1:23–268. Paris: Gallimard, 1951.

Larbaud, Valéry. *A. O. Barnabooth, ses œuvres complètes.* Paris: Gallimard, 1995.

Manzoni, Alessandro. *I romanzi.* Edited by Salvatore Silvano Nigro. Vol. 1, *Fermo e Lucia. Appendice storica sulla colonna infame.* Vol. 2, bk. 1, *I promessi sposi (1827).* Vol. 2, bk. 2, *I promessi sposi (1840). Storia della colonna infame.* Milan: Mondadori, 2002.

———. *Tutte le opere.* Edited by Alberto Chiari and Fausto Ghisalberti. Vol. 5, bk. 3, *Scritti letterari,* edited by Carla Riccardi and Biancamaria Travi. Milan: Mondadori, 1991.

———. *Tutte le opere.* Vol. 7, *Lettere,* edited by Cesare Arieti. 3 bks. Milan: Mondadori, 1970.

Mathews, Harry. *The Journalist.* Boston: Godine, 1954.

Melville, Herman. "Bartlebly." In *Billy Budd and Other Stories,* 1–46. New York: Penguin, 1986.

Pavic, Milorad. *Dictionary of the Khazars: A Lexicon Novel.* Translated by Christina Pribicevic-Zoric. New York: Vintage, 1989.

Perec, Georges. *Un cabinet d'amateur.* Paris: Balland, 1979.

———. *Cahier des charges de "La Vie mode d'emploi."* Edited by Hans Hartje, Bernard Magné, and Jacques Neefs. Paris: Zulma, 1993.

———. *Les Choses.* Paris: Juillard, 1965.

———. *Un homme qui dort.* Paris: Denoël, 1967.

———. *L'infra-ordinaire.* Paris: Seuil, 1989.

———. *Je me souviens.* Paris: Hachette, 1978.

———. *Life: A User's Manual.* Translated by David Bellos. Boston: Godine, 1987.

———. *Penser/Classer.* Paris: Hachette, 1975.

———. *Tentative d'épuisement d'un lieu parisien.* Paris: Bourgois, 1975.

———. *La Vie mode d'emploi.* Paris: Hachette, 1978.

———. *Voeux.* Paris: Seuil, 1989.

Poniatowska, Elena. *La noche de Tlatelolco.* Mexico City: Era, 1971.

Rabelais, *Le quart livre.* In *Œuvres complètes,* 515–720. Paris: Gallimard, 1994.

Roa Bastos, Augusto. *Yo el supremo.* Madrid: Cátedra, 1987.

Saramago, José. *Todos os Nomes.* Lisbon: Caminho, 1997.

Sarmiento, Domingo F. *Facundo: Civilización y barbarie.* Madrid: Alianza Editorial, 1988.

Sciascia, Leonardo. *Il Consiglio d'Egitto.* Milan: Adelphi, 1989.

Scott, Walter. *Ivanohe.* Oxford: Oxford University Press, 1996.

———. *Waverley.* Oxford: Oxford University Press, 1986.

Sterne, Laurence. *The Life and Opinions of Tristram Shandy.* London: Penguin, 1967.

Ugresic, Dubravka. *The Museum of Unconditional Surrender*. Translated by Celia Hawkesworth. New York: New Directions, 1999.
Vassalli, Sebastiano. *La chimera*, Turin: Einaudi, 2005.
Vigny, Alfred de. *Cinq-Mars*. Paris: Gallimard, 1980.

Archival Theory

Behrmann, Thomas. "Genoa and Lübeck: The Beginnings of Communal Record-Keeping in Two Medieval Trading Metropolises." In *Archives and the Metropolis*, edited by M. V. Roberts, 11–21. London: Guildhall, 1998.
Blouin, Francis X., Jr. "History and Memory: The Problem of the Archive." *PMLA* 119, no. 5 (2004): 296–98.
Brothman, Brien. "Declining Derrida: Integrity, Tensegrity, and the Preservation of Archives from Deconstruction." *Archivaria* 48 (Fall 1999): 64–88.
Casanova, Eugenio. *Archivistica*. Siena: Lazzeri, 1928.
Cook, Terry. "Fashionable Nonsense or Professional Rebirth: Postmodernism and the Practice of Archives." *Archivaria* 51 (Spring 2001): 14–35.
———. "Mind over Matter: Toward a New Theory of Archival Approach." In *The Archival Imagination*, edited by Barbara L. Craig, 38–70. Ottawa: ACA, 1992.
———. "What Is Past Is Prologue: A History of Archival Ideas since 1898, and the Future Paradigm Shift." *Archivaria* 43 (Spring 1997): 17–63.
Derrida, Jacques. *Mal d'archive: Une impression freudienne*. Paris: Galilée, 1995.
Gränström, Claes. "The Janus Syndrome." In *The Principle of Provenance*, edited by Kerstin Abukhanfusa and Jan Sydbeck, 11–22. Borås: Centraltryckeriet, 1994.
Ham, Gerald F. "Archival Strategies for the Post-Custodial Era." *The American Archivist* 44, no. 3 (Summer 1981): 207–16.
Horsman, Peter. "Taming the Elephant: An Orthodox Approach to the Principle of Provenance." In *The Principle of Provenance*, edited by Kerstin Abukhanfusa and Jan Sydbeck, 51–63. Borås: Centraltryckeriet, 1994.
Jenkinson, Hilary. *A Manual of Archive Administration*. London: Percy Lund, Humphries & Co., 1937.
MacNeil, Heather. "Trusting Records in a Postmodern World." *Archivaria* 51 (Spring 2001): 36–47.
———. *Trusting Records: Legal, Historical and Diplomatic Perspective*. Dordrecht: Kluwer Academic Publishers, 2000.
Muller, S. Fz., J. A. Feith, and R. Fruin Th. Az. *Manual for the Arrangement and Description of Archives*. Translated by Arthur H. Leavitt. New York: The H. W. Wilson Company, 1940.
Pearce-Moses, Richard, ed. *A Glossary of Archival and Records Terminol-*

ogy. The Society of American Archivists, 2005. http://www.archivists.org/glossary/index.asp.

Posner, Ernst. "Max Lehmann and the Genesis of the Principle of Provenance." In *Archives & Public Interest: Selected Essays by Ernst Posner*, edited by Ken Munden, 36–44. Washington, DC: Public Affairs Press, 1967.

———. "Some Aspects of Archival Development since the French Revolution." In *Archives & Public Interest: Selected Essays by Ernst Posner*, edited by Ken Munden, 23–35. Washington, DC: Public Affairs Press, 1967.

Schellenberg, T. R. *Modern Archives: Principles and Techniques.* Chicago: The University of Chicago Press, 1956.

Sekula, Allan. "The Body and the Archive." *October* 39 (Winter 1986): 3–64.

Taylor, Hugh A. "The Collective Memory: Archives and Libraries As Heritage." *Archivaria* 15 (Winter 1982–83): 118–30.

Zelenyj, Dan. "Archivy Ad Portas: The Archives-Records Management Paradigm Re-Visited in the Electronic Information Age." *Archivaria* 47 (Spring 1999): 66–84.

Literary Theory, Media Theory, History, and Philosophy

Agamben, Giorgio. *Quel che resta di Auschwitz. L'archivio e il testimone.* Turin: Bollati Boringhieri, 1998.

Anderson, Benedict. *Imagined Communities.* London: Verso, 1991.

Aristotle. *Poetics.* Translated by Richard Janko. Indianapolis, IN: Hackett, 1987.

Barthes, Roland. *S/Z.* Paris: Gallimard, 1970.

Brooks, Peter. *Reading for the Plot.* New York: Knopf, 1984.

Curtius, Robert. "Goethe as Administrator." In *Essays on European Literature*, 58–72. Princeton, NJ: Princeton University Press, 1973.

Davis, Lennard J. *Resisting Novels: Ideology and Fiction.* New York: Methuen, 1987.

Dimock, Wai Chee. "Genre as World System: Epic and Novel on Four Continents." *Narrative* 14, no. 1 (January 2006): 85–101.

Foucault, Michel. *The Archaeology of Knowledge.* New York: Pantheon, 1972.

———. *Power/Knowledge: Selected Interviews and Other Writings, 1972–1977.* Edited by Coling Gordon. Translated by Colin Gordon, Leo Marshall, John Mepham, and Kate Soper. New York: Pantheon Books, 1980.

———. *Surveiller et punir: Naissance de la prison.* Paris: Gallimard, 1975.

Freud, Sigmund. "Beyond the Pleasure Principle." In *The Standard Edition of the Complete Psychological Works of Sigmund Freud*, translated by James Strachey, 18:7–64. London: The Hogarth Press, 1955.

Frow, John. *Genre.* London: Routledge, 2006.

Ginzburg, Carlo. "Morelli, Freud and Sherlock Holmes: Clues and Scientific Method." *History Workshop Journal* 9, no. 1 (1980): 5–36.

González Echevarría, Roberto. *Myth and Archive: A Theory of Latin American Narrative*. Durham, NC: Duke University Press, 1998.

Goody, Jack. *The Domestication of the Savage Mind*. Cambridge: Cambridge University Press, 1977.

Harrison, Robert Pogue. *The Dominion of the Dead*. Chicago: University of Chicago Press, 2004.

Hayles, Katherine N. *The Cosmic Web*. Ithaca, NY: Cornell University Press, 1984.

Hegel, G. W. F. *Encyclopedia of Philosophical Sciences in Outline and Critical Writings*. Translated by A. V. Miller, Steven A. Taubeneck, and Diana I. Behler. New York: Continuum, 1990.

Hutcheon, Linda. *The Politics of Postmodernism*. New York: Routledge, 1989.

Kittler, Friedrich A. *Gramophone, Film, Typewriter*. Translated by Geoffrey Winthrop-Young and Michael Wutz. Stanford, CA: Stanford University Press, 1999.

Kundera, Milan. *L'art du roman*. Paris: Gallimard, 1986.

Lukács, Georg. *The Historical Novel*. Translated by Hannah and Stanley Mitchell. Lincoln: University of Nebraska Press, 1983.

Manovich, Lev. *The Language of the New Media*. Cambridge, MA: The MIT Press, 2001.

Matsuda, Matt K. *The Memory of the Modern*. New York: Oxford University Press, 1996.

Noiriel, Gérard. "L'identification des citoyens: Naissance de l'état civil républicain." *Genèses* 13 (Fall 1993): 3–28.

———. *La Tyrannie du national*. Paris: Calmann-Levy, 1991.

Ong, Walter. *Orality and Literacy: The Technologizing of the World*. London: Routledge, 1988.

Ranke, Leopold von. *The Secret of World History*. Edited and translated by Roger Wines. New York: Fordham University Press, 1981.

Ricœur, Paul. *La mémoire, l'histoire, l'oubli*. Paris: Seuil, 2000.

———. *Temps et récit*. Vol. 1, *L'intrigue et le récit historique*. Paris: Seuil, 1983.

Salsano, Alfredo. "Enciclopedia." In *Enciclopedia*, edited by Ruggiero Romano, 1:3–62. Turin: Einaudi, 1977–84.

Snyder, Alice D., ed. *S.T. Coleridge's Treatise on Method as Published in the Encyclopedia Metropolitana*. London: Constable, 1934.

Sontag, Susan. *On Photography*. New York: Anchor Books, 1990.

Spang, Kurt. "Apuntes para una definición de la novela histórica." In *La novela histórica: Teoría y comentarios*, edited by Kurt Spang, Ignacio Arellano, and Carlos Mata, 51–87. Pamplona: EUNSA, 1995.

Spieker, Sven. *The Big Archive: Art from Bureaucracy.* Cambridge, MA: The MIT Press, 2008.

Stille, Alexander. *The Future of the Past.* Picador: New York, 2003.

Secondary Sources on the Eighteenth-Century Novel

Bastian, F. "Defoe's *Journal of the Plague Year* Reconsidered." *The Review of English Studies* 16, no. 62 (May 1965): 151–73.

Celati, Gianni. *Finzioni occidentali: fabulazione, comicità e scrittura.* Turin: Einaudi, 1986.

Congreve, William. *Incognita and The Way of the World.* Edited by A. Norman Jeffares. Columbia: University of South Carolina Press, 1970.

Davis, Lennard J. *Factual Fictions: The Origins of the English Novel.* New York: Columbia University Press, 1983.

Day, Geoffrey. *From Fiction to the Novel.* London: Routledge, 1987.

Ellis, Frank H. "Defoe's *Journal of the Plague Year.*" Review of *A Journal of the Plague Year*, by Daniel Defoe, edited by Paula R. Backscheider. *The Review of English Studies* 45, no. 177 (February 1994): 76–82.

Hunter, J. Paul. *Before Novels: The Cultural Contexts of Eighteenth-Century English Fiction.* New York: Norton, 1990.

Mayer, Robert, "The Reception of *A Journal of the Plague Year* and the Nexus of Fiction and History in the Novel." *ELH* 57, no. 3 (Autumn 1990): 529–55.

McDowell, Paula. "Defoe and the Contagion of the Oral: Modeling Media Shift in *A Journal of the Plague Year.*" *PMLA* 121, no. 1 (2006): 87–106.

McKeon, Michael. *The Origins of the English Novel: 1600–1740.* Baltimore: The Johns Hopkins University Press, 1987.

Rambuss, Richard. "'A Complicated Distress': Narrativizing the Plague in Defoe's *Journal of the Plague Year.*" *Prose Studies* 12, no. 2 (1989): 115–31.

Richetti, John J. *Defoe's Narratives: Situations and Structures.* Oxford: Clarendon, 1975.

Schonhorn, Manuel. "Defoe's *Journal of the Plague Year*: Topography and Intention." *The Review of English Studies* 19, no. 76 (November 1968): 387–402.

Watt, Ian. *The Rise of the Novel.* Berkeley: University of California Press, 1962.

Williams, Ioan, ed. *Novel and Romance, 1700–1800: A Documentary Record.* New York, Barnes & Noble, 1970.

Secondary Sources on *I Promessi Sposi (1840)*. *Storia della colonna infame*

Bruni, Francesco. "Manzoni, l'anonimo, la storia." In *Le donne, i cavalier, l'arme, gli amori: poema e romanzo, la narrativa lunga in Italia,* edited by Francesco Bruni, 197–210. Venice: Marsilio, 2001.

Caputo, Rino. "La 'Colonna infame': tra 'Fermo e Lucia' e 'I promessi sposi.'" In *Omaggio ad Alessandro Manzoni nel bicentenario della nascita*, edited by Giuseppe Catanzaro, Francesco Santucci, and Salvatore Vivona, 337–60. Assisi: Accademia properziana del Subasio, 1986.

Codebò, Marco. "Records, Fiction, and Power in Alessandro Manzoni's *I promessi sposi* and *Storia della colonna infame*." *MLN* 121, no. 1 (2006): 187–206.

———. "Scomodi compagni di banco: scrittori e notai fra Boccaccio e Manzoni." *Italica* 84, no. 2–3 (Summer/Fall 2007): 187–98.

Gladfelder, Hal. "Seeing Black: Alessandro Manzoni between Fiction and History." *MLN* 108, no. 1 (January 1993): 59–86.

Menton, Seymour. *La nueva novela histórica de la America Latina, 1973–1992*. Mexico City: Fondo de cultura económica, 1993.

Nigro, Salvatore. *La tabacchiera di don Lisander: saggio sui "Promessi sposi."* Turin: Einaudi, 1996.

Pupino, Angelo R. *"Il vero solo è bello": Manzoni tra retorica e logica*. Bologna: il Mulino, 1982.

Puppo, Mario. *Poesia e verità: interpretazioni manzoniane*. Messina: D'Anna, 1979.

Raimondi, Ezio. *Il romanzo senza idillio: saggio sui "Promessi sposi."* Turin: Einaudi, 1983.

Repossi, Cesare, and Angelo Stella. Commentary on *I promessi sposi. Storia della colonna infame*, by Alessandro Manzoni, 673–1165. Turin: Einaudi-Gallimard, 1995.

Toschi, Luca. *La sala rossa: biografia dei "Promessi sposi."* Turin: Bollati Boringhieri, 1989.

Secondary Sources on *La Comédie humaine*

Becker, Peter. "The Standardized Gaze: The Standardization of the Search Warrant in Nineteenth-Century Germany." In *Documenting Individual Identity: The Development of State Practices in the Modern World*, edited by Jane Caplan and John Torpey, 139–63. Princeton, NJ: Princeton University Press, 2001.

Brooks, Peter. "Narrative Transaction and Transference (Unburying 'Le Colonel Chabert')." *NOVEL: A Forum on Fiction* 15, no. 2 (Winter 1982): 101–10.

———. *Realist Vision*. New Haven: Yale University Press, 2005.

Caruth, Cathy. "The Claims of the Dead: History, Haunted Property, and the Law." *Critical Inquiry* 28, no. 2 (Winter 2002): 419–41.

Garval, Michael D. "Balzac's *La Comédie humaine*: The Archival Rival." *Nineteenth-Century French Studies* 25, no. 1–2 (Fall 1996–Winter 1997): 30–40.

Good, Graham. "*Le Colonel Chabert*: A Masquerade with Documents." *The French Review* 42, no. 6 (May 1969): 846–56.

Kaluszynski, Martine. "Republican Identity: Bertillonage as Government Technique." In *Documenting Individual Identity: The Development of State Practices in the Modern World*, edited by Jane Caplan and John Torpey, 123–38. Princeton, NJ: Princeton University Press, 2001.

Moretti, Franco. *Atlas of the European Novel, 1800–1900.* London: Verso, 1998.

Pasco, Allan H. "Ursule through the Glass Lightly." *The French Review* 65, no. 1 (October 1991): 36–45.

Prendergast, Christopher. *The Order of Mimesis: Balzac, Stendhal, Nerval, Flaubert.* Cambridge: Cambridge University Press, 1986.

Robb, Graham. *Balzac: A Life.* New York: Norton, 1994.

Torpey, John. *The Invention of the Passport: Surveillance, Citizenship and the State.* Cambridge: Cambridge University Press, 2000.

Tozzi, Federigo. *Pagine critiche.* Pisa: ETS, 1993.

Woloch, Isser. *The New Regime: Transformations of the French Civic Order, 1789–1820s.* New York: Norton, 1994.

Zola, Émile. *Le Roman expérimental.* Paris: Carpentier, 1923.

Secondary Sources on *Bouvard et Pécuchet*

Comte, Auguste. *Philosophie première: Cours de philosophie positive, leçons 1 à 45.* Edited by Michel Serres, François Dagognet, and Allal Sinaceur. Paris: Hermann, 1975.

D'Alembert. *Discours préliminaire de l'Encyclopédie.* Paris: Colin, 1929.

Deléage, Jean-Pierre. "Acquisition et transmission des savoirs au XIXe siècle." In *Analyses & réflexions sur . . . "Bouvard et Pécuchet,"* 98–103. Paris: Ellipses, 1999.

Descharmes, René. *Autour de "Bouvard et Pécuchet."* Paris: Librairie de France, 1921.

Donato, Eugenio. *The Script of Decadence: Essays on the Fictions of Flaubert and the Poetics of Romanticism.* New York: Oxford University Press, 1993.

Foucault, Michel. "La bibliothèque fantastique." In *Travail de Flaubert*, edited by Gérard Genette and Tzvetan Todorov, 103–22. Paris: Seuil, 1983.

Gleize, Joëlle. *Le double miroir: Le livre dans les livres de Stendhal à Proust.* Paris: Hachette, 1992.

A History of Paper. New York: Fraser Paper, 1964.

Ippolito, Christophe. "Critique du positivisme et fictions d'un gai savoir dans *Bouvard et Pécuchet*." *The Romanic Review* 91, no. 1–2 (Jan–Mar 2000): 61–75.

Kliebenstein, George. "L'encyclopédie minimale." *Poétique* 22, no. 88 (November 1991): 447–61.

Lalonde, Normand. "Une alliance anormale: Roman et dictionnaire dans

Bouvard et Pécuchet." Rivista di letterature moderne e comparate 45, no. 2 (1992): 145–55.

———. "La somme et le récit: l'exemple de *Bouvard et Pécuchet.*" *Littératures* 29 (Fall 1993): 73–85.

Leclerc, Yvan. *La Spirale et le monument: Essai sur "Bouvard et Pécuchet" de Gustave Flaubert.* Paris: SEDES, 1988.

Neefs, Jacques. "Noter, classer, briser, montrer, les dossiers de *Bouvard et Pécuchet.*" In *Penser, Classer, Écrire de Pascal à Perec,* edited by Béatrice Didier and Jacques Neefs, 69–90. Saint-Denis: Press Universitaires de Vincennes, 1990.

Secondary Sources on *La Vie mode d'emploi*

Bellos, David. *Georges Perec: A Life in Words.* Boston: Godine, 1993.

Burgelin, Claude. *Georges Perec.* Paris: Seuil, 1988.

———. *Les Parties de dominos chez Monsieur Lefèvre: Perec avec Freud, Perec contre Freud.* Strasbourg: Circé, 1996.

Chassay, Jean-François. *Le jeu des coïncidences dans "La Vie mode d'emploi" de Georges Perec.* Pantin: Le Castor Astral, 1992.

Genette, Gérard. *Narrative Discourse: An Essay in Method.* Translated by Jane G. Lewin. Ithaca, NY: Cornell University Press, 1980.

Magné, Bernard. "Lavis mode d'emploi." In *Cahiers Georges Perec 1: Colloque de Cerisy,* 232–46. Paris: P.O.L., 1985.

———. *Perecollages: 1981–1988.* Toulouse: Presses Universitaires du Mirail-Toulouse, 1989.

Peperoni, Laura, and Marina Zuccoli. "Georges Perec e l'invenzione bibliografica." *Intersezioni* 22, no. 3 (December 2002): 441–59.

Pomart, Paul-Dominique. "Georges Perec et la documentation. Questions à notre métier." *Documentaliste. Sciences de l'information* 29, no. 6 (1992): 243–49.

Secondary Sources on *Libra*

Carmichael, Thomas. "Lee Harvey Oswald and the Postmodern Subject: History and Intertextualiy in Don DeLillo's *Libra, The Names,* and *Mao II.*" *Contemporary Literature* 34, no. 2 (1993): 204–18.

Civello, Paul. "Undoing the Naturalistic Novel: Don DeLillo's *Libra.*" *Arizona Quarterly* 48, no. 2 (1992): 33–56.

Courtwright, David T. "Why Oswald Missed: Don DeLillo's *Libra.*" In *Novel History: Historians and Novelists Confront America's Past (and Each Other),* edited by Mark C. Carnes, 77–91. New York: Simon and Shuster, 2001.

De Curtis, Anthony. "'An Outsider in This Society': An Interview with Don

DeLillo." In *Introducing Don DeLillo*, edited by Frank Lentricchia, 43–66. Durham, NC: Duke University Press, 1991.

Johnston, John. "Superlinear Fiction of Historical Diagram? Don DeLillo's *Libra*." *Modern Fiction Studies* 40, no. 2 (Summer 1994): 319–42.

Simon, Art. *Dangerous Knowledge: The JFK Assassination in Art and Film.* Philadelphia, Temple University Press, 1996.

Thomas, Glen. "History, Biography, and Narrative in Don DeLillo's *Libra*." *Twentieth Century Literature: A Scholarly and Critical Journal* 43, no. 1 (Spring 1997): 107–24.

U.S. President's Commission on the Assassination of President Kennedy. *Report.* Washington, DC: GPO, 1964. http://www.archives.gov/research/jfk/warren-commission-report/index.html.

———. Select Committee on Assassinations of the U.S. House of Representatives. *Report.* Washington, DC: GPO, 1979. http://www.archives.gov/research/jfk/select-committee-report/

Willman, Skip. "Art after Dealey Plaza: DeLillo's *Libra*." *Modern Fiction Studies* 45, no. 3 (Fall 1999): 621–40.

———. "Traversing the Fantasies of the JFK Assassination: Conspiracy and Contigency in Don DeLillo's *Libra*." *Contemporary Literature* 39, no. 3 (1998): 405–33.

Index

Agamben, Giorgio, 18; and the witness, 163–64 n. 34
Ambrière-Fargeaud, Madaleine, 172 n. 30
archival novel: definition of, 13; and the digital database, 20; and the encyclopedia, 19; epistemology of, 33; and the found manuscript, 42; and genre, 13–19; and historical novels, 19; and hybridity, 19; and the identification of citizens, 19; and the law, 19; and libraries, 19; and literary realism, 19, 51, 57, 115, 136; and memory, 20; and the paradigm of challenge, 19, 53–54, 56, 102, 119, 136, 137; and the paradigm of legitimation, 19, 50–51, 56, 79, 80, 101–2, 136; and plot, 14; and postmodernism, 18, 19, 54, 57, 136, 142, 154; and post-Newtonian science, 20; prehistory of, 36–37; rhetorical structure of, 14–15; as a self-reflexive genre, 158; thematic content of, 15; and the verification of truth, 24
archive: and appraisal, 53, 57; and apprehension through localization, 45, 49, 86, 121, 135; bureaucratic, 15, 17, 120, 138, 159; and the Canadian macroappraisal model, 57; definition of, 13; and dislocation, 102; in the eighteenth century, 36; epistemic crisis of, 120; epistemology of, 45, 52, 53, 56, 138, 157; French reform of, 37, 43, 157; and historiography, 60; and human sciences, 48–49; hypertrophy of, 53, 142; and the identification of citizens, 46, 98; and information overload, 120; in late modernity, 137, 148; and the law, 90, 94–95; and Newtonian physics, 155, 157; and nineteenth-century realism, 49, 57, 86; and organicism, 148; and the origin of law and power, 55; and paper, 137, 146, 149, 157, 159, 160; and postmodernism, 56–57, 142, 151; and the principle of pertinence, 44; and the principle of provenance, 44–45, 56, 58, 143, 145–154, 155, 165 n. 15; as radical desorder, 101, 138; and le "Respect de fonds," 43–44; and the search for the origin, 132, 133, 149; and self-destruction, 131, and totality, 118, 133, 135, 138, 147–48, 151
Aristotle: *Poetics*, 120
Austen, Jane, 22

Balzac, Honoré de, 19, 27, 37, 42, 46, 51, 115, 121, 128, 135, 138, 147, 154, 176 n. 40; and the Bentham's Panopticon, 82; and the bureaucratic archive, 86; and bureaucratic identity, 88–89, 99; and the celebration of bureaucracy, 93; and *La Comédie humaine* as an archival project, 94, 100; and the état civil, 80–81, 100, 121, 136, 154; and the *mise en intrigue*, 84; and notaries, 83–84; and realism, 85, 100; as the sender of *La Comédie humaine*, 79
—Works of: *Le Colonel Chabert*, 95–100, 159; *La Comédie humaine*, 19, 79–86, 94–95, 121, 128, 135, 138; *Le Contrat de Mariage*, 84; *Le*

Cousin Pons, 84; *Un début dans la vie*, 173 n. 43; *Les Employés*, 173 n. 43; *Une Fille d'Ève*, 46; *Modeste Mignon*, 81; *La Muse du department*, 172 n. 27; *Œuvres diverses*, 170 n. 10; *Le Père Goriot*, 86–88, 121; *Splendeurs et misères des courtisanes*, 81; *Ursule Mirouët*, 90–93
Barthes, Roland, 108, 125, 175 n. 28
Bastian, F., 26, 162 n. 15, 163 n. 24
Beattie, James, 22
Becker, Peter, 171–72 n. 25
Behrmann, Thomas, 178 n. 19
Bellos, David, 177–78 n. 13
Bertillon, Alphonse, 51, 166 n. 31
Blouin, Francis, 180 n. 43
Boccaccio, Giovanni, 32, 178 n. 14
Bollème, Geneviève, 173 n. 5
Borges, Jorges Luis, 151
Brooks, Peter, 30, 94, 173 n. 42
Bruni, Francesco, 168 n. 9
Burgelin, Claude, 129, 132
Butor, Michel: *Passage de Milan*, 171 n. 17

Capote, Truman: *In Cold Blood*, 30
Caruth, Cathy, 98
Casanova, Eugenio, 165 n. 13
Celati, Gianni, 31
Civello, Paul, 182 n. 24
Coleridge, Samuel Taylor, 107, 108, 175 n. 26
Comte, Auguste, 108, 110, 175 n. 26
Congreve, William, 22, 162 n. 2
Consolo, Vincenzo: *Il sorriso dell'ignoto marinaio*, 18, 169 n. 18
Cook, Terry, 56, 156

Da Cunha, Euclides: *Os Sertões*, 16
D'Alembert, Jean, 107, 108, 110, 175 nn. 24 and 26
database: digital, 17, 20, 123, 137, 157, 159, 160; paper-made, 119
Davis, Lennard J., 40, 41, 59, 162 n. 18, 163 n. 25, 164 nn. 1 and 10
Day, Geoffrey, 161 n. 1 [chap. 1]
death drive, 99–100, 132
DeCurtis, Anthony, 152, 182 n. 28

Defoe, Daniel, 19, 22, 25, 42, 119; and the archivization of narrative in the *Journal*, 27; and bureaucratic language, 31–33; and the *Journal* as a forerunner of the archival novel, 35; and H. F. as archivist, 30–31; and print as purveyor of truth in the *Journal*, 163 n. 27; and the use of a master record in the *Journal*, 34–35; and the use of paste-ins in the *Journal*, 32–33, 164 n. 40; and writing as recycling in the *Journal*, 29
—Works of: *A Journal of the Plague Year*, 25–37, 60; *Moll Flanders*, 26; *Robinson Crusoe*, 26
Deléage, Jean-Pierre, 175–76 n. 30
DeLillo, Don, 19, 20, 42; and audiovisual records, 150–51; and the boundlessness of the Dallas Archive, 148; and conspiracy, 138–39; and contingency, 138–39; and disorder in the Dallas archive, 141–42, 146; and the Einstenian context of the Dallas archive, 156; and *Libra* as a postmodern novel, 154; and Nicholas Branch as a desperate writer, 154–55; and Nicholas Branch as a Newtonian archivist, 155–56; and patterns, 156; and secrecy, 146–47; and technology in recordmaking, 148; and the *Warren Commission Report*, 152–54; and the Zapruder film, 149–51
—Works of: *Libra*, 20, 29, 137–57; *Underworld*, 181 n. 11
Derrida, Jacques, 18, 55, 131, 149, 173 n. 2; and the *archiviolithique*, 131–32
Descharmes, René, 112, 176 n. 34
Dimock, Wai Chee, 16
Donato, Eugenio, 117, 177 n. 43
Doughty, Arthur G., 58
Dunton, John, 24

Eco, Umberto: *Il nome della rosa*, 18, 42, 44
Edwards, Magdalena, 173–74 n. 6

Ellis, Frank H., 163 n. 33, 164 n. 36
Eloy Martínez, Tomás: *El cantor de tango*, 18; *Santa Evita*, 18, 169 n. 18
encyclopedia, 107–10, 116–18

Faulkner, William: *Go Down Moses*, 54, 166 n. 40
Fielding, Henry, 22, 38, 46, 47, 50, 56, 89, 165 n. 19, 171 n. 16; and the storing of records in *Tom Jones*, 41–42; *Tom Jones*, 38–42; and the use of public records in novels, 39–40
Flaubert, Gustave, 19, 32, 51, 161 n. 5; and the archivization of the novel, 104; and *Bouvard et Pécuchet* as an avant-garde archive, 116; and *Bouvard et Pécuchet* as a critique of the encyclopedia, 104–5; and bureaucratic writing, 106, 108; and copying, 107, 114; and the difficulties of narrative, 111, 113; and duplication 115, 176 n. 36; and plot in *Bouvard et Pécuchet*, 111–12; and rhetoric, 106, 174–75 n. 17; and social stupidity, 114; and time in *Bouvard et Pécuchet*, 112–13
—Works of: *Bouvard et Pécuchet*, 19, 51, 100, 101–18, 120, 161 n. 5; *Madame Bovary*, 91; *Salammbô*, 175 n. 20; *La Tentation de Saint Antoine*, 176 n. 41
Foucault, Michel, 13, 18, 47, 48, 82, 94, 176 n. 41
Freud, Sigmund, 99, 132
Frow, John, 14, 16, 161 n. 1 [Intro.]

Garval, Michael D., 80–81
Ginzburg, Carlo, 166 n. 32
Gladfelder, Hal, 170 nn. 23 and 28
Gleize Joëlle, 106
González Echevarría, Roberto, 95, 161 n. 11, 166 nn. 39 and 42, 167 n. 52, 172 nn. 39 and 40
Good, Graham, 173 n. 50
Goody, Jack, 128

Gothot-Mersch, Claudine, 103
Gough, Richard, 26

Harrison, Robert, 167 n. 54
Hayles, Katherine N., 156; and the field model, 155
Hegel, G. W. F., 108
Hunter, J. Paul, 24, 158
Hutcheon, Linda, 167 n. 47

Jenkinson, Hilary, 52, 53, 77
Johnston, John, 20

Kaluszynski, Martine, 171–72 n. 25
Kittler, Friedrich A., 150, 158
Kundera, Milan, 58

Lalonde, Normand, 177 n. 44
library, 116–18
Lukács, Georg, 18, 27; and H. F. as a world-historical individual, 28

Mabillon, Jean: *De re diplomatica*, 55
Magné, Bernard, 177 n. 6, 180 n. 41
Manovich, Lev, 157
Manzoni, Alessandro, 19, 27, 42, 51, 96, 115, 155, 159, 171 n. 14, 174 n. 10; as anticipator of the "new historical novel," 71; and the antifiction agenda in *Storia della colonna infame*, 74; and anti-illusionism, 67; and the archival historical novel, 72; and the archive as the structuring principle of plot in *I promessi sposi*, 70; as dossier creator, 63; and the found manuscript, 65–66; and Goethe's criticism on *I promessi sposi*, 169 n. 16; and invention, 75; and his judgment on Scott's fiction, 168 n. 11; and the pratice of archive as an act of power, 72–73, 75–76; and records as texts, 76; and the theory of *fatto positivo*, 63; and the validation of records in *I promessi sposi*, 66; and the writer as a copyist/researcher, 70–71

—Works of: *Adelchi*, 63; *I promessi sposi (1840)*, 19, 60–74, 77–78, 96, 97, 155, 174 n. 10; *Del romanzo storico*, 169 n. 19; *Storia della colonna infame*, 19, 62, 72–78, 174 n. 10
Marra, Michele, 182 n. 4
Mathews, Harry: *The Journalist*, 18
Matsuda, Matt, 51
Mayer, Robert, 37
McDowell, Paula, 163 n. 27
McKeon, Michael, 22
Menton, Seymour, 169 n. 17
mimesis, 85, 171 n. 15
Moretti, Franco, 79
museum, 116–18

narratives: digital, 160
Neefs, Jacques, 175 n. 20
Nigro, Salvatore Silvano, 5, 19
Noiriel, Gérard, 166 n. 28
novel: archival foundation of, 96; and bureaucratic writing, 31; and the cell phone, 160; and characters' names, 86; and the digital era, 159–60; in early modern England, 23–25, 158; and the eighteenth-century debate on genres and truth 22–24, 30; as an eighteenth-century project, 158, 159; epistemology of, 52; epistolary, 40; and inclusivity, 32; and history, 37; in the modern age, 120; nonfictional, 30; and postmodernism, 142; realist, 86, 109, 112, 116, 118, 171 n. 16; and the urge to record, 24, 30, 34, 37

OuLiPo, 121–22, 178 n. 16

paper age, 17, 29, 138, 157, 159, 160
Parrish, Timothy L., 181 n. 12
Pasco, Allan H., 172 n. 27
Pavic, Milorad: *Dictionary of the Khazars: A Lexicon Novel*, 18, 42
Pearce-Moses, Richard, 161 n. 2, 165 n. 16
Peperoni, Laura, 177 n. 2
Perec, Georges, 19, 42, 137, 159; and the archive as a game, 135–36; and archive-related materials in *La Vie mode d'emploi*, 128–29; and bureaucratic writing, 123, 125, 127, 128; and compulsive archivists, 130–32, 135; and copying, 123, 127, 179 n. 27; and descriptions, 125–27; and indexes, 123–25; and the layout of *La Vie mode d'emploi*, 120–21; and lists, 128, 179 n. 29; and memory, 129–30, 180 n. 38; as a professional archivist, 119, 129, 179 n. 36; and the rules for composing *La Vie mode d'emploi*, 121–23; and utopian archivists, 132–34, 135
—Works of: *Cahier des charges de "La Vie mode d'emploi,"* 122; *Les Choses*, 128; *Un homme qui dort*, 179 n. 35; *Penser/Classer*, 178 n. 11, 179 n. 33; *Tentative d'épuisement d'un lieu parisien*, 129; *La Vie mode d'emploi*, 20, 33, 119–36, 137, 159, 161 n. 5, 175 n. 21
Petrey, Sandy, 87
Pomart, Paul-Dominique, 179–80 n. 36
Poniatowska, Elena: *La noche de Tlatelolco*, 16, 30
Prendergast, Christopher, 171 n. 15
Proust, Marcel, 126, 129

Rabelais, François, 175 n. 21
Raimondi, Ezio, 169–70 n. 20
Ranke, Leopold von, 27, 165 n. 19
Richardson, Samuel, 22, 40, 171 n. 16
Richetti, John J., 164 n. 35
Ricœur, Paul: and the *mise en archive*, 28; and the *mise en intrigue*, 170–71 n. 12
Roa Bastos, Augusto: *Yo el supremo*, 18, 167 n. 50, 169 n. 18

Saramago, José: *Todos os Nomes*, 18, 161 n. 5
Sarmiento, Domingo F: *Facundo*, 16
Schonhorn, Manuel, 163 n. 31
Sciascia, Leonardo: *Il consiglio*

d'Egitto, 54–56; and the contextualization of the archive, 55
Scott, Walter, 22, 26, 27, 61, 67; and his paradigm of historical fiction, 71; and illusionism, 67–68
Sekula, Allan, 166 n. 28
Simon, Art, 181 n. 3
Smollett, Tobias, 22
Sontag, Susan, 171–72 n. 25
Spieker, Sven, 44, 120
Stille, Alexander, 53

Taylor, Hugh, 58, 156
Thomas, Glen, 180 n. 2
Tozzi, Federigo, 171 n. 14

Ugresic, Dubravka: *The Museum of Unconditional Surrender*, 16

Vassalli, Sebastiano: *La chimera*, 18, 169 n. 18
Verri, Pietro: *Osservazioni sulla tortura*, 72, 76
Vigny, Alfred de: *Cinq-Mars*, 68

Wailly, Natalis de, 43, 44
Watt, Ian, 21, 86, 162 nn. 6 and 11, 171 n. 16
Willman, Skip, 182 n. 19
Woloch, Isser, 171 n. 18

Zelenyj, Dan, 56
Zola, Émile, 182 n. 24; *Pot bouille*, 171 n. 17
Zuccoli, Marina, 177 n. 2